*xperience*

J. M. COHEN · J.-F. PHIPPS

The Common Experience

RIDER AND COMPANY
LONDON

201.1

Rider and Company
3 Fitzroy Square, London WIP 6JD

An imprint of the Hutchinson Publishing Group

London Melbourne Sydney Auckland
Wellington Johannesburg and agencies
throughout the world

First published 1979
© Selection and commentary J. M. Cohen and J.-F. Phipps 1979

Set in Monotype Bembo

Printed in Great Britain by
The Anchor Press Ltd, and bound by
Wm Brendon & Son Ltd, both of
Tiptree, Essex

ISBN 0 09 136810 3   cased
0 09 136811 1   paperback

2002604 2

Contents

Foreword

The subject of this book is the way to enlightenment, and its purpose is to show that the way starts not in some distant monastery, but at our own door. 'Lift up the stone and you will find me there', says Jesus in the fragmentary Gospel of Thomas.

As evidence, we have assembled an anthology of thoughts and experiences grouped under various headings and all concerned with the entrance to that way. In assembling these many passages from writings of east and west, we have at the same time developed our own argument and endeavoured to show their relevance to the problems and questions of those who may read us. For this purpose we have set side by side the experiences of contemporary people living very much in the everyday world, and those of monks, teachers and philosophers primarily concerned with the quest for enlightenment. Hence our title, *The Common Experience*. For all men record and pass through the same stages on the slowly mounting path, whatever their creed, epoch or station in life. The landmarks are unchanging, although they may be variously named and described. We set out to plot them in the words of those who have passed before us. Our commentary is no more than the small print in a lavishly illustrated guidebook. In this instance, it is more important to read our authorities.

The book is divided into nine sections, each treating one aspect of the way. But the writings we have selected are seldom confined to a single theme. Although they appear in one section, their significance spreads to others. We have aimed at a shape, but a rigid structure would be both impossible and undesirable. 'The Way is like an empty vessel that yet may be drawn from', says the

Tao Te Ching (Lao Tzu). The same is true of a would-be guide to the way.

This is primarily an anthology and may be treated purely as a bedside book. Those who require no argument to convince them may confine themselves to our extracts and quotations, any of which may provide themes for discursive reflection, even for meditation in the strict sense of the term.

This book is the product of two men's experiences and consequently reflects their own mental and spiritual journeys. They are of different generations, started from very different standpoints, have led very different lives, and have reached different, though not entirely dissimilar, conclusions. Whereas the one would lay greater stress on the need for a specific method taught by a specific teacher, the other would tend to regard everyday life as our greatest teacher and every moment an opportunity to experience the 'eternal now'.

Our approach, therefore, is personal, but we have endeavoured to speak from a level beyond that of the everyday ego. We do not aim to stress contradictions but to indicate the unity of all true thought.

We are particularly grateful to the Religious Experience Research Unit of Oxford, which has generously put at our disposal numerous accounts of moments of enlightenment sent to the Unit by the public at large. We have indicated by the abbreviation RERU those quotations which we owe to them.

J.M.C.

J.-F.P.

1 Meditation

The mystical path is not mysterious. It is not the private path of monks and yogins. It is open to all and has been liberally signposted by writers familiar with its various stages, men and women who have used the language of their own traditions – Christian, Buddhist, Sufi, Hindu, Taoist, Platonic or Jewish – to describe experiences which are not easily reduced to words, but which are sufficiently clear for anyone to understand who has a practical interest in exploring this universal path. The signposts are visible. There are even detailed maps of the terrain, which stretches from the bordering hills whence a preliminary vista may be obtained, as through a break in the mist, to the sunlit plains of enlightenment and beyond them to that paradoxical sea where being and non-being, selfhood and unity are one, to Nirvana or the heavenly state at the end of the journey.

The purpose of this book is to note the signposts by the choice of passages written by travellers, ancient or contemporary, who have followed this path. Since their signpost language will not be equally clear to all enquirers, it will be necessary to offer some comments, even explanations, as the book proceeds. We have chosen these passages not only for their individual significance, but for the light they throw on one another. Moreover, readers will no doubt find some passages more appealing than others, may profit from some but find others baffling. Although the writings are variously coloured by their separate eras or traditions, our aim is to reflect in the book as a whole the white light that combines the rainbow hues of the different mystical traditions, which we believe to be essentially one.

The beginning of the path is marked for many by sporadic

glimpses of states of being that will become permanent, perhaps after many years, if the path is seriously pursued. Many people have known, perhaps in childhood, perhaps in adolescence, perhaps at reflective moments, perhaps in periods of stress, sudden foretastes of enlightenment or unity, or indeed of both together. For a moment, the world has seemed different, brighter and more significant. Time has seemed to stop. The truth has seemed just within reach. Then the moment has passed, as it came, remaining memorable but almost indescribable. To some these moments have acted as pointers along a way that they will henceforth follow with greater confidence. But others have found them embarrassing, even alarming, and have devised various means of explaining them away.

Many today are afraid of what they take to be a 'religious' urge, which they feel may alienate them from the common way of life. Lord Clark's reaction, in the incident from his autobiography quoted below, typifies this attitude. This book will cite many such accounts of sporadic mystical experiences, given in the words of the (usually anonymous) people who have written their stories in response to appeals by investigators. Some of the anecdotes that we shall quote will be drawn from published autobiographies, some from early investigators such as William James, and a considerable number from the records of the Religious Experience Research Unit at Oxford, which has amassed an extensive archive over the last few years.

Here follow four descriptions of such moments, two of which appear to have had positive results on the future lives of the experiencers, and two of which appear to have left no lasting trace:

Vauxhall Station on a murky November Saturday evening is not the setting one would choose for a revelation of God! . . . The third-class compartment was full. I cannot remember any particular thought processes which may have led up to the great moment . . . For a few seconds only (I suppose) the whole compartment was filled with light . . . I felt caught up into some tremendous sense of being within a loving, triumphant and shining purpose. I never felt more humble. I never felt more exalted. A most curious, but overwhelming, sense possessed me and filled me with ecstasy. I felt that all was well for mankind ... All men were shining and glorious beings who in the end would enter incredible joy. Beauty, music, joy, love immeasurable and a glory unspeakable, all this they would inherit ...

This happened over fifty years ago, but even now I can see myself in the corner of that dingy third-class compartment, with the feeble lights of inverted gas mantles overhead and the Vauxhall Station platforms outside with milk cans standing there. In a few moments the glory had departed – all but one curious, lingering feeling. I loved everybody in that compartment. It sounds silly now, and indeed I blush to write it, but at that moment I think I would have died for any one of the people in that compartment. I seemed to sense the golden worth in them all.

(RERU 385)

This experience profoundly affected the whole course of the life of the person concerned, who went on to become a famous preacher, spiritual counsellor and writer.

Next follows an example of an intimation that apparently led nowhere:

Went to St Peter's, Rome. Enter hall, see Pietà on right, Raffaelo things on left, organ playing Bach, come forward into main hall under dome and look up. Conscious of wonder, beauty, marvel of art. Then, looking up at dome, some spell took me. Couldn't move. From far away, something happening; whisper of wind, strange sensation, apprehension – what's going to happen? Wonder, beauty, body rooted, brain quite coldly commenting to me on experience like BBC sports commentator ... Then like tremendous wind tearing through me, powerful, overwhelming, like Aladdin's genie escaping from bottle, tearing up into that dome in ecstasy, brain saying, 'Don't kid yourself, this is art, aesthetic not religious, it's all geared to make you feel this, human genius, not God,' etc. But great expansion from inside fills dome, out of body and at height, yes, orgasm of experience, this escaped exultant 'soul' (what better?) says to my brain, 'I don't care what you say, I am *immortal*; I have come home!' My brain replied, 'Alright, you think so now, but this will pass, you will go out the door you came in by, take up the burden of your mortality again, for that is the human reality, this is a marvellous, beautiful illusion, effect of great art,' etc.

That is what happened. Gradually the storm subsided, I came back down to myself, my cynical brain took over again, not unkindly but sympathetically, as with a child that's lost its toys or has to live with the fact that mummy or daddy is dead . . . The experience made no difference to my behaviour.

(RERU 1789)

It was about 1948, when I often spent half an hour in the National Gallery at lunchtime. One day I stopped before Gerard David's 'Deposition from the Cross', a picture that made no special appeal to me. Suddenly I found myself inside that picture, standing on the left beside the ladder, with the other spectators and witnessing the taking down of that pale collapsed body. I was moved by an emotion to which I cannot give a name. It was shared with the other witnesses.

A few seconds later I was once more outside the scene, moved, though not surprised, for such 'moments' had come to me before. I returned to the Gallery next day, and found only the faint echo of that experience. On subsequent visits, even the echo had disappeared, and Gerard David was once more for me a rather stiff and mannered painter, too much concerned with physical suffering . . .

I was studying the ideas of the Russian thinker, P. D. Ouspensky, at the time of this experience, but found it tantalizingly unrelated to those ideas. The incident linked on, however, with some childhood experiences and with one from my Cambridge days, to be related later.

(J.M.C.)

Such experiences are not always welcome, as Lord Clark shows in the following extract from his autobiography:

I lived in solitude, surrounded by books on the history of religion, which has always been my favourite reading. This may help to account for a curious episode that took place on one of my stays at the villino. I had a religious experience. It took place in the church of San Lorenzo, but did not seem to be connected with the harmonious beauty of the architecture. I can only say that for a few minutes my whole being was radiated by a kind of heavenly joy, far more intense than anything I had known before. This state of mind lasted for several months, and, wonderful though it was, it posed an awkward problem in terms of action. My life was far from blameless: I would have to reform. My family would think I was going mad, and perhaps after all it *was* a delusion, for I was in every way unworthy of receiving such a flood of grace. Gradually the effect wore off, and I made no effort to retain it. I think I was right; I was too deeply embedded in the world to change course. But that I had 'felt the finger of God' I am quite sure, and although the memory of this experience has faded, it still helps me to understand the joy of the saints.

(*The Other Half*)

Such glimpses of the land of Canaan may occur at the outset of the journey. In the initial stages of the journey itself they are rare indeed. Later, as we shall see, they come in the form of intuition less disturbing and more meaningful. Today the journey often begins in confusion. Indeed, it is sometimes a prolonged state of anxiety and bewilderment that impels a person to seek a way of life or scale of values that will make some sense of our contemporary situation. But, having decided to seek a path, the anxious explorer will soon be confronted with yet another form of confusion.

In the last twenty years the entrance to the path has been blocked by a vast market of clamorous stallholders, each offering his own special form of guidance through the dangers of the journey, his own map, complete with staging posts and short cuts and a detailed survey of the terrain. Esoteric teachings, meditations, psychological methods, scientifically proven specifics are offered, often for hard cash. The seeker is asked to surrender his or her freedom to a society or a guru, but has little opportunity of testing the claims or even the honesty of would-be guides. The choice appears to be between the inflated promises of the noisier stallholders and the more respectable claims of the established religions, whose representatives hardly bother to man their stalls. While they claim to possess reliable maps of the terrain ahead, the prospective traveller may well feel that they have long since lost them.

At this moment of bewilderment, one might recall the gospel promise: 'Ask, and it shall be given you; seek, and ye shall find; knock, and it shall be opened unto you.' In the area of confusion, the traditional signposts are of supreme value. Earlier guides have left records of their teachings; earlier travellers have left pictures of the road. A guide is needed. But to choose a guide it is necessary to study the methods of previous guides, to observe their sense of responsibility and judge by this the reliability of those persons or organizations offering their guidance today. A guide may not be hard to find. He may only be one who has progressed a little further than oneself along the way.

The first section of this book is devoted to preliminary methods, first of all to meditation, the meaning of which must be clarified by reference to experts in the art. These are primarily the monks, Catholic and Orthodox, the teachings of the Hindu master Patanjali and the Buddhists, for whom meditation has far more aspects and practices than for Patanjali or the early Fathers. The Christian categories were defined once and for all in the twelfth century by Richard of Saint-Victor, one of the first theorists of western mysticism:

Thinking, slow-footed, wanders hither and thither along bypaths, caring not where they will lead. Meditation, with great mental industry, plods along the steep and laborious road keeping the end in view. Contemplation, on a free wing, circles around with great nimbleness wherever the impulse takes it. Thinking crawls along, meditation marches and sometimes runs, contemplation flies around and when it wills, it hovers upon the height. Thinking is without labour and bears no fruit. Meditation labours and has its fruit. Contemplation abides untoiling and fruitful. Thinking roams about; meditation investigates; contemplation wonders.

(Richard of Saint-Victor)

For Richard, thinking is the product of imagination, meditation is based on reason, while contemplation rests on the intelligence, which is a spiritual quality. But we will now turn to the last of the great Spanish mystics, Miguel de Molinos, who was at the same time the first modern meditational guide.

The mystical teaching of the Roman Catholic Church from its twelfth-century beginnings to the great Spanish school of the sixteenth century was essentially institutional. Teaching was given by priests to priests under the supervision of 'spiritual directors' – church dignitaries who were often ignorant of mystical technique and higher forms of meditation but expert in detecting dangerous thoughts and incipient heresies. In fact individual pursuit of the path was not encouraged by the institutional Church and many outstanding mystics fell under suspicion of heresy. Meister Eckhart, the German mystic, died while under prosecution for heresy. Some of his followers, the Friends of God, were patently heretical, while others were careful to avoid in their writings language too closely recalling that of Eckhart. In the Spanish school, Santa Teresa had to justify herself to her superiors by writing an account of her life (from which extracts will be given in later sections of this book), and St John of the Cross even suffered a short imprisonment for his allegedly dangerous statements.

Miguel de Molinos, who at the end of the seventeenth century followed John of the Cross closely, was in one important way an innovator. Church authority did not forbid the teaching of advanced techniques of prayer to laymen; there were always exceptional cases. But the view was, as it still is today, that meditational practice is suitable only for the recluse life. Molinos, a Spanish priest living in Rome, did not contest this view. He was no revolutionary. Indeed, at the beginning of his career he was on close terms with Pope Innocent XI. He merely stated in his very popular *Spiritual Guide* that when conventional prayer ceased to satisfy, or actively dissatisfied a person, this was a sure sign that he or she should advance to a more subtle form of prayer:

In order to know when God is raising the soul from the state of meditation to that of contemplation, so that he may not remain in meditation too long or abandon it prematurely, we need wait for no miracles nor the arrival of an angel with instructions. There are enough signs and symptoms for the soul to be quite certain of the divine call. The saints and masters are in general agreement on the means of knowing when God wishes a soul to give up meditation (discursive prayer) and pass on to the prayer of faith. These are, firstly, that he derives no pleasure or spiritual nourishment from meditation, but rather finds dwelling on particular subjects difficult, tedious and repugnant. His inclination is to stay still. His only pleasure is to remain calm and silent, calmly and lovingly aware that he is with God and attending only to Him.

(Defence of Contemplation)

Initially, the influence of Molinos spread rapidly among priests, in monasteries and convents, where meditational practice had fallen into decline, and among the influential laity of Rome. But he quickly found enemies, especially among the Jesuits. His teaching, later labelled 'Quietism', clearly made demands on the conventional and complacent clergy that they were unable to fulfil. He went so far as to suggest that the contemplative would be justified in neglecting church rituals if he found them of no benefit to his spiritual life. The campaign against the Spanish priest gathered momentum. Suddenly he found himself deserted by his influential friends and facing a trial for heresy before the Holy Inquisition. The trial was a staged drama. Yet the counts of heresy which he faced were never proved and the prosecution resorted to sexual accusations, which were not substantiated either. Molinos behaved with great dignity throughout his trial and even his judges ended by treating him courteously. Nevertheless they sentenced him to perpetual imprisonment and he spent the last nine years of his life in the dungeons of the Holy Office.

Quietism persisted for a while in France. But Molinos' chief influence was in the Protestant countries, where his *Spiritual Guide* was much translated. His second book, the *Defence* of his spiritual position, submitted at his trial as evidence of his orthodoxy, remained unpublished in Vatican archives until a few years ago. It cites as proof of his scrupulous orthodoxy precedents for all his beliefs and teachings, drawn from the Church Fathers and John of the Cross.

The following extract from the book makes clear not only his own position as a teacher, but his understanding of the differences between the initial stages of prayer. Meditation is for him, as for the Catholic tradition, dwelling on some sacred subject. Contemplation, or the prayer of quiet, is a more abstract practice known as meditation in Hindu and Buddhist tradition:

According to the saints, the prayer of quiet is a raising of the mind to

God. And in order to keep the mind fixed on God – this is contemplation – it is necessary to leave behind all rational and discursive thinking, however exalted – that is meditation. Meditation, say the saints, is the seeking, discussing, ruminating and chewing of the divine food. And if this food is always ruminated, if it is perpetually chewed, it remains in the mouth and is never swallowed. Thus it cannot be quietly held and digested in the stomach and it brings no life or nourishment to a man. Indeed, he gains nothing from it. Meditation is a means of reaching an end and the end of meditation is contemplation. Contemplation is finding; it is the enjoyment and retention of the divine food in the stomach. It is the goal, the end of the road where a person understands and knows God.

(Defence of Contemplation)

Molinos' trial marks the end of Roman Catholic mystical teaching. But among the Greek Orthodox the tradition of the Church Fathers has continued almost to this day, and among the most influential writings on the subject was that of an Italian priest of the sixteenth century, Lorenzo Scupoli. His work, largely forgotten in the west, circulated widely in a Russian translation under the title of *Unseen Warfare*. Scupoli bases his teaching on the Prayer of Quiet and on an attitude of detachment known in the Greek tradition as 'sobriety':

There is yet another form of prayer, which is called standing in the presence of God, when the man who prays is wholly concentrated in his heart and inwardly contemplates God as being present to him and within him, with corresponding feelings – either of fear of God and the feeling of wonder and awe before His greatness, or of faith and hope, or of love and submission to His will, or of contrition and readiness for any sacrifice. Such a state comes when a man becomes deeply immersed in prayer by word, mind and heart. If a man prays in the right way and for a long time, these states come to him more and more often, and finally this state can become permanent; then it is called walking before God and is constant prayer.

Thus, my brother, if you wish your prayer to bring much fruit, never be content by oral prayer alone, but pray also with your mind and heart – using your mind to understand and be conscious of all that is said in words, and your heart to feel it all. Above all, pray with your heart. Prayer bursting from the heart is like a streak of lightning which takes but a moment to cross the heavens and appear before the throne of the all-merciful God. God hears it and inclines towards this most of all.

(*Unseen Warfare*)

But how is attention to be preserved?

Tsai-an studied the Vinaya texts at Huang-po Shan, which, however, failed to satisfy him, for he had as yet no approach to the ultimate meaning of Buddhist truth. He went about on his disciplinary pilgrimage and came to Pai-chang. Tsai-an remarked, 'I have been seeking for the Buddha, but do not yet know how to go on with my research.'

Said the master, 'It is very much like looking for an ox when riding on one.'

'What shall a man do after knowing him?'

'It is like going home on the back of an ox.'

'May I be further enlightened as to the care I shall have to bestow on the whole matter?'

Pai-chang said, 'It is like a cowherd looking after his cattle, who using his staff keeps them from wandering into another's pasture.'

(quoted in D. T. Suzuki, *Essays in Zen Buddhism, 2*)

A Zen-like parable, noticed by Molinos, occurs in the Old Testament:

Interior recollection is symbolized in Scripture by the story of the patriarch Jacob who wrestled all night with God till the dawn broke and he gave him his blessing. For the soul must persevere in the struggle, whatever difficulties it may find in inner recollection, till the light breaks and God gives him his blessing.

(*Spiritual Guide*)

Among those influenced by Molinos was the eighteenth-century divine, William Law:

Now there is but one possible way for man to attain this salvation or life of God in the soul. There is not one for the Jew, another for a Christian, and a third for the heathen. No; God is one, human nature is one, salvation is one, and the way to it is one; and that is, the desire of the soul turned to God. When this desire is alive and breaks forth in any creature under Heaven, then the lost sheep is found and the shepherd has it upon his shoulders. Through this desire the poor

Prodigal Son leaves his husks and swine and hastes to his father: it is because of this desire that the father sees the son while yet afar off, that he runs out to meet him, falls on his neck and kisses him. See here how plainly we are taught that no sooner is this desire arisen and in motion towards God, but the operation of God's Spirit answers to it, cherishes and welcomes its first beginnings – signified by the father's seeing and having compassion on his son whilst yet afar off, that is, in the first beginnings of his desire. Thus does this desire do all, it brings the soul to God and God to the soul, it unites with God, it co-operates with God, and is one life with God. Suppose this desire not to be alive, not in motion, either in a Jew or a Christian, and then all the sacrifices, the service, the worship either of the Law or the Gospel are but dead works that bring no life into the soul nor beget any union between God and it. Suppose this desire to be awakened and fixed upon God, though in souls that never heard either of the Law or Gospel, and then divine life or operation of God enters into them, and the new birth in Christ is formed in those who never heard of His name. And these are they that shall come from the East, and from the West, and sit down with Abraham and Isaac in the Kingdom of God.

(S. Hobhouse, *Selected Mystical Writings of William Law*)

In our own day, Krishnamurti, who comes from the east and has spent much of his life in the west, perhaps fulfils Law's ideal of a new unity of tradition:

What is important in meditation is the quality of the mind and the heart. It is not what you achieve, or what you say you attain, but rather the quality of a mind that is innocent and vulnerable. Through negation there is the positive state. Merely to gather, or to live in, experience, denies the purity of meditation. Meditation is not a means to an end. It is both the means and the end. The mind can never be made innocent through experience. It is the negation of experience that brings about that positive state of innocency which cannot be cultivated by thought. Thought is never innocent. Meditation is the ending of thought, not by the meditator, for the meditator is the meditation. If there is no meditation, then you are like a blind man in a world of great beauty, light and colour.

Wander by the seashore and let this meditative quality come upon you. If it does, don't pursue it. What you pursue will be the memory of what it was – and what was is the death of what is. Or when you wander among the hills, let everything tell you the beauty and the pain of life, so that you awaken to your own sorrow and to the ending of it. Meditation is the root, the plant, the flower and the fruit. It is words that divide the fruit, the flower, the plant and the root. In this separation action does not bring about goodness: virtue is the total perception.

(*The Second Penguin Krishnamurti Reader*)

For Krishnamurti, dualism is rooted in thought. Thus the absence of thought leads to the absence of discrimination. Neither Law nor Krishnamurti, however, is prepared to give precise guidance for the attainment of the state of non-discrimination. Molinos and the Zen masters are more precise, and so is the *Lankavatara Sutra*, a classic of Buddhism:

Among human beings, enlightenment appears in varying degrees of purity. Just as soon as a common person is conscious of a difference between right thoughts and false thoughts, between good thoughts and evil thoughts, it can be said that he has become enlightened, but it is a very rudimentary form of enlightenment. Hinayana disciples as they begin their practice of meditation are conscious of their discriminating thoughts and at the same time are conscious that they have no validity; they are said to have attained enlightenment but it is a very crude form of enlightenment. As they restrain their discriminative concepts, being conscious of their falsity, their enlightenment becomes more refined. As they become Bodhisattvas, becoming more conscious of the grasping nature of discriminative thoughts and yet reminding themselves that even discriminative thoughts have no grasping quality in their self-nature, their enlightenment has become partly accommodating. As Bodhisattvas advance along the stages, they more and more become sensitive to the arising of these false discriminations and more and more quickly react against them, and become more and more skilful in employing expedient means for checking them arising and ignoring them if they arise. Until at last they come to a state of awareness in which they are able to keep far away from even the most refined conceptions, knowing that Essential Mind is permanent and abiding in its purity. This is a state of perfect accommodation; it can truly be called enlightenment. Therefore it is said in the Sutras, if any sentient being is able to keep free from all discriminative thinking, he has attained to the wisdom of a Buddha.

(*Lankavatara Sutra*)

The writer distinguishes Mahayana or northern Buddhism, in his view the more subtle and developed teaching, from the southern Hinayana, which is more moralistic. The *bodhisattva* is one who, having attained compassion for all sentient beings, refuses to leave the wheel of rebirth until all are rescued from the realm of suffering.

Many people in brief moments find themselves free from discriminative thought. Here is one example from many in the RERU archives:

I had travelled up to Keswick for a short holiday alone. I was sitting eating dinner in my small boarding house. The dining room was filled with a lively group of students, but I sat alone, looking out over Lake Derwentwater. I was thinking at the time about the problem of the existence of God, and was trying purposely to direct, even to force, my thoughts along certain tracks, instead of allowing them to come to mind haphazardly as usual . . .

[I asked myself] 'Why, if there is no God, should anything exist in the first place? Indeed, how *could* anything exist? Why not just nothing?'

At this moment in my reasoning it was as if suddenly a door had been opened in the mind . . . I glimpsed what I can only call the Kingdom of Heaven. For a moment all time seemed to stand still. It was as if I was looking down into a great hall, but unlike an earthly hall it defies description. It was like an intuition of infinity and pure reason. I had caught sight of Truth, which the human faculties in their frailty are unable to grasp. There were the answers to the mysteries of human life and of the existence of the universe. And if I could not understand those mysteries, at least I could know that there is something beyond . . .

Then the door was closed quietly and the vision slipped away like a dream. It took me a moment to catch my breath and to remember where I was. I had no doubts about the significance of what I had experienced and felt elated. My interest in the material world, however, was not noticeably diminished, and I continued with my meal and my cabbage, boiled as only the English know how.

(RERU 1153)

Another moment of clarity occurred in the totally different setting of the western desert during a lull in the battle of el Alamein:

The time was 02.10 a.m. on the 5th November 1942. The place: Tel el Eisa, in the Western Desert just west of el Alamein. I was wireless officer with a tank regiment ... Although very tired I was content to lie on the sand on my back and soak up the unaccustomed silence ...

For the first time since before the battle I was lying *on* the ground, rather than in a slit trench or inside a tank or armoured car. The dust of battle which had obscured the sky had quite gone, and the stars were enormous and magnificent. A slight breeze came from the warm sea nearby and the air seemed to be slightly perfumed, from what source I could not imagine.

Suddenly my train of thought accelerated and vastly improved in quality. New and convincing ideas came into my head in a steady torrent ... I was immediately aware that this was important to me as nothing had been before. The impact was so powerful that for a split second I felt something akin to fear, but this I rejected quickly, because simultaneously I was enjoying an almost, nay actual, physical thrill of delight ... a small, everyday, critical part of my brain was standing apart observing with astonishment what was going on in the rest of my thinking apparatus ...

That small watch-dog part of my brain marvelled at this as it happened. This ability to experience thought on two quite different levels simultaneously is something I have never heard mentioned as being possible ...

There was no specific 'religious' aspect in the pattern of ideas which presented itself to me. It had to do with man's (my) position in the universe; with eternity, which became readily understandable; with infinity ... and so on until, as suddenly as it had started, the train of thought passed and added, as a definite statement, 'That's quite enough to be going on with.' I remember taking a deep breath and exclaiming aloud, 'You can say that again!'

I had pleasurable thrills running across underneath my skull; almost like a cold shower in hot weather, but as it were in a higher octave and champagne, not water.

I stood up and stretched, rested and elated. I am as sure as anyone can be about such things, that I had not been asleep; in fact I had never been so wide awake, so conscious. I crawled into my armoured car, switched on the light and made notes on the back of signal forms, because I knew it was important not to forget ...

(RERU 947)

A method of inducing such moments is suggested by a wandering Russian monk of the nineteenth century:

So I began by searching out my heart in the way Simeon the New Theologian teaches. With my eyes shut I gazed in thought, i.e., in imagination, upon my heart. I tried to picture it there in the left side of my breast and to listen carefully to its beating. I started doing this several times a day, for half an hour at a time, and at first I felt nothing but a sense of darkness. But little by little after a fairly short time I was able to picture my heart and to note its movement, and further with the help of my breathing I could put into it and draw from it the Prayer of Jesus in the manner taught by the saints, Gregory of Sinai, Callistus and Ignatius. When drawing the air in I looked in spirit into my heart and said, 'Lord Jesus Christ', and when breathing out again, I said, 'Have mercy on me'. I did this at first for an hour at a time, then for two hours, then for as long as I could, and in the end almost all day long.

(*The Way of a Pilgrim*)

This is a triple technique, involving attention to the breath, the heartbeat, and the repetition of a short prayer or mantra.

Followers of Sufism – a mystical tradition within the Muslim faith – also knew the efficacy of the brief prayer, which is described by the outstanding eleventh-century theorist of the movement, al Ghazali:

With the Sufis, repose and movement, exterior or interior, are illumined with the light which proceeds from the central radiance of inspiration. And what other light could shine on the face of the earth? In a word, what can one criticize in them? To purge the heart of all that does not belong to God is the first step in their cathartic method. The drawing up of the heart by prayer is the keystone of it, as the cry 'Allahu Akbar' ('God is great') is the keystone of prayer, and the last stage is the being lost in God. I say the last stage, with reference to what may be reached by an effort of will; but, to tell the truth, it is only the first stage in the life of contemplation, the vestibule by which the initiated enter.

(*Confessions*)

The practice of meditation appears so far to hinge on watching the breath, on placing attention at the level of the heart, on repetition of a sound, on the rejection of discriminative thinking or on all these combined. Each method has its followers. Some further excerpts from eastern and western writers may help to clarify the problem.

Whereas Christian meditation in general starts from the consideration of a given theme drawn from scripture or theology, there are exceptions. Both the anonymous author of *The Cloud of Unknowing* and St John of the Cross follow a negative way, akin to the Buddhist concept of *sunyata* (the void). The 'Cloud of Unknowing' is perfectly described in the following extract:

By 'darkness' I mean 'a lack of knowing' – just as anything that you do not know or may have forgotten may be said to be 'dark' to you, for you cannot see it with your inward eye. For this reason it is called a 'cloud', not of the sky of course, but of 'unknowing', a cloud of unknowing between you and your God.

If ever you are to come to this cloud and live and work in it, as I suggest, then just as this cloud of unknowing is as it were above you, between you and God, so you must also put a cloud of forgetting beneath you and all creation. We are apt to think that we are very far from God because of this cloud of unknowing between us and him, but surely it would be more correct to say that we are much farther from him if there is no cloud of forgetting between us and the whole created world. Whenever I say 'the whole created world' I always mean not only the individual creatures therein, but everything connected with them. There is no exception whatever, whether you think of them as physical or spiritual beings, or of their states or actions, or of their goodness or badness. In a word, everything must be hidden under this cloud of forgetting.

(The Cloud of Unknowing)

Patiently accepting the darkness of non-vision, the meditator is instructed to pierce it with a succession of prayers or invocations, similar perhaps to mantra repetition:

Why does it penetrate heaven, this short little prayer of one syllable? Surely because it is prayed with a full heart, in the height and depth and length and breadth of the spirit of him that prays it. In the height, for it is with all the might of his spirit; in the depth, for in this little syllable is contained all that the spirit knows; in the length, for should it always feel as it does now, it would always cry to God as it now cries; in the breadth, for it would extend to all men what it wills for itself.

(The Cloud of Unknowing)

John of the Cross also speaks of darkness in which the soul must abide, and which separates him both from the common life of the senses below him and the heavenly vision, still veiled from him, which lies above:

What we here call the dark night is the absence of pleasure in all things. For as night is an absence of light and consequently, of all things visible by means of light, whereby the powers of sight are obscured and nullified, so it can be said also that the mortification of the appetites is night for the soul. For when the soul is deprived of its pleasure in all things, when its appetites fail, it is left, so to speak, in darkness and alone.

The soul that has denied and abandoned its pleasure in all things, mortifying its appetite for them, can be said to be in a sort of night, in darkness, which is simply an emptiness, an absence of all things within her.

The cause of this is, according to the philosophers, that once God is instilling soul into the body, that soul is like a smooth blank board with nothing painted on it, except so much as it learns through the senses. Otherwise, naturally, nothing is communicated to it. For so long as it remains in the body it is in a kind of dark prison. It knows nothing except what it manages to see through the windows of its cell, and if it cannot see through them it will see nothing in any other way. So if the soul receives no communication by way of the senses, which are the windows of its prison, naturally it can receive nothing by any other way.

(The Dark Night)

John of the Cross takes a more ascetic view of this sojourn in the void than the author of *The Cloud of Unknowing*. He speaks of mortifying where his English predecessor speaks more abstractly of 'self-noughting'. But John adds an explanation of this state, suggesting that its true cause is that God is feeding the soul with spiritual nourishment and that during the process of nourishment there must perforce be a separation both from the pleasures of the world and of human attachments, and from the vision that is to come.

The term 'dark night of the soul' is often used loosely today as being synonymous with depression or alienation. It is certainly true that there are many, like the girl whose narrative follows, who are described by doctors and psychiatrists as 'depressives' or 'mentally unstable', but who are in fact undergoing a profound spiritual crisis:

Up until I was thirteen I had experiences of transcendence – a great warmth and power beyond, which touched me. At about the age of thirteen I went through a period of nihilism and despair – the world felt a closed circuit, deserted by this presence, and I did not know how to reach 'God' amid urban life and the rat-race . . .

At fifteen I began to re-experience, more intensely than before, a feeling of blissful transcendence: light, life and joy mingled with pain, darkness and death, until the idea of a transcendent being no longer held. 'God' seemed personal, intimately connected with the world and ever-present. I saw things as an ever-flowing stream, with 'God' as the source and the current . . .

After months of intense mental concentration and intellectual synthesis I had a breakthrough: I suddenly 'saw' the world as if it had always been there. There was no gap, no barrier, all was inextricably bound, continuing, one great being. I cannot describe the extreme simplicity of what I saw – the plainness and unity . . .

No one about me understood the experience . . . When I left school I went to Israel for a year. I returned amid another rush of intense mystical experiences, which did not fit with the military situation in Israel . . . My GP, to whom I tried to express some of my disturbing experiences of being about to 'die', diagnosed me dangerously ill with schizophrenia! I was rushed into hospital and totally misunderstood for two months until my present husband appeared on the scene and re-diagnosed me as 'more of a mystic' and not at all schizophrenic, and discharged me.

(RERU 593)

The following example of rapid transition from darkness to light would seem to involve some form of self-abandonment to 'providence', with, in this instance, extremely positive results:

Often during my late twenties and early thirties I had a good deal of depression, not caused by any outward circumstances . . . at the age of thirty-three I felt I must be going mad. I felt shut up in a cocoon in complete isolation and could not get in touch with any-one . . . things came to such a pass and I was so tired of fighting that I said one day 'I can do no more. Let nature, or whatever is behind the universe, look after me now.'

Within a few days I passed from a hell to a heaven. It was as if the cocoon had burst and my eyes were opened and I saw.

The world was infinitely beautiful, full of light as if from an inner radiance. Everything was alive and God was present in all things; in fact, the earth, all plants and animals and people seemed to be made of God. All things were one, and I was one with all creation and held safe within a deep love. I was filled with peace and joy and with deep humility, and could only bow down in the holiness of the presence of God . . . if anyone had brought news that any member of my family had died, I should have laughed and said 'There is no death'. It was as if scales had fallen from my eyes and I saw the world as it truly was. How had I lived for thirty-three years and been so blind? This was the secret of the world, yet it all seemed so obvious and natural that I had no idea that I should not always see it so. I felt like going round and telling everyone that all things were one and that knowledge of this would cure all ills . . .

Psychologically, and for my own peace of mind, the effect [of the experience] has been of the greatest importance.   (RERU 388)

Among those who come to the various groups teaching medi-tation are many who have suffered from profound depressions, who have resorted to drugs or who have even attempted suicide. Such people of course need careful guidance, but it may reassure them to learn from John of the Cross that even in their darkest moments they are being nourished by an unseen force.

The darkness of the Christian tradition, first described by the sixth-century Syrian who wrote under the name of Dionysius the Areopagite, differs from the Buddhist *sunyata* in that it always carries some connotation of suffering. The void of Mahayana Buddhism is a state of egolessness – there is in it no self capable of suffering, no duality – a state in which the experiencer and the experienced are one.

Whereas for the author of *The Cloud of Unknowing* and John of the Cross the cloud represents a state which befalls a person and which will eventually be dispersed by the use of prayer or mantra, for the Buddhist it is a positive state to be attained by meditation. In the form of meditation recommended by Lama Govinda – a Buddhist monk of German birth – the meditator consciously visualizes the forms of the world and deliberately disperses them:

Sunyata is not 'nothingness' but rather no-*thing*-ness. It is the beginning and end of all things. If we want to make *sunyata* an experience instead of a mere concept . . . we must consciously go through the process of creation and dissolution, of becoming and dissolving and reintegrating in meditation. We must *experience* that form is emptiness and emptiness is form by consciously creating form, until it is visible to the inner eye and filled with life and significance, in order to reabsorb it bit by bit and stage by stage into *sunyata*, the all-embracing inner space. This is the dual process of meditation; it does not consist merely in the reversal of the creative process or in the negation of form, but contains both form-creation and form-dissolution, because *sunyata* can never become a living experience unless we have realised both poles of its incommensurable nature.

(Creative Meditation and Multi-dimensional Consciousness)

The Buddhist method of meditation begins with a simple exercise: the watching of the breath. Breathing leads to 'inspiration'; breathing is the one bodily activity that can be raised to the level of conscious action. This is not foreign to western tradition, in which *pneuma* (the breath) is also the soul. At first, the control of breath induces calm. This makes possible the opening of the inner eye by visualization; of the inner ear by mantras; and of the heart, in which the vital warmth is kindled. This too has its western parallel in the Jesus Prayer of the wandering Russian monk already quoted. Visualization of a Buddha figure involves no belief in superhuman beings, only an awareness of an enlightened state attainable by everybody. The Buddha is the meditator himself. Christian and Buddhist methods of meditation differ principally in the importance attributed to Christ and the Buddha respectively. Christ *is* the way; the Buddha *points* the way. As a historical figure he stands for the enlightenment that he attained. He has no special relationship to God. Indeed, God the Creator lies outside Buddhism, for which the highest good is the enlightenment of all sentient beings. Each person who attains enlightenment must dedicate his enlightenment to the benefit of the rest. For the Mahayana Buddhist at least there is no personal attainment. The Sangha, or community of saints, devotes itself to universal salvation.

But even this idea is not final. For, as the following extract from the *Diamond Sutra* explains, ultimately there are no separate beings at all:

Any good pious disciple who undertakes the practice of concentrating his mind in an effort to realize most perfect knowledge, should cherish only one thought, namely, when I attain this highest perfect wisdom, I will deliver all sentient beings into the eternal peace of Nirvana. If this purpose and vow is sincere, these sentient beings are already delivered. And yet, if the full truth is realized, one would know that not a single sentient being has ever been delivered. And why? Because if the great Bodhisattvas have kept in mind any such arbitrary conceptions as one's own self, other selves, living beings, or a universal self, they could not be called perfectly enlightened ones. And what does this mean? It means that there are no sentient beings to be delivered and there is no selfhood that can begin the practice of seeking to attain most perfect knowledge.

(Diamond Sutra)

Buddhist and Christian alike postulate a process of enlightenment that requires special actions and special guidance. Contrary to both, the Sufi cuts short the whole cycle of union and separation, of fullness and void, by concentrating on love. For him, the soul's adoration of God, God's desire for the individual soul, eliminates all process of gradual approach through darkness.

Two ecstatic poems from the *Diwan* of Mansur Hallaj proclaim the immediacy of enlightenment:

I have two watchers (my ears) who observe who I love; two more (my eyes) who observe that Your eyes are upon me. No thought but of You crosses my secret heart; my tongue speaks no word but of Your love. If I look to the east, You are the risen sun; to the west, You are straight before me. If I look up, You are what stretches above; or down, You are everywhere. You give everything its place but have Yourself no place. You are in all things perishable, but You are not perishable. You are my heart, my spirit, my inspiration, the rhythm of my breath and the kernel of my organic being.

(Diwan, lxiv)

You have left me? No, You have not left my consciousness, whose joy and delight You have become. And separation falls apart of itself, and the state of abandonment is again transformed to presence in the mysterious depths of my thought. In my consciousness You precede the power of thought. By day You are truly my companion. You hold converse with me in the darkness.

(Diwan, xxv)

Jakob Boehme, the seventeenth-century Protestant mystic, in his dialogue *Of the Supersensual Life*, gives a more specific explanation concerning the way beyond thought. He clearly recommends no action on the part of the meditator, but a cessation of action, such as his Sufi predecessor achieved in a moment of love:

The disciple said to his master: 'Sir, how may I come to the supersensual life, so that I may see God, and hear my God speak?'

The master answered and said: 'Son, when thou canst throw thyself into that, where no creature dwelleth, though it be but for a moment, then thou hearest what God speaketh.'

Disciple 'Is that where no creature dwelleth near at hand; or is it afar off?'

Master 'It is in thee. And if thou canst, my son, for a while but cease from all thy thinking and willing, then thou shalt hear the unspeakable words of God.'

Disciple 'How can I hear him speak, when I stand still from thinking and willing?'

Master 'When thou standest still from the thinking of self, and the willing of self; when both thy intellect and will are quiet, and passive to the impressions of the Eternal Word and Spirit; and when thy soul is winged up, and above that which is temporal, the outward senses and the imagination being locked up by holy abstraction, then the eternal hearing, seeing, and speaking will be revealed in thee; and so God heareth and seeth through thee, being now the organ of his spirit; and so God speaketh in thee, and whispereth to thy spirit, and thy spirit heareth his voice. Blessed art thou therefore if that thou canst stand still from self-thinking and self-willing, and canst stop the wheel of thy imagination and senses; forasmuch as hereby thou mayest arrive at length to see the great salvation of God, being made capable of all manner of divine sensations and heavenly communications.

(The Signature of All Things)

Krishnamurti, who resolutely refuses to regard himself as a teacher, takes a short cut. He holds that there is no need for any special practice, or course of instruction in meditation, no need for a teacher or a teaching. 'There is nowhere to go', he says in effect. 'If you do not seek to travel, you are there already':

Meditation is a never-ending movement. You can never say that you are meditating or set aside a period for meditation. It isn't at your command. Its benediction doesn't come to you because you lead a systemized life or follow a particular routine or morality. It comes only when your heart is really open. Not opened by the key of thought, not made safe by the intellect, but when it is as open as the skies without a cloud; then it comes without your knowing, without your invitation. But you can never guard it, keep it, worship it. If you try, it will never come again: do what you will, it will avoid you. In meditation, you are not important, you have no place in it; the beauty of it is not you, but in itself. And to this you can add nothing. Don't look out of the window hoping to catch it unawares, or sit in a darkened room waiting for it; it comes only when you are not there at all, and its bliss has no continuity.

(The Second Penguin Krishnamurti Reader)

How many people who have never consciously practised meditation have in fact known meditation in Krishnamurti's sense of the term?

We conclude the section with an example of what Krishnamurti would, in our opinion, regard as 'spontaneous meditation':

I was sitting on a low wall on the outskirts of the town of Chittagong. Across the road was a wayside teashop stall, with the proprietor in full view serving two customers. The branches of two small trees next to the stall waved in the moderately strong breeze and the sun shone with some glare on the white dusty road, along which came some fishermen with baskets of fish on their heads. From the second storey of a nearby building I could hear a nautch tune. Then, as the fishermen came abreast of me, one fish still alive, flapped up and seemed to stand on its tail and bow. I felt great compassion for the fish.

Suddenly everything was transformed, transfigured, translated, transcended. All was fused into one. I was the fish. The sun sang and the road sang. The music shone. The hands of the stall-keeper danced. All in time with the same music. They were the music and I was the music and I was the fish, the fishermen, the hands of the stall-keeper, the trees, the branches, the road, the sun, the music; all one and nothing separate. Not parts of the one but the one itself.

(RERU 1284)

2 Right Action

Meditational practice can occupy only a small proportion of a person's day. Unless one is a monk or nun living in a recluse community, the greater part of the day is spent in actions which bring one into the company of other people. One is concerned with one's job and with family relations. During the greater part of the day one seldom thinks of meditation, being fully immersed in the superficial world, which then seems the only reality. Far ahead lies that state when meditation will be present throughout the actions of the day. This is the beginning of enlightenment, of which most people have had no more than a premonitory glimpse.

The attitude of religious teachers to the world of action differs widely. Some Hindus regard it as entirely illusory and seek to spend their whole lives withdrawn from it. Some modern schools of meditation suggest that the things of this world will easily fall into place for the meditator: 'Meditate', says the Maharishi Mahesh Yogi, 'and nature will support you.' Transcendental Meditation has nothing to say about right actions, except that experience of meditation will lead automatically to right behaviour.

The principal religions, in their present formalized state, are greatly concerned with rules of action. They prescribe what a person should eat and when, what prayers or rituals he should perform on what days, whom he should regard as his neighbour and how he shall treat him. Such concerns with the details of action have led to religious schisms and wars.

Neither the Buddhists nor the Christian mystics have ignored the field of action. But perhaps the outstanding description of action, correctly performed, occurs in the Hindu scripture, the

Bhagavad Gita. Arjuna, a warrior, is irresolute; he cannot decide to take part in a battle which, whatever its results, will lead to the death of friends and relatives whom he sees in both opposing armies. At this juncture, his charioteer, who is in fact the god Krishna in disguise, gives him the following advice:

Set thy heart upon thy work, but never on its reward. Work not for a reward; but never cease to do thy work.

Do thy work in the peace of Yoga and, free from selfish desires, be not moved in success or in failure. Yoga is evenness of mind – a peace that is ever the same.

Work done for a reward is much lower than work done in the Yoga of wisdom. Seek salvation in the wisdom of reason. How poor are those who work for a reward!

In this wisdom a man goes beyond what is well done and what is not well done. Go thou therefore to wisdom: Yoga is wisdom in work . . .

When thy mind leaves behind its dark forest of delusion, thou shalt go beyond the scriptures of times past and still to come.

When thy mind, that may be wavering in the contradictions of many scriptures, shall rest unshaken in divine contemplation then the goal of Yoga is thine.

(Bhagavad Gita)

A person must not hold back in the name of meditation from performing his duty; nor must he be deluded into the thought that it is his actions that have led to the apparent results. His responsibility is limited to his own field of decision, and his power of decision is limited to his choice of attitude towards what are in fact necessary actions. Right action is disinterested action without desire for self-aggrandizement, fame, profit or power. The perfect action is one performed with attention to the action alone. In this spirit, Prince Wen Hui's cook in the Taoist parable of Chuang Tzu perfected the cutting up of meat:

Prince Hui's cook was cutting up a bullock. Every blow of his hand, every heave of his shoulders, every tread of his foot, every thrust of his knee, every *whshh* of rent flesh, every *chhk* of the chopper, was in perfect harmony – rhythmical like the dance of the Mulberry Grove, simultaneous like the chords of the Ching Shou.

'Well done!' cried the Prince; 'yours is skill indeed.'

'Sire,' replied the cook. 'I have always devoted myself to Tao. It is better than skill. When I first began to cut up bullocks, I saw before me simply *whole* bullocks. After three years' practice, I saw no more whole animals. And now I work with my mind and not with my eye. When my senses bid me stop, but my mind urges me on, I fall back upon eternal principles. I follow such openings or cavities as there may be, according to the natural constitution of the animal. I do not attempt to cut through joints; still less through large bones. A good cook changes his chopper once a year – because he cuts. An ordinary cook, once a month – because he hacks. But I have had this chopper nineteen years, and although I have cut up many thousand bullocks, its edge is as if fresh from the whetstone.'

(*Musings of a Chinese Mystic*)

From Chuang Tzu we learn that right action is almost effortless. There is a telling application here to our modern condition, in which so many people complain of tension and exhaustion, anxiety and restlessness. Are they perhaps performing their everyday actions with too little attention and minds bent not on the action itself, but on the hoped-for or expected results? Their knives are blunted by the first lump of unexpected gristle. The same lesson is drawn by an anonymous Hassidic rabbi, probably of the eighteenth century:

Once Rabbi Hayyim of Krosno, a disciple of the Baal Shem's, was watching a rope dance together with his disciples. He was so absorbed in the spectacle that they asked him what it was that riveted his gaze to this foolish performance. 'This man', he said, 'is risking his life, and I cannot say why. But I am quite sure that while he is walking the rope, he is not thinking of the fact that he is earning a hundred gulden by what he is doing, for if he did, he would fall.'

(Martin Buber, *Tales of the Hassidim*)

Arjuna, the prince's cook, the rope dancer – each was, or was enjoined to be, single-pointed, mindful only of the action in hand, never of its possible outcome. Everything hinges not so much on the right action as on the right attitude. This thought was particularly stressed by the Sufis who, being for the most part merchants, craftsmen and officials in the Muslim cities of the early Middle Ages, paid due attention to the market place of the world. The congregation should attend the mosque at the proper hour. But he who comes late with the right thought in his heart causes the prayers of all the others to be acceptable to God. This we learn from one of those beautiful parables inset in the long and rather tedious poems of the thirteenth-century Persian poet, Jalal-uddin Rumi:

> A certain man was going into the mosque as the people were coming out. He began to ask one of them, saying, 'What ails the congregation that they are coming out of the mosque so soon?'
>
> That person said to him, 'The Prophet has prayed with the congregation and finished his communion. Why art thou going in, O foolish man, when the Prophet has already given the blessing?'
>
> He cried, 'Ah!' and smoke issued from that burning sigh: his sigh was giving forth the smell of blood from his heart.
>
> One of the congregation said, 'Give me this sigh and my prayers are thine.'
>
> He answered, 'I give the sigh and accept the prayers.' He, the other, took that sigh with a hundred yearnings towards God.
>
> At night whilst he was asleep, a voice said to him, 'Thou hast bought the water of life and salvation. In honour of this choice and this appropriation the prayers of all the people have been accepted.'
>
> *(Mathnawi)*

Sufi writings frequently express an intoxication with the love of God. They are seldom sober in their imagery, or technical like the Buddhists in their instructions to the seeker after righteousness. Yet their message does not essentially differ from that of the Buddhist who extols the virtues of mindfulness with all the sobriety of a teacher dealing with an attentive pupil. The Buddhist has no contempt for the fool. It is the enlightened man's duty to deliver all, wise and fools alike, from the wheel of repeated lives; and to save him he enjoins him to mindfulness. He may not fear the fool nor condemn him, but he is nevertheless on his guard against the wandering and unrestrained mind:

So you should preserve mindfulness and self-possession in all actions such as sitting, looking round and speaking. He who has established mindfulness as a doorkeeper at the gate cannot be overpowered by sins, even as enemies cannot conquer a well-guarded town. He who lacks the defensive armour of mindfulness is indeed a target for sins, even as a warrior in battle who has no armour, is exposed to the arrows of his foes.

(*The Bodhicaryavatara of Shantideva*)

The Greek Church Fathers are equally specific concerning the methods of achieving mindfulness or sobriety. Hesychius of Jerusalem, a fifth-century monk, is writing, like the Buddhist author just quoted, for monks who are following a rule of prayer and silence:

Sobriety is the steadfast setting up of the thought of the mind and posting it at the door of the heart, so that it sees alien thoughts as they come, those thieves and robbers, and hears what these destroyers say and do; and sees what is the image inscribed and figured in them by the demons, who are trying thus to seduce the mind by fantasy. For this work, when it is done with loving effort, reveals to us very fundamentally and clearly by experience, the art of mental war and brings skill in it.

(*Philokalia*)

Both the Church Fathers and the Buddhists regard the attitude of watchfulness as an essential protection against wandering thoughts, which are like wild animals. Right action is seen to lie not in the choice of behaving in this or that way, but in preserving a mindful attitude in all eventualities. The accent throughout is on the moment. What may follow should not be dwelt upon. Desire for results is a sure and destructive enemy of mindfulness.

Right action is the complement of meditation. Without it, meditation may produce illusions. According to their enemies in the Church, some heretical sects of the Middle Ages believed that to the perfect or enlightened all actions are permissible. A similar delusion has recently appeared among groups in California who, believing themselves to be enlightened, have even committed murder.

Mindfulness without meditation also leads into great dangers, not in the realm of criminality or unprincipled actions by the self-styled elect, but rather in the field of psychological imbalance.

The teachings of Gurdjieff and Ouspensky in the present century are a prime example of this danger. It is significant that several of the quotations chosen to demonstrate the theme of right action can be found in an anonymous anthology, privately printed during the war years under the title *Values*. It was compiled by one of Gurdjieff's earliest followers in the west, the scientist J. G. Bennett.

The philosophical system of Gurdjieff and Ouspensky originated in the near east and its first appearance was in Moscow in the early years of the First World War. Gurdjieff was mysterious about the source of these ideas, which he taught to small groups under the pledge of secrecy. Sometimes he claimed to have learnt them from some 'remarkable men' during travels in central Asia; sometimes he even claimed to have invented them himself.

Gurdjieff was a Georgian of little formal education, who adopted the pose of a magician and certainly appeared at times to possess supernormal powers. His pupil, P. D. Ouspensky, was a scientific journalist, an intellectual and a gentleman. Learning 'the System' from Gurdjieff, he taught it in London and America between the late twenties and his death in 1949. For those years 'The Work', as it was called by its disciples, was perhaps the most important source of new thought concerning man's place in the universe available in the west. On analysis it can be seen to contain elements of theosophy, sufism and the popular science of the nineteenth century. From the start, Gurdjieff relied more on his power to dominate than his capacity to teach. Ouspensky, taking the system more seriously as a vehicle of teaching, saw its defects and endeavoured to remedy them.

What for many people Ouspensky failed to see was that the system lacked an essential feature, some teaching on prayer or meditation, without which it was a useless intellectual construction. Whether those unknown men from whom Gurdjieff learnt it practised meditation but did not teach it to him, or whether he left them too soon thinking that he had the essential secret and could now set up as a teacher, is not known and never will be. Gurdjieff's system was flawed from the start. But not until the end of his life did Ouspensky himself see that interpreting the world from a philosophical diagram, without any practical methods of spiritual working, was not merely ineffective but psychologically dangerous.

The central theme of Gurdjieff's system was the necessity for right action. Man was, according to him, an automaton, a machine that worked entirely from 'negative emotions': self-love, fear, hate, jealousy. In order to be real he must wake up from his negative dreams, although, according to the System, all the powers of nature were geared against his doing so. The analysis was not unlike that of Buddhism:

Now the Exalted One thus addressed the brethren: 'Through not understanding, through not penetrating the Four Noble Truths, brethren, we have run on and wandered round this long, long journey [of rebirth], both you and I. What are those four?

The Noble Truth of ill: the Noble Truth of the arising of ill: the Noble Truth of the ceasing of ill: the Noble Truth of the way leading to the ceasing of ill.

But, brethren, when these four noble truths are understood and penetrated, then is uprooted the craving for existence, cut off is the thread that leadeth to rebirth, then is there no more coming to be.

(*Some Sayings of the Buddha*)

The System did not allow such a possibility of escape from the wheel of rebirth except in the rarest of cases. Most people, in Gurdjieff's view, were fools. But a person's foolish or limited vision may suddenly be dispelled:

One day I was in an art gallery looking with great absorption at a picture. Suddenly I felt that my consciousness was not only in me but all around me in the room. I felt that not only had the lid been taken off my head, but that I had escaped outside, where I belonged. There was an experience of great peace and contentment, also heightened awareness. I really 'saw' the room for the first time – the picture, floors, walls, light, shade and the three-dimensional effect of the seats and cases. Also I saw that the other people in the room were 'sleep-walking' compared to my condition. I did not want to return to my normal condition, as it seemed so easy and natural to stay happy as I was. At that point the warden of the room, who must have noticed that I was standing still as a statue, came over and offered me a sweet, saying it

would help me concentrate. I took one and spoke to him for some time
while the ecstatic experience gradually slipped away . . .

I tried to bring back this experience by concentration and meditation,
without results. It seemed the harder I tried to get this experience the
less likely I was to achieve it.

(RERU 1228)

Gurdjieff purported to offer secrets of the universe hidden
from common men. His method was to shock his disciple into
wakefulness by stripping him of all his protective armour of
personality, to strip him of his mask. This may suggest the
methods of Zen, but *satori* – the sudden illumination that over-
takes a Zen adept after long reflection on a seemingly illogical and
insoluble problem – does not arise from a 'system of thought'. It
gives him a new method of thinking:

When Chao-chou came to study Zen under Nan-ch'uan, he asked,
'What is the Tao (or the Way)?' Nan-ch'uan replied: 'Your everyday
mind, that is the Tao.'

The way to self-realization is presumed by many to start somewhere outside everyday thought and action, in an esoteric system
perhaps to be learnt from a magician. But in fact it starts in the
midst of life. The Zen *koan* just quoted brings to mind Ouspensky's last meetings with his followers, when, as a dying man, he
tried to tell them that Gurdjieff's system on which they relied was
valueless. 'Be simpler', he told them. 'Start from something you
know.' His followers were bewildered and continued to ask him
questions in the language of Gurdjieff's system, all of which he
stonewalled.

'Be simple. Start from what you know' is the fundamental rule
for right thought, which will lead to right action. Prayer and
meditation will expand the area of the known. The way begins
from some quite familiar place in the mind. The twofold entrance
to the way by reason and conduct is in essence one:

There are many ways to enter the Path, but briefly speaking they are
of two sorts only. The one is 'Entrance by Reason' and the other is
'Entrance by Conduct'. By 'Entrance by Reason' we mean the realization of the spirit of Buddhism by the aid of the scriptural teaching.

We then come to have a deep faith in the true nature which is the same in all sentient beings. The reason why it does not manifest itself is due to the overwrapping of external objects and false thoughts. When a man, abandoning the false and embracing the true, in singleness of thought practises wall-gazing he finds that there is neither self nor other, that the masses and the worthies are of one essence, and he firmly holds on to this belief and never moves away therefrom. He will not then be a slave to words, for he is in silent communion with the reason itself, free from conceptual discrimination; he is serene and not-acting. This is called 'Entrance by Reason'.

By 'Entrance by Conduct' is meant the four acts in which all other acts are included. What are the four? 1. To know how to requite hatred. 2. To be obedient to karma. 3. Not to crave anything. 4. To be in accord with the Dharma.

(D. T. Suzuki, *Manual of Zen Buddhism*)

This 'Twofold entrance to the Way' is no doubt visible to one who has resolved to follow Zen. Such a person may have in his heart some inkling of what it is to be a *bodhisattva* – one who has passed beyond the self-cherishing stage of life and who can dedicate the merits earned by his practice to the benefit of others. Most of these others, by contrast, are still deep in attachment to self. But what is self? Central to the practices of the Gurdjieff system was the attempt at 'self-remembering'. But the self to be remembered was swathed in thick layers of 'false personality'. According to the system, this unreal self-image with which we attempt to convince ourselves and our neighbours of our only reality obscures that true self which we wish to remember. 'The nearest we come to self-remembering', Ouspensky would repeat in the days of his attachment to the system, 'is when we know that we do not remember ourselves.' He valued those sporadic experiences of a deeper reality of which we have given many instances in this book. But he did not attach great importance to them, comparing them to the chance picking up of a sixpence.

Attempts at 'self-remembering' by people in 'the Work' were occasional and unrewarding. Attention to breathing was discouraged, since Ouspensky had himself had a bad experience during some such experiments, and meditation was unknown.

Experiments with the Jesus Prayer, even with drugs, were not conspicuously successful.

The twofold entrance was in those days hidden, yet 'know thyself' had been the cardinal watchword of every teaching. Let us illustrate the chance confrontation with self by an elderly man's recollection of a childhood incident in an Ipswich barber's shop:

I recall several 'moments' in childhood. I see these now as flashes of self-consciousness (consciousness of the true Self). It was a sense of otherness rather than of freedom of responsibility. It was not associated with religion, but rather with such strange moments as sitting in a barber's shop at the age of seven and seeing the back of my head reflected in the mirror in front of me and a further reflection of my face and so on. If I am not clear, let me add that there were two lines of mirrors, one on either side of the shop. I can visualize this experience today, some sixty-eight years later.

(J.M.C.)

What is most remarkable about this very common incident is that the boy had no memory of self at all. 'Self' was unreal, a mere sequence of diminishing reflections in receding mirrors. It was an intimation of his essential unreality.

A far more vivid description of such a confrontation – the picking up not of sixpence but of a golden sovereign – is given by J. A. Symonds in a well-known narrative reproduced in William James's *Varieties of Religious Experience*. This provides a far more circumstantial account of the emergence of the true self in adult life:

Suddenly, at church, or in company, or when I was reading, and always, I think, when my muscles were at rest, I felt the approach of the mood. Irresistibly it took possession of my mind and will, lasted what seemed an eternity, and disappeared in a series of rapid sensations which resembled the awakening from anaesthetic influence. One reason why I disliked this kind of trance was that I could not describe it to myself. I cannot even now find words to render it intelligible. It consisted of a gradual but swiftly progressive obliteration of space, time, sensation, and the multitudinous factors of experience which seem to qualify what we are pleased to call our Self. In proportion as these conditions of ordinary consciousness were subtracted, the sense of an underlying or essential consciousness acquired intensity. At last nothing remained but a pure, absolute, abstract Self. The universe became without form and void of content. But Self persisted, formidable in its vivid keenness, feeling the most poignant doubt about reality, ready, as it seemed, to find existence break as it breaks a bubble about it. And what then? The apprehension of a coming dissolution, the grim conviction that this state was the last state of the conscious Self, the sense that I had followed the last thread of being to the verge of the abyss and had arrived at demonstration of eternal Maya or illusion, stirred, or seemed to stir me up again. The return to ordinary conditions of sentient existence began by my first recovering the power of touch, and then by the influx of familiar impressions and diurnal interests.

(quoted in *The Varieties of Religious Experience*)

Dr Crichton-Browne, who fills William James's footnotes with unlikely physical explanations of the experiences collected by the American philosopher, suggests that Symonds' 'higher nerve centres' were to some extent 'enfeebled'. James himself passes on from the consideration of Symonds' 'trances' to examine certain similar accounts of experiences under drugs. But Symonds himself analysed the situation quite clearly; and his judgement would have been reinforced had he read any of the Hindu or Buddhist scriptures which Dr Max Müller was translating in the latter part of the nineteenth century.

Symonds was not the only Victorian writer to record such 'trances', but what distinguishes his repeated lapses from the phenomenal world is his fear that if the experience were ever to be completed he would never get back. He does not seem to have regarded the revelations of 'essential consciousness' as fundamentally religious, and he did not welcome them. Tennyson, on the other hand, used a rough and ready form of mantra meditation to induce them. We quote his son's *Memoir*:

It was a kind of waking trance which I have frequently had, quite up from boyhood, when I have been all alone. This has generally come upon me through repeating my own name two or three times to myself silently, till all at once, as it were out of the intensity of the consciousness of individuality, the individuality itself seemed to dissolve and fade away into boundless being, and this not a confused state, but the clearest of the clearest, the surest of the surest, the weirdest of the weirdest, utterly beyond words where death was an almost laughable impossibility, the loss of personality (if so it were) being no extinction but the only true life . . . This might be the state which St Paul describes. Whether in the body I cannot tell or whether out of the body I cannot tell.

Tennyson made the necessary connection with the form of 'self-discovery' mentioned by St Paul. But there is no doubt that in the age of agnosticism Symonds' reaction to such momentary encounters with the true self is the more typical. At best, the subject may be puzzled, and even attempt with Crichton-Browne to discover some physical explanation. This was the case with the boy of the Ipswich barber's shop when a similar experience occurred some twelve years later, by which time he was a Cambridge undergraduate:

Once, crossing the college court late at night, I had one of those experiences of timelessness that I'd had, though less intensely as it seemed to me, as a child. It was a moonless night, without clouds, the vault of the stars was vast and still. As I came out into the dark, something changed inside me – almost with a click, like the adjustment of a mechanism – that related me – or rather something that was not the habitual me – to the night and something beyond it. I cannot describe this *moment* more precisely . . .

Tennyson was able to recognize his state of waking trance – it is really nothing like a trance – as that of very clear consciousness. He understood that true individuality is only present when common individuality has faded. The experience had occurred by apparent chance, but he knew how to lay himself open to its return. When I learnt mantra meditation I recognized that Tennyson had half – but only half – guessed the secret. But in my Cambridge days, I did not know what my experience was, or how to find it again. I looked up into the sky again and again, night after night, and nothing came. Hardly even the memory of that surprising state of other consciousness was to be found. Perhaps, I thought, it was just some trick of the digestion, or the effect of coming out of a hot room into the cold night air. But the experience did recur several times in the next months –

though not so intensely, since I only remember that it came but have
no picture of the time or scene.

(J.M.C.)

Common to this and many such experiences of the last hundred
or so years is that they arouse no religious associations in the subject. Many of those recorded by William James occurred to
clergymen or other committed Christians and resulted in a
strengthening or confirmation of religious belief. But latterly
these experiences have frequently been recorded by agnostics.
Among those persons already quoted, several specifically deny
religious belief. The occurrence is seen as a strange psychological
happening from which no deductions can be made.

Ouspensky relates an experiment on himself, possibly under
drugs, in the deliberate expansion of consciousness:

Once, I remember, in a particularly vividly expressed new state,
that is, when I understood very clearly all I wished to understand, I
decided to find some formula, some key, which I should be able, so to
speak, to throw across to myself for the next day. I decided to sum up
shortly all I understood at that moment and write down, if possible in
one sentence, what it was necessary to do in order to bring myself into
the same state immediately, by one turn of thought without any
preliminary preparation, since this appeared possible to me all the time.
I found this formula and wrote it down with a pencil on a piece of
paper.
On the following day I read the sentence, 'Think in other categories'.
(A New Model of the Universe)

In his final meetings with his followers, Ouspensky insisted on
this need to think afresh. We have already mentioned his dictum
to 'be simpler; start from what you know'. But his followers
tended to think of 'new categories' as no more than old categories
revived. 'Let us start', said one of his intimates, 'by looking at the
Sankya system of Indian philosophy.' Within a few months of
his death, everyone seemed to have forgotten his answer to the
surgeon, Kenneth Walker, who asked painfully during one of
those last meetings: 'Mr Ouspensky, are you not going to resume
teaching the System?' 'There is no system', Ouspensky answered.
But systems of thought are hypnotic. Within a few months of

his death, most of his followers had either joined Gurdjieff in Paris or Mme Ouspensky in America, or were laboriously re-formulating the system in slightly different language.

'Be simpler', demanded Ouspensky, and waited for a question that would enable him to speak. Once when we came for a meeting we were greeted with the message that since there were no questions there would be no meeting. Perhaps the questions he had hoped for were like those asked of the great Tibetan yogi of the eleventh century, Milarepa, on his deathbed. For his disciples' questions enabled him to make a clear statement of his final testimony:

'As to how ye are to carry the religious teachings into practice in your everyday life, bear in mind the following: some there may be among you who are proud of their apparent sanctity, but who, at heart, are really devoted to acquiring name and fame in this world; they dispense a hundred necessary and unnecessary things in charity, hoping thereby to reap a liberal return. This, though displeasing to the divinities gifted with divine vision, is persevered in by selfish beings of obscured vision. The hypocrisy of thus hankering after the rich juices of this world, while outwardly appearing pious and devout, because unable to face the ridicule of the world is like partaking of delicacies and rich food mixed with deadly aconite. Therefore, drink not the venom of desire for worldly fame and name; but casting aside all the fetters of worldly duties, which but lead to this desire, devote yourselves to sincere and earnest devotion.'

The disciples then inquired if they could engage in worldly duties, in a small way, for the benefit of others, and he said: 'If there be not the least self-interest attached to such duties, it is permissible. But such detachment is indeed rare; and works performed for the good of others seldom succeed if not wholly freed from self-interest. Even without seeking to benefit others, it is with difficulty that works done even in one's own interest are successful. It is as if a man helplessly drowning were to try to save another man in the same predicament. One should not be over-anxious and hasty in setting out to serve others before one hath oneself realized Truth in its fullness; to be so, would be like the blind leading the blind. As long as the sky endureth, so long will there be no end of sentient beings for one to serve; and to everyone cometh the opportunity for such service. Till the opportunity come, I exhort each of you to have but the one resolve, namely, to attain Buddhahood for the good of all living things.'

(Evans-Wentz, *Tibet's Great Yogi, Milarepa*)

Milarepa reduces the whole of a person's duty to a single formula: that Buddhahood must be sought not for personal salvation, but for the benefit of all sentient beings. The hope for a 'liberal return' for deeds of kindness is, from the Buddhist standpoint, the greatest stumbling-block of would-be travellers on the path. Krishna preached to Arjuna the virtues of detachment, the necessity for disinterested action. Yet, however disinterested an action, however simply it is performed, with however little thought for its success or failure, its very performance does bring 'merit' – in the Buddhist term – to the performer. It is here that to think in new categories becomes essential. The accent must be on the deed not the doer.

One can see disinterested action at work in the person of the French lay brother Lawrence, who worked in the kitchen or went out to buy wine for his community. Brother Lawrence was almost certainly the spiritual superior of the monks whom he served. But having started life as a footman he was their social inferior, compelled to carry out tasks that he did not like and actually found difficult on account of his lameness. A small book about him entitled *The Practice of the Presence of God* has, like the *Spiritual Guide* of Molinos, circulated in Protestant rather than Catholic countries. A very personal flavour is conveyed by such passages as the following, in which the writer of the memoir is reporting Brother Lawrence's account of his recent occupations:

That he had been lately sent into Burgundy, to buy the provision of wine for the society, which was a very unwelcome task for him, because he had no turn for business and because he was lame, and could not go about the boat but by rolling himself over the casks. That however he gave himself no uneasiness about it, nor about the purchase of the wine. That he said to God, it was His business he was about, and that he afterwards found it very well performed. That he had been sent into Auvergne the year before upon the same account; that he could not tell how the matter passed, but that it proved very well.

So likewise, in his business in the kitchen (to which he had naturally a great aversion), having accustomed himself to do everything there for the love of God, and with prayer, upon all occasions, for His grace to do the work well, he had found everything easy, during the fifteen years that he had been employed there.

That he was very well pleased with the post he was now in; but that he was as ready to quit that as the former, since he was always pleasing himself in every condition, by doing little things for the love of God.

(The Practice of the Presence of God)

Brother Lawrence's was an ordinary life. If he had not met the anonymous author of the memoir, he would have worked and died quite unknown. Similarly with Molinos, were it not for some gossip-loving visitors to Rome who attended his trial, his behaviour before the inquisitors would not have been recorded. The truly humble remains at rest in the quietude of his heart.

Up to the moment of sentence, Molinos had knelt impassively before the court holding a burning candle. The attitude was one of contrition. But to the last, he was confident that he was no heretic. In the end, as he left the court for his last nine years of oblivion, he is reported to have said to the priest who accompanied him: 'On the Judgement Day we shall see which of us is right, you or I.' We do not have to wait so long. Throughout the two years of his intermittent trial, Molinos observed a continuous rightness of action which was clearly based on rightness of thought, grounded in meditation; and this at least persuaded his judges to treat him with respect.

Socrates, confronting compulsory suicide by poison for the teaching of ideas considered dangerous to Athenian orthodoxy, spoke with a similar withdrawn objectivity in his final conversation with his friends:

'Someone had better bring in the poison, if it is ready prepared; if not, tell the man to prepare it.'

'But surely, Socrates,' said Crito, 'the sun is still upon the mountains; it has not gone down yet. Besides, I know that in other cases people have dinner and enjoy their wine, long after they receive the warning; and only drink the poison quite late at night. No need to hurry; there is still plenty of time.'

'It is natural that these people whom you speak of should act in that way, Crito,' said Socrates, 'because they think that they gain by it. And it is also natural that I should not; because I believe that I should gain nothing by drinking the poison a little later – I should only make myself ridiculous in my own eyes if I clung to life and hugged it when it has no more to offer. Come, do as I say and don't make difficulties.'

(The Last Days of Socrates)

Andrew Marvell's lines on the execution of Charles I give a poetic, not a literal, account of the king's 'right action' as another victim of political expediency:

> That thence the Royal Actor borne
> The tragic scaffold might adorn:
> While round the armèd bands
> Did clap their bloody hands.
>
> He nothing common did or mean
> Upon that memorable scene,
> But with his keener eye
> The axe's edge did try;
>
> Nor call'd the gods with vulgar spight
> To vindicate his helpless right;
> But bow'd his comely head
> Down, as upon a bed.
>
> (from *Ode upon Cromwell's Return from Ireland*)

This is perhaps reminiscent of Thomas More's encouragement to his executioner as he mounted the scaffold:

'I beseech you, good Master Pope, to be a mean unto his Highness that my daughter Margaret may be at my burial.'

'The King is content already', quoth Master Pope, 'that your wife, children, and other your friends shall have liberty to be present thereat.'

'O how much beholden then', said Sir Thomas More, 'am I to his Grace, that unto my poor burial vouchsafeth to have so gracious consideration.' Pope burst into tears. More comforted him:

'Quiet yourself, good Master Pope, and be not discomforted; for I trust that we shall, once in Heaven, see each other full merrily where we shall be sure to live and love together, in joyful bliss eternally.'

(R. W. Chambers, *Thomas More*)

Some who have suffered similar or even more terrible ends have lacked that essential rightness of thought that one sees in Socrates, Molinos, Charles I and Thomas More – that certainty and composure that comes of a mind at one with the Self. Joan of Arc, who likewise suffered a political execution for behaviour that was disturbing to the thought-censors of the day, was bewildered, faced as she was by inquisitors far more intelligent than she, and informed that the inner voice on which she had relied was perhaps no more than the prompting of the devil. Yet the brief eye-witness account of her death by burning testifies to an inner certainty which moved many hardened participants in her ugly trial and execution to tears:

... Master Pierre Maurice visited her that morning, before she was led to the sermon in the Vieux Marché; and Joan said to him: 'Master Pierre, where shall I be tonight?' And Master Pierre answered her: 'Do you not trust in God?' She said that she did and that, with God's aid, she would be in Paradise. This I have from Master Pierre himself. When Joan saw the fire set to the wood, she began to cry aloud: 'Jesus! Jesus!' and right up to her death she went on crying: 'Jesus!' And when she was dead, being afraid that it might be said that she had escaped, the English told the executioner to push the fire back a little so that the spectators could see her dead, and no one could say that she had escaped ...

... I heard Master Jean Alepée, then Canon of Rouen, who was present at Joan's death and wept abundantly, say in my presence and in the presence of those around me: 'I wish that my soul were where I believe the soul of that woman to be.'

(R. Pernoud, *The Retrial of Joan of Arc*)

There are innumerable instances of courage under martyrdom. The church calendar abounds in well-authenticated tales of impassiveness under torture and in the face of death, made possible by a form of 'recollection' which enables the sufferer to witness his or her ordeal without being fully immersed in it. This control is attained by a change in the level of thought which the religious would call an access of faith.

But this acquisition of strength under desperate conditions has come also to irreligious people. A few years ago an elderly communist of the Bela Kun era described her long and solitary imprisonment under the Stalinist regime in Hungary. She kept herself sane until her eventual release by deliberate exercise of thought, reconstructing in her mind every detail of places and events from before her imprisonment. Unwittingly, she was following a little-known technique of Buddhist meditation. This carefully planned withdrawal to a deeper level of experience enabled her to withstand the cross-examination of her inquisitors and her long isolation. Going back to a more real epoch in her life, she may be said to have practised a form of 'self-remembering', though with no esoteric or spiritual overtones.

Others who have resisted solitary confinement and brain-washing in recent times have resorted to similar practices to preserve their sanity. Arthur Koestler, for example, while under sentence of death in one of Franco's prisons, devised similar exercises in mindfulness which saved him from the worst on-slaughts of fear and despair. He was in fact practising a form of mantra meditation:

One of my magic remedies was a certain quotation from a certain work of Thomas Mann's; its efficacy never failed. Sometimes, during an attack of fear, I repeated the same verse thirty or forty times, for almost an hour, until a mild state of trance came on and the attack passed. I knew it was the method of the prayer-mill, of the African tom-tom, of the age-old magic of sounds. Yet in spite of my knowing it, it worked . . .

The healing power . . . was derived from the device of merging that stark image of the firing-squad with the general problem of life and death, of merging my individual misery with the biological misery of the universe; just as the vibrations and tensions of a wireless-receiver are conducted to earth, where they disperse, I had 'earthed' my distress.

In other words I had found out that the human spirit is able to call upon certain aids of which, in normal circumstances, it has no know-ledge, and the existence of which it only discovers in itself in abnormal circumstances. They act, according to the particular case, either as merciful narcotics or ecstatic stimulants. The technique which I developed under the pressure of the death sentence consisted in the skilful exploitation of these aids. I knew, by the way, that at the decisive moment when I should have to face the wall, these mental devices would act automatically, without any conscious effort on my part. Thus I had actually no fear of the moment of execution; I only feared the fear which would precede that moment. I relied on . . . that dream-like feeling of having one's consciousness split in two, so that with one half of it one observes oneself with comparative coolness and aloofness, as though observing a stranger. The consciousness sees to it that its complete annihilation is never experienced. It does not divulge the secret of its existence and its decay. No one is allowed to look into the darkness with his eyes open. He is blindfolded beforehand.

This is why situations lived through are never so bad in reality as in imagination. Nature sees to it that trees do not grow beyond a certain height, not even the trees of suffering.

(Dialogue with Death)

Alexander Solzhenitsyn tells in *The Gulag Archipelago* of an imprisoned Russian astronomer who saved himself in a labour camp by meditating on a theme from his own previous work:

If the first thing you see each and every morning is the eyes of your cellmate who has gone insane, how then shall you save yourself during the coming day? Nikolai Aleksandrovitch Kozyrev, whose brilliant career in astronomy was interrupted by his arrest, saved himself only by thinking of the eternal and infinite: of the order of the Universe – and of its Supreme Spirit; of the stars; of their internal state; and what time and the passing of time really are.

(The Gulag Archipelago)

A final example of such a withdrawal, in this case unpremeditated, is given by Laurens van der Post in his well-known account of his imprisonment in a Japanese prisoner-of-war camp:

. . . my turn came to face Mori. I walked towards him suddenly feeling strangely calm. It was as if I had become another person and somewhere far down within me, someone far wiser and with the the benefit of having had to face this kind of thing ever since the beginning of man on earth, took command of me. I faced Mori, and this other self gauged Mori's blows and anticipated his kicks so accurately that it was able to make me move my head and body at the last moment before the blows fell in a manner not perceptible to the enraged man and his satellites, yet sufficient to rob them of their severity – to such an extent that I hardly felt them.

Indeed the physical impact of what Mori was trying to do to me seemed so irrelevant that, during the whole time of his assault on me, this process within me of appraising the full meaning of the incident and searching my imagination for a way of putting an end to it all before it developed into something worse, even something which Mori himself might possibly not have intended, went on unimpeded, and if possible with greater clarity than before. The result was that, when Mori delivered his final kick and pushed me back to my place in the line and I once more caught a glimpse of the machine-gun at the gates, it was as if I heard from deep within myself very clearly a voice of command from this other self, ordering me as with the authority of life itself: 'Turn about! Go back and present yourself to Mori for another beating.'

Rationally, everything was against such a course of action. If there were normally anything which provoked the Japanese to extremes of punishment it was any action on our part that broke their rules and sense of order. Yet this voice that rang out almost like a bell within me was so clear and insistent that I turned about without hesitation, walked back and once more stood to attention in front of Mori before the next officer could take my place.

Mori was already in a position to beat up his next victim. He was on the point of attacking again when the realization came to him that he was being confronted with the very person whom he had beaten just a moment before. The shock of this slight variation in a process which he had taken for granted was great, and showed immediately in his eyes. He looked at me over his raised cudgel, arrested in its downward move, as a cliché would have it, like someone who was seeing a ghost in broad daylight. Indeed, so grave was the shock that it utterly broke the accelerating rhythm of passion and anger in which he had been imprisoned. Slight as the irregularity was, it began drawing him out of the preconditioned processes of collective and instinctive reaction in which he had been involved and made him, I believe, suddenly aware of himself as an individual being. He stood there glaring at me, a strange inner bewilderment at this unexpected turn of events showing in the sombre glow of his dark eyes. Then, taking another sort of half-hearted swipe at my head, he grumbled with a kind of disgust that he thought the whole matter utterly incomprehensible and beneath contempt. He gave me a shove in the direction of our line, turned about, and still muttering tensely to himself walked away and out of sight . . .

(*The Night of the New Moon*)

Thus while change of thought is generally prepared by a long process of deliberate training, as prescribed by religious teachings, it may come suddenly under the impact of violent or tragic circumstances. A further example of an unexpected transition from a negative to a positive attitude, even under the most unbearable circumstances, is provided by an account of a woman's change of heart under bereavement:

I had a most happy married life, ending abruptly with the unexpected deaths, within a brief period, of my mother, baby son and finally my husband. I wanted to pray but did not know how to begin.

One afternoon when I was hurrying to the Underground to fetch my two little girls from school, I found that I had forgotten to bring a book to read and was annoyed. Something inside me urged me to pray instead. When I thought that I did not know how to do so, 'it' pointed out that there was always a first time, and I must start then. I got into the Underground train at Westminster and tried.

I had no sooner begun to pray haltingly than I seemed to be overwhelmed with loving warmth – not physical warmth, but so tremendous that I felt I would die if it lasted any longer – and to be right outside time and space. I managed to stumble out at South Kensington station, drunk with happiness, and the assurance that God existed, and that He was the one reality. It was like a homecoming – like finding something I had been unconsciously looking for all my life. Kind friends were then still coming round to pay visits of condolence and what they thought when they saw me looking years younger and gloriously happy, I don't like to think.

While I was still wondering what to do next, the same experience but still more awe-inspiring, happened to me one morning just as I was getting breakfast and about to switch on the seven o'clock news. Both experiences took place in the most prosaic circumstances and not when I could have been affected by a beautiful sunset, a sublime concert or a moving sermon (I am not a churchgoer). (RERU 1212)

Ignorance, say the Buddhists, is the principal cause of all our illusions. This ignorance is not the same as lack of knowledge, let alone lack of learning. Molinos, it is true, was a learned man, and his *Defence of Contemplation* sets out an argument that should certainly have refuted all charges of heresy, if the basis of his trial had not been fundamentally political. Not only did he find precedent for his beliefs and actions in the great mystics of the past, but he adequately showed himself to have been the devoted follower of John of the Cross, a hundred years dead and soon to be canonized. Lacking all learning, Joan of Arc on the other hand was driven back on her inner certainty that she had done God's work. Her lack of learning was not ignorance; her defence was to call on Christ's help in the face of a cruel and lonely death. But the Hungarian communist did not even do that; she did not call on Marx, or seek to justify her purer Marxism against the corruptions of Stalinist bureaucracy. She fell back on the reality of life as she had known it outside prison, switching her attention by 180 degrees. In the same way Laurens van der Post reaffirmed a reality truer than the Japanese camp. All turned from the level of bewilderment, pain and confusion to another level of thought of a more permanent reality.

But what are we to say of the lady who suddenly found herself able to accept what by any standards was a succession of most grievous losses? How could she find the strength to confront the friends who came to commiserate with her in her secret mood of acceptance? She does not seem to have had any comforting belief that the dead have not suffered extinction but are instead moving into a new life. She simply knew that, in the words of the medieval anchorite, Julian of Norwich, all things, including sin and loss, occupy their proper place in the world and are therefore an acceptable part of a divine pattern. 'In my folly', Julian wrote, 'I wondered why God had not in the beginning prevented the arising of sin.' The answer came in a revelation:

But I saw not sin: for I believe it has no manner of substance nor no part of being, nor could it be known but by the pain it is cause of.

And thus pain, it is something, as to my sight, for a time; for it purgeth, and maketh us to know ourselves and to ask mercy. For the passion of our Lord is comfort to us against all this, and so is his blessed will. And for the tender love that our good Lord hath to all that shall be saved, he comforteth readily and sweetly, signifying thus: 'It is sooth that sin is cause of all this pain; but all shall be well, and all shall be well, and all manner of thing shall be well.'

(Revelations of Divine Love)

Ignorance can be summarized in the single idea, 'It might be otherwise'. The Sufi poet Rumi reduced it to the single word 'if':

See that you are not made captive by 'if', saying, 'If I had done this or the other thing'. For the sincere prophet forbade people to say 'if' and said, 'That is a form of hypocrisy'. For the hypocrite died in saying 'if' and in saying 'if' he won nothing but remorse.

A certain stranger was hastily seeking a house; a friend took him to a house in ruins. He said to the stranger 'If this house had a roof, it would be a home for you beside me; your family too would be comfortable if it had another room in it.'

'Yes,' said he, 'it is nice to be beside friends, but my dear soul, one cannot lodge in "if".'

(Rumi, *Mathnawi*)

Right thought, therefore, lies in acceptance. Right action is that of the prince's butcher who, following the grain of the meat and finding the joints between the bones, found no resistance. His knife remained sharp, whereas those of less adroit cooks are continually at the whetstone.

At a deeper and more abstract level, the Buddhist scriptures attribute all discrimination to the mind itself. The world contains no alternatives. The choice is simply between dwelling in the illusion of 'if' in attachment to desire, regret and self-pity, or the acceptance of Molinos, Julian of Norwich and a thousand travellers in the Métro, the New York subway or the London Underground who, by a 180 degree switch of the mind, accept the unacceptable. To quote the *Lankavatara Sutra* again:

When the existence and the non-existence of the external world are recognized as rising from the mind itself, then the Bodhisattva is prepared to enter into the state of imagelessness and therein to see into the emptiness which characterizes all discrimination and all the deep-seated attachments resulting therefrom. Therein he will see no signs of deep-rooted attachment nor detachment; therein he will see no one in bondage and no one in emancipation, except those who themselves cherish bondage and emancipation, because in all things there is no 'substance' to be taken hold of.

But so long as these discriminations are cherished by the ignorant and simple-minded they go on attaching themselves to them and, like the silkworm, go on spinning their thread of discrimination and enwrapping themselves and others, and are charmed with their prison. But to the wise there are no signs of attachment nor of detachment; all things are seen as abiding in solitude where there is no evolving of discrimination.

(*Lankavatara Sutra*)

It is more difficult to find this refusal to discriminate among Christian writers. For the Christian mystic finds himself always at war with the devil, who not only tempts him to sin but cunningly conceals sin in the guise of virtue, or tempts the virtuous to take pride in their good deeds. Few see as clearly as Julian of Norwich that sin too must be accepted as part of the world picture. Of those few, Meister Eckhart stands apart; and he faced accusations of heresy which made his successors reluctant to quote him by name. For although he was not condemned, it was only because his trial was still unconcluded at his death. Having seen beyond duality he was more closely akin to the non-Christian Greeks such as Plotinus, whom he read, and to Vedantists and Buddhists, of whom of course he knew nothing. This section on right thought and right action cannot end better than with a passage from this thirteenth-century German scholar and mystic:

The saints declare that all things are in God as they have been in God eternally; not that we were in God in the gross nature we have here; we were in God eternalwise, like art in the artist. God saw himself and saw all things. God was not therefore manifold as things are here in separation. Though creatures here are manifold they are but one idea in God. God in himself is just the *one alone*. When creature goes back to her first cause she knows God simply as one in form and essence and threefold in operation. What intellect knows is knowledge and knowledge stops at what is known, with what is known becoming one. Into the simple idea no knowledge ever entered, for this impartible exemplar after which God created all creatures towers God-high above creatures. Creature in pursuing God to his eternal heights must mount above all creatures, nay, beyond her very self, her own wont and uses, and follow agnosia (knowledgelessness) into the desolate Godhead. St Dionysius says, 'God's desert is God's simple nature.' A creature's desert is her simple nature. In the desert of herself she is robbed of her own form and in God's desert, leading out of hers, she is bereft of name; there she is no more called soul, she is called God with God.

(Eckhart, I)

Here multiplicity is reduced to unity, God's abundance to God's 'desert'. Knowledge is carried to the stage beyond know-ledge, which is *agnosia*. Thought passes beyond thought to the supreme level where thinker and thought are one. There is no more discrimination. All is God. And Meister Eckhart, a travelling Dominican scholar who read sermons in their own language to semi-literate nuns, delivered truths as bare and homely as any Zen master. It is not surprising that his enemies instituted that prosecution for heresy. But what was his effect upon his hearers? One, Sister Katrei, as we shall see later, gained illumination and was able to teach her own master. Others were later convicted of heresy. For their master's thought went beyond the accepted theological level at which man and God are forever divided and can be brought together only through a mediator, who was both God and man. 'That man', said an Indian teacher after some passages from Eckhart had been read to him, 'knew the Vedanta'. He refused to believe that this statement was historically impossible.

3 Compassion

'The shifting of the emotional centre', wrote William James, 'brings . . . increase of charity, tenderness for fellow creatures.' The need for compassion is stressed again and again in the First Epistle to the Corinthians: 'Though I speak with the tongues of men and of angels, and have not charity, I am become as sounding brass or a tinkling cymbal . . .' Meditation and even right thought and action may, at root, be self-regarding. A person may ultimately be concerned with his own salvation, his own release from the wheel. Hence the Buddhist insistence that all merits gained by action or meditation must be dedicated to the release of all beings from the wheel of rebirth.

The word charity has long ago lost its meaning and there is no equivalent broad enough to embrace it. Charity is *caritas*, 'dearness'. It is love. But love presumes an object; and a selected object presumes the exclusion of other objects. Commonly it also entails the desire for a return of love by the loved one. The mother's love for her child may come near to charity; and the love of the child for the mother is used by Buddhists as an example to stimulate compassion (they remind us that every living being has been our mother in some past life).

Charity is fundamentally an attitude of mind. It is the same whether directed towards fellow beings, animals, one's teacher or towards God in any aspect. 'Charity suffereth long and is kind . . . asketh not for her own and is not easily provoked, thinketh no evil . . .' Buddhists recommend in particular that it shall be turned towards those who have treated us badly, to those who have disappointed our hopes, and to wandering discarnate spirits. William Law speaks of it as love, but expands the word's common meaning; for him it knows no difference of time, place or person:

This is the ground and original of the spirit of love in the creature: it is, and must be, a will to all goodness; and you have not the spirit of love until you have this will to all goodness, at all times, and on all occasions.

You may indeed do many works of love, and delight in them, especially at such times as they are not inconvenient to you, or contradictory to your state, or temper, or occurrences in life. But the spirit of love is not in you until it is the spirit of your life, until you live freely, willingly, and universally, according to it.

For every spirit acts with freedom and universally according to what it is. It needs no command to live its own life, or be what it is, no more than you need bid wrath be wrathful. And therefore, when love is the spirit of your life, it will have the freedom and universality of a spirit; it will always live and work in love, not because of this or that, here or there, but because the spirit of love can only love, wherever it is or goes, or whatever is done to it.

As the sparks know no motion but that of flying upwards, whether it be in the darkness of the night, or in the light of the day; so the spirit of love is always in the same course; it knows no difference of time, place or persons; but whether it gives or forgives, bears or forbears, it is equally doing its own delightful work, equally blessed from itself. For the spirit of love, wherever it is, is its own blessing and happiness, because it is the truth and reality of God in the soul.

(Selected Mystical Writings)

Walter Hilton, an English priest of the fourteenth century, sees love as a force acting secretly within one, and observes that it is 'a great mystery' to a person who lives only by the light of his reason. If this was true in his time, then it is certainly even more true today. Hilton is kind to those who, lacking the full warmth of charity, yet act with patience and forbearance in trying circumstances:

Love worketh wisely and softly in a soul where he will, for he slayeth mightily ire and envy and all passions of angriness and melancholy in it, and bringeth into the soul virtues of patience and mildness, peaceability and amity to his even-christian. It is full hard and a great mastery to a man that standeth only in working of his own reason for to keep patience, holy rest and softness in heart, and charity to his even-christian if they trouble him unreasonably and do him wrong, that he shall not somewhat do again to them through stirring of ire or of melancholy, either in speaking or in working or in both.

And nevertheless though a man be stirred or troubled in himself and made unrestful, so be that it be not too mickle, passing over the bounds of reason, and that he keep his hand and his tongue and be ready for to forgive the trespass when mercy is asked, yet this man hath the virtue of patience, though it be but weakly and nakedly; for as mickle as he would have it, and travaileth busily in refraining of his unreasonable passions, that he might have it, and also is sorry that he hath it not as he should.

(The Scale of Perfection)

The Christian mystics – and for that matter the Sufis also – see no essential difficulty in stimulating the growth of love or charity by means of prayer. The Buddhists are not so sanguine and offer far more practical guidance to modern man. The aim is to cultivate equanimity, or unlimited friendliness. After some discussion about who is the most suitable person to start with – a friend, an enemy, some dear person of the other sex, someone lost by death – one treatise on meditation concludes:

First of all friendliness should again and again be developed for *oneself*, 'May I be happy, free from ill', or, 'May I be free from enmity, free from injury, free from disturbance, and may I preserve myself at ease.'

(Conze, *Buddhist Meditation*)

From such a basis of freedom from self-hate the practice can be extended, first to the teacher, whose generous help makes the whole endeavour possible, then to 'a very dear person', then to 'an indifferent person', then towards an enemy. If at this point aversion arises, the meditator should turn back to his earlier subjects – teacher, friend, neutral person – thus dispelling his aversion.

This, like other Buddhist meditations, may seem to be no more than a mental exercise, requiring much effort and surface thinking. Those who practise meditation on a mantra or on the breath may wonder whether this can ever lead to *samadhi* or transcendence of surface reality. Although aiming at an emotional result – love not merely of one's neighbour but of one's enemy – it appears to be an emotionally dry process. But experience demonstrates the contrary:

Immediately together with the breaking down of the barriers, the monk has acquired the mental image and access to concentration. But when he has broken down the barriers, and then tends, develops and cultivates that mental image, he attains full concentration without much trouble.

(Buddhist Meditation)

Concentration in this sense does not involve effort, but rather the focussing of attention.

The meditator is now radiating friendliness – the Christian would say love – and he sees himself to be at one with all beings. This leads him to unlimited compassion, directed first to the sick, then to the unfortunate and finally even to happy people (for is not their happiness transitory?). From compassion the meditator passes to rejoicing in the joy of others, and to the final state of equanimity towards all men, his friends and former enemies, those who rejoice and those who grieve. Not until he has reached this condition of even-minded calm can he look on all men with equal compassion. And here *samadhi* is attained.

It is surely evident that although this meditation appears to be intellectual it is in fact a process of opening the heart. 'Equanimity' is rather a colourless word: 'compassion' conveys greater warmth. 'Friendliness', again, is a cool word compared with 'love'. Yet the Sufis knew no higher attribute for God than the character of friend:

A certain man came and knocked at a friend's door: his friend asked him, 'Who art thou, O trusty one?' He answered, 'I'. The friend said, 'Begone, 'tis not the time for thee to come in: at a table like this there is no place for the raw.'

Save the fire of absence and separation, what will cook the raw one? What will deliver him from hypocrisy?

The wretched man went away, and for a year in travel, and in separation from his friend, he was burned with sparks of fire.

That burned one was cooked: then he returned and again paced to and fro beside the house of his comrade.

He knocked at the door with a hundred fears and respects, lest any disrespectful word might escape from his lips. His friend called to him, 'Who is at the door?' He answered, ' 'Tis thou art at the door, O charmer of hearts.'

'Now,' said the friend, 'since thou art I, come in, O myself: there is not room in the house for two I's.'

(Mathnawi)

Thus Rumi sees that the final stage of 'friendliness' is union with the divine.

The outstanding difference between Christian practice and the eastern tradition lies in the Christian concern with sin. The legend of man's initiation into sin in the Garden of Paradise, and his need for redemption by the bloody sacrifice, first of a lamb and in the end of a divine being, hangs like a baleful star over the Christian mystic's head. He can only gain access to the way by paying blood money. Only by austerities that often involve self-torture can he win the friendship of that angry God to whom he must atone in person for the sin of Adam.

Henry Suso, a contemporary and follower of Meister Eckhart, has a Sufi-like delight in the beauties of the world, but is unable to see them as a reflection of supernal beauty. For him they are a snare; to enjoy them is to deflect one's thoughts from the essential subject of the redeemer's sacrifice. In his *Little Book of Wisdom* he debates, in the person of the Servant, with a master, personified as Eternal Wisdom. At the outset the Servant tells of his boyhood's yearning for he knows not what. But soon the discussion reaches the subject of 'love of the world':

The Servant: Beloved One, if I leave Thee even for a short time, I am like a roe that has left its mother, and is being hard pressed by the hunt; it flees with sudden twists and turns, until it escapes to its lair. Lord, I am fleeing, I rush to Thee with fervent, burning zeal, as the stag to the living waters. Lord, one single hour without Thee is a whole year. To be a stranger to Thee for one day is a thousand years to a loving heart. Ah, then, Thou branch of salvation, Thou May bough, Thou red blossoming rose bush, open up Thy arms, scatter and spread the blossoming branches of Thy divine and human nature!

(The Little Book of Eternal Wisdom)

The vision that follows is of a pilgrim approaching a ruined city, which Suso paints with the detail of a Flemish artist of his own day, the fourteenth century. The pilgrim is Christ; the ruined city is that of a religious unity now shattered. We are in a dualistic territory, in which it is necessary to renounce in order to gain.

Suso views the world's beauty, which so pleases him as a poet (for his descriptive power is poetic), with horror. To start cultivating 'eternal wisdom' by the exercise of mere worldly love or 'friendliness' would seem to him a betrayal of that 'pilgrim' who sacrificed himself for men. Suso practised the most extreme forms of self-torture, as he relates in his autobiography, wearing for years a hair shirt studded with nails whose points pierced his flesh. When he fell down in ecstatic vision, joy was mingled with pain, as he himself relates, and even when in this vision he was bidden to abandon these cruel penances, he yet persisted for some time, going about and even preaching in self-inflicted physical pain.

One cannot say whether Suso was advanced or retarded on the way by his austerities. Perhaps, by some such methods as those adopted by yogins, he became impervious to them. But this is unlikely, because he cherished his suffering as a method of atoning for sin.

Christ's compassion for man is expressed in his suffering; and the physical torture of the scourging, the raising on the cross and the crucifixion obsess the Christian mystics. If he suffered, then they must share or imitate his suffering. His apparent abandonment on the cross when he called on his Lord in vain, can be matched, in small, by their spells of desolation. Almost alone of the mystics, Eckhart sees that suffering may not be the same for those who have lived a holy life as for others. They may 'reach oblivion of its travail':

Folks tell us of the holy life, how they have suffered. To tell the tale of what our Lord's friends suffered time would be all too short. I say: they did not suffer. The least suspicion of God-consciousness and sufferings would be all forgot. This may well happen while the soul is in the body. I say more: while yet in the body a soul may reach oblivion of its travail not to remember it again.   (*Eckhart, I*)

But Eckhart concludes, 'to him who suffers not for love, to suffer is suffering and hard to bear'.

One may assert that Christ's physical suffering cannot have been the same as that of the common robber who hung beside him. Furthermore, his apparent abandonment could not have been the same as it would have been for one on a lower plane. Enlightened men are not to be judged by the standards of the unenlightened. Nonetheless, Christian orthodoxy continually stresses the common humanity assumed by the redeemer, and bids its followers assume his physical suffering.

The Gnostics alone saw Christ as more than human, a divine emissary, a *bodhisattva*. Their influence on Christianity was considerable until it was expunged in a series of early Church Councils. The Gnostics presented Jesus purely as a preacher of enlightenment, which was to be found by a series of 'repentances' or changes of heart. In the second-century document called the *Pistis Sophia* he speaks in this vein to his disciples:

'When I shall have gone into the Light, then herald it unto the whole world and say unto them: Cease not to seek day and night and remit not yourselves until ye find the mysteries of the Light-kingdom, which will purify you and make you into refined light and lead you into the Light-kingdom.

'Say unto them: renounce the whole world and the whole matter therein and all its cares and all its sins, in a word all its associations which are in it, that ye may be worthy of the mysteries of the Light and be saved from all the chastisements which are in the judgements.

'Say unto them: Renounce murmuring, that ye may be worthy of the mysteries of the Light and be saved from the fire of the dog-faced one.

'Say unto them: renounce eavesdropping, that ye may be worthy of the mysteries of the Light and be saved from the judgements of the dog-faced one.'

(Pistis Sophia)

The dog-faced demons of the last judgement vividly recall the angry deities of *The Tibetan Book of the Dead* (a book of instruction in the art of dying). In the form of preoccupation with sin and suffering, they came to bedevil the orthodox and to inspire

c

sectarian feuds and wars, persecutions and heresy-hunts, which distinguish Christianity from the other great religions.

Preoccupation with sin is the exact opposite of the Buddhist practice of forgiving oneself before exercising compassion towards one's neighbours. To forgive oneself is not the equivalent of 'self-cherishing'. We are warned against this by innumerable Buddhist writings, and also by the anonymous author of the *Theologia Germanica*:

It is said, it was because Adam ate the apple that he was lost, or fell. I say, it was because of his claiming something for his own, and because of his I, Mine, Me and the like. Had he eaten seven apples, and yet never claimed anything for his own, he would not have fallen: but as soon as he called something his own, he fell, and would have fallen if he had never touched an apple. Behold! I have fallen a hundred times more often and deeply, and gone a hundred times farther astray than Adam; and not all mankind could amend his fall, or bring him back from going astray. But how shall my fall be amended? It must be healed as Adam's fall was healed, and on the self-same wise. By whom, and on what wise was that healing brought to pass? Mark this: man could not without God, and God should not without man . . .

Again in this bringing back and healing, I can, or may, or shall do nothing of myself, but just simply yield to God, so that He alone may do all things in me and work, and I may suffer Him and all His work and His divine will. And because I will not do so, but I count myself to be my own, and say 'I', 'Mine', 'Me' and the like, God is hindered, so that He cannot do His work in me alone and without hindrance; for this cause my fall and my going astray remain unhealed. Behold! this all cometh of my claiming somewhat for my own.

(*Theologia Germanica*)

In forgiving oneself one humbly acknowledges one's position at a great distance from the divine consciousness one longs for. One's 'sin' is proportionate to one's distance from this goal. It has been suggested that the root word for sin in New Testament Greek implies only distance from the divine – a condition, surely, to be acknowledged and remedied, but not a reason for self-hate. Moreover, self-hate is not merely an internal poison; it is projected on the world outside. We habitually dislike in others those shortcomings of our own that we try hardest to conceal from ourselves. In fact hatred of our neighbour is usually a projection of self-hate.

Certainly this acceptance of ourselves must not lead to the indulgence of our own desires and prejudices. On the subject of these hindrances, Buddhism is as categorical as Christianity. The following simple code was given by the Buddha in his advice to a householder:

'Now what are those four vices of action which he has put away? They are these, young master: the vice of taking the life of creatures; of taking what is not given; of wrong practice in sexual acts of passion; and falsehood. These four.'

Thus spake the Exalted One. When the Happy One had thus spoken the Master added this further:

'Who taketh life, who steals, who telleth lies, who defiles another's wife – him wise men blame.

'And what are the four motives of evil-doing, free from which he does no evil deed?

'A man does evil deeds by going on the wrong path through desire, through hatred, through delusion and through fear. But since the disciple does not go on these four wrong paths, he does no evil deed through these four motives of evil-doing.'

(*Some Sayings of the Buddha*)

An essential constituent of Buddhist meditation is the practice of 'checking' – the examination of past actions and motives. This introspection is the counterpart of the Christian preoccupation with sin. In all traditions, self-knowledge is accounted a virtue.

A modern westerner might object that while it may be easy enough to renounce hatred, envy and the other vices, it is quite another matter to prevent them. The Gurdjieff system attempted to overcome this difficulty by enjoining, as a first step, that those in the Work should try not to express their 'negative emotions' – the equivalent of the Buddha's vices. Then, it was hoped, they would disappear of themselves. Frequently they merely festered within, bursting out at some unwary moment in unexpected form. There is no defence against the vices except the opening of the heart in love, or, as in the Hassidic tale that follows, in grief:

Once the Baal Shem had his disciple Rabbi Wolf Kitzes learn the ritual of blowing the ram's horn, so that, on New Year's Day, he might announce before him the order of the sounds. Rabbi Wolf learned the directions but, for greater security, noted everything down on a slip of paper which he hid in his bosom. This paper, however, dropped out soon after and he never noticed it. They say that this was the work of the Baal Shem. Now when it was time to blow, Rabbi Wolf looked for his slip in vain. Then he tried to remember the directions, but he had forgotten everything. Tears rose to his eyes, and weeping, he announced the order of sounds quite simply without referring to the directions at all. Later the Baal Shem said to him: 'There are many halls in the king's palace and intricate keys open the doors, but the axe is stronger than all of these, and no bolt can withstand it. What are all the directions compared to one really heartfelt grief!'

(*Tales of the Hassidim*)

The vice of forgetfulness was thus shattered by the axe of loving contrition.

The Buddhist meditation on unlimited friendship towards all creatures is calculated to dispel the vices, but it is at the same time an act of devotion towards that spirit or breath which informs them and thus leads to the awakening of the heart. At the same time as he accepts himself, the disciple can even-handedly accept both friends and those to whom he has once felt indifference or hatred; and in particular he turns in gratitude to his teacher, in whom he sees reflected the supreme teacher.

Guru meditation, however, forms a category of its own. The disciple dedicates himself entirely to the master, anticipating his wishes, however seemingly unreasonable, acting as his cook and his body servant until the moment when the master finds him worthy and confers on him the gift of his teaching. An extreme example of guru devotion is told in the autobiography of Mila-repa. He tells how, having sought out the great yogi Marpa, he was subjected to a series of ordeals. First Marpa offers to give the lad the teaching and support him during the period of instruction, on condition that he should build him a house for his son. There follows some bargaining, but the youth is satisfied:

He took me to a mountain ridge having an eastern aspect, and, pointing out a particular place, described a circular structure and ordered me to begin building it there; and this I at once did. When I had finished about half of it, he came along and said that, when giving me my orders at the outset, he had not well considered the matter, and that I must stop work on the building and carry back to the place whence I had taken them the earth and stones I had used.

When I had carried out this order, the Lama, appearing to me to be intoxicated, took me to a ridge having a western aspect and, ordering me to build another house there, after describing a crescent-shaped ground-plan, went away. When I had built this house up to about half the height required, the Lama again came to me while I was working and said that even this house would not do, and that I must restore the clay and the stones to the places whence I had taken them. Again I obeyed his commands.

Once more the Lama took me away, this time to a ridge with a northern aspect, and there addressed me . . .   (*Tibet's Great Yogi*)

Three more houses were built and demolished and the disciple's back was worn sore from carrying stones. But still Marpa prevaricated, and although his wife did her best to intercede, Milarepa was as far as ever from receiving the teaching. The ordeal was long, but finally Milarepa gained his reward and became a far greater teacher than his own master.

Guru devotion has its parallels in other faiths. A western Christian may harbour a devotion to a saint, to Christ, or to some quality of the Saviour's. The Mahayana Buddhist will contemplate the Buddha in one of his aspects, chosen by his teacher according to the disciple's temperament. Of these aspects, Avalokitesvara, embodying compassion, is associated with the awakening of the heart through equanimity.

Such awakening may occur spontaneously in a person habitually dry and inhibited. It is perhaps the most frequent form of spontaneous 'mystical experience'. Two contemporary examples demonstrate such experiences in people who, although of a religious nature, had drifted away from belief. The first, a young girl, appears to have been in a state of some distress when the event occurred:

At seventeen I was confused and questing. Nothing made a lot of sense; the world seemed so unfair and people unreliable. However, I had not forgotten how to pray; and I prayed with unashamed sincerity that if God existed, could He show me some sort of light in the jungle.

One day, I was sweeping the stairs, down in the house in which I was working, when suddenly I was overcome, overwhelmed, saturated . . . with a sense of most sublime and living *love*. It not only affected me, but seemed to bring everything around me to *life*. The brush in my hand, my dustpan, the stairs, seemed to come alive with love. I seemed no longer me, with my petty troubles and trials, but part of this infinite power of love, so utterly and overwhelmingly wonderful that one knew at once what the saints had grasped. It could only have been a minute or two, yet for that brief particle of time it seemed eternity . . .   (RERU 1753)

This unexpected wave of love brought everything in the girl's surroundings to life. She was no longer herself but 'part of this infinite power of love', which extended to such commonplace objects as the brush and dustpan. Do we call this love, this apprehension of the unity of all things of which we are one?

The next narrator speaks rather of compassion:

Although religion had meant a lot to me, at the time I was going through a period of doubt and of disillusion with life and was torn by conflict . . . On this particular June day I had time to fill in. It was a glorious sunny evening and I walked through St James's Park and sat down by the water intending to read. I never opened my book.

It was very beautiful, with the sun glinting through the trees and the ducks swimming on the water, and quite suddenly I felt lifted beyond all the turmoil and the conflict. There was no visual image and I knew I was sitting on a seat in the park, but I felt as if I was lifted above the world and looking down on it. The disillusion and cynicism were gone and I felt compassion suffusing my whole being, compassion for all people on earth. I was possessed by a peace that I have never felt before or since and – what is to me most interesting and curious of all – this whole state was not emotional; it was as if I was not without emotion but beyond it. The experience passed off gradually and I suppose it lasted twenty to thirty minutes.

At the time I felt it was an experience of God, because I interpreted it according to my own religious framework.   (RERU 363)

Again we note the 'doubt and disillusion' that preceded this experience. From cynicism, this woman was moved to 'compassion for all people on earth'; and with this she felt herself lifted, although with no accompanying visual imagery, above the park seat on which she was sitting. In this very acute narrative she notes with some surprise that she was 'not without emotion but above it'. What is commonly taken for inspiration is usually adulterated: desire, excitement, expectation are habitually mingled with it and at the end it is often clouded by disappointment and regret. But such emotional feelings as come in these moments, these foretastes of *samadhi*, are associated with more profound experiences: the 'infinite power of love' in the first example, and 'a peace that I have never felt before' in the second.

These experiences, though less extensive, are clearly of the same kind as the rapture of Henry Suso, who, like these two experients, had undergone a period of trouble or suffering beforehand. Even some of the descriptive writing is similar. Suso's experience, however, does not seem to have led him to compassion, but rather to an intensification of his religious practice:

'In the first days of his conversion it happened upon the Feast of St Agnes, when the Convent had breakfasted at midday, that the servant went into the choir [Suso refers to himself as the servant]. He was alone, and he placed himself in the last stall on the prior's side. And he was in much suffering, for a heavy trouble weighed upon his heart. And being there alone, and devoid of all consolations – no one by his side, no one near him – of a sudden his soul was rapt in his body, or out of his body. Then did he see and hear that which no tongue can express.

'That which the servant saw had no form neither any manner of being; yet he had of it a joy such as he might have known in the seeing of the shapes and substances of all joyful things. His heart was hungry, yet satisfied; his soul was full of contentment and joy: his prayers and hopes were all fulfilled. And the Friar could do naught but contemplate this Shining Brightness; and he altogether forgot himself and all other things. Was it day or night? He knew not. It was, as it were, a manifestation of the sweetness of Eternal Life in the sensations of silence and of rest. Then he said "If that which I see and feel be not the Kingdom of Heaven, I know not what it can be: for it is very sure that the endurance of all possible pains were but a small price to pay for the eternal possesssion of so great a joy."'

(quoted in Evelyn Underhill, *Mysticism*)

Most experiences of this kind are unshared. Indeed the subject is often reluctant to speak of them even to a close friend. He may fear that in reducing them to words, in exposing them to another's comment or criticism, however kind, one is smudging their outline, bringing them down to the level of the commonplace.

These experiences may on occasions, however, be shared between close friends, in this instance husband and wife:

Perhaps the deepest mystical experience I have had was just before my husband's death ... One day we were alone together when suddenly a complete change came over him and I had a sense of a singing, surging, mighty power surrounding us ... For about half an hour we were able to talk almost normally about ourselves and the family and the future with a great sense of unity and purpose and undying love without possessiveness. Then he lapsed into unconsciousness and died a day or two later. There have been times when my husband has been vividly alive and present since ...

(RERU 871)

'Love without possessiveness' is the keynote of this brief but moving account. It is an emotion perhaps more often expressed in actions than in words. Few people discuss an approaching death, or what will follow. To apprehend death one must be lifted to a higher emotional level than is usual in the hospital or the sick room. Viewed from such a plane, death wears a different look.

The shared experience is no doubt a principal reason for communal prayer or joint meditation. 'Where two or more are gathered together in My name' there will be greater power than where the single worshipper prays or meditates alone. St Catherine of Genoa and her friends appear to have shared ecstatic experiences during their conversations, the exact nature of which does not emerge clearly from her account:

This soul remained henceforth many a time in company with its many spiritual friends, discoursing of the Divine Love, in such wise that they felt as though in Paradise, both collectively, and each one in his particular way . . . He who spoke and he who listened, each one fed on spiritual food of a delicious kind; and because the time flew so swiftly, they never could attain satiety, but all on fire within them, they would remain there, unable at last to speak, unable to depart, as though in ecstasy.

(St Catherine of Genoa, Dialogue)

But such stories are rare; Catherine of Genoa seems to have had a kind of sensitiveness bordering on the psychic.

The opening of the heart to the 'fire of love' is the pervasive and lyrical theme of the fourteenth-century English mystic Richard Rolle of Hampole:

The burning of love truly taken into a soul purges all vices; it voids both too mickle and too little, and plants the beauty of all virtues. It never stands with deadly sin, and if it do with venial yet nevertheless the moving and desire of love in God can be so burning that they waste all venial sins; for whilst the true lover is borne to God with strong and fervent desire, all things displease him that withdraw him from the sight of God. Truly whiles he is gladdened by songly joy, his heart may not express what he feels of heavenly things, and therefore he languishes for love.

(Richard Rolle of Hampole, The Fire of Love)

And the state that arises from this burning joy, once even the venial sins are consumed, is proclaimed in the last revelation of Julian of Norwich, in which she received an answer to her request for meaning:

And from that time that it was shewed I desired oftentimes to learn what was our Lord's meaning. And fifteen years after, and more, I was answered in ghostly understanding, saying thus: 'Woudst thou learn our Lord's meaning in this thing? Learn it well: love was his meaning. Who shewed it thee? Love. What shewed he thee? Love. Wherefore shewed it he? For love. Hold thee therein and thou shalt learn and know more in the same. But thou shalt never know nor learn therein other thing without end.' Thus was I learned that love was our Lord's meaning.

(Revelations of Divine Love)

The fervour of Rolle and Julian is matched by that of the Sufis, lovers of God who become nothing but his attributes:

> We are the flute, our music is all Thine;
> We are the mountains echoing only Thee;
> Pieces of chess Thou marshallest in line
> And movest to defeat or victory;
> Lions emblazoned high on flags unfurled –
> Thy wind invisible sweeps us through the world.
>
> (Rumi, *Persian Poets*)

Obvious though it is that light and fire have always been stock correlatives for sexual passion, and that the Christian use of sexual analogy was encouraged by the perhaps fortuitous inclusion in the Bible of a secular love poem, the Song of Songs, more cogent reasons must be sought for the erotic parallels so fervently drawn by Christian and also Sufi mystics. What is there in the transcendent experience that can be called fire? Fire and song combine to form a double analogy for the rapture of Richard Rolle:

> Truly the lover of Almighty God is not raised in mind to see into high things withouten skill, and to sing the song of love that springs up in the soul, the which is ardently and openly burnt with the fire of love, and spread out in sweet devotion, abiding in songs that yield honey from our fairest Mediator. Therefore the singer is led into all mirth, and, the well of endless heat breaking forth in mirth, he is received into halting and singular solace, and the lover is arrayed with the might of the most lovely passage and refreshed in sweet heat.
>
> He joys, truly glistening whiter than snow and redder than a rose; for he is kindled by God's fire, and going with clearness of conscience he is clad in white. Therefore he is taken up thereto above all others; for in his mind melody abides and sweet plenty of heat tarries; so that not only shall he offer a marrow offering in himself and pay Christ praise in ghostly music, but also he shall stir others to love, so that they hie to give themselves devoutly and perfectly to God; the which vouchsafes to make glad His lovers, cleaving to him with all their heart, in this exile also.
>
> (*The Fire of Love*)

One may think of this passage as no more than an extended

poetic analogy. Rolle was certainly a poet, although he himself says in the heading to the chapter from which this quotation is drawn that this experience of rapture 'neither can be said nor written'. But if one turns to the meditational practice of the east, one realizes that this fire in the heart, this burning of the soul in love, is not a mere poetic flight of language. Even the practitioner of simple meditation will sometimes recognize the relevance of this fire in the heart to his own experience.

Most meditational practice prescribes a moving of the attention as it proceeds, from the head to the heart. A mantra may begin as an unspoken repetition in the head or in the throat, not perhaps strictly localized, but with time it can be moved to the heart – not of course to the physical heart but to its counterpart, the *chakra* or psychic centre at the level of the heart. This is the beginning of an elementary form of Tantric meditation:

The Light of the eyes must shine quietly, and, for a long time, neither sleepiness nor distraction must set in. The eyes do not look outward, they drop their lids and light up what is within. There is Light in this place. The mouth does not speak or laugh. One closes the lips and breathes inwardly. Breathing is at this place. The nose smells no odours. Smelling is at this place. The ear does not hear things outside. Hearing is at this place. The whole heart watches over what is within. Its watching is at this place. The thoughts do not stray outwards; true thoughts have continuity in themselves. If the thoughts are lasting, the seed is lasting; if the seed lasts, the power lasts; if the power lasts, then will the spirit last also. The spirit is thought; thought is the heart; the heart is the fire; the fire is the Elixir.

(The Secret of the Golden Flower)

No Christian prescriptions for the opening of the heart are as specific as this Taoist treatise. In the Christian mystic the alchemy takes place, if not unseen, at least uncharted. The tantric process whereby sexual energy is deliberately transmuted into higher energy is only loosely conveyed by Christian love imagery.

The theme first appeared in Christian thought during the eleventh century, which saw the flowering of western mysticism. One possible cause was the humanizing influence of the Sufis, transmitted to a more barbarous Europe at the time of the

Crusades. From the Sufis came the cult of courtly love. It was the Arabic poetry of Spain that inspired the troubadour lyric. And indeed, one of the first Spanish mystics, Ramon Lull, intending to be a missionary to the Moslems, learnt Arabic and made contact with Muslim scholars in Majorca. Out of this eastern idealization of erotic love grew the western cult of Mary the virgin mother and the sexual metaphor of the holy marriage between the soul – feminine in all western languages – and the heavenly bridegroom.

This lyrical influence did not touch the Greek Church, whose inspiration remained that of the desert hermits and the monks of Sinai, for whom sin always took a female form. The prescription of the eleventh-century St Simeon, the 'New Theologian', for what corresponds to the opening of the heart is as direct as any Buddhist instructions, but has a harsh quality of its own. The idea of 'friendliness' is absent; and for self-forgiveness he, like his master St John of the Ladder, substitutes a rigid attention to thoughts and instant extirpation of any promptings of lust: 'He who does not have attention in himself, and does not guard his mind, cannot become pure in heart, and so cannot see God. If he does not have attention on himself, he cannot be poor in spirit.'

The self is never forgiven and must be scrupulously searched like an enemy for sinful thoughts. This self-observation may correspond to the Buddhist checking or the Catholic examination of conscience, but the pouncing on dangerous thoughts before they are able to arise appears obsessive. Moreover, Simeon goes on to postulate a 'freedom from cares' that would seem to anyone with any psychological knowledge more likely to be an end-product than a reasonable prerequisite of meditational practice. Ironically, he warns the reader not to start at the top of the ladder by attempting contemplation, but on the lowest rung of vocal prayer. Indeed Molinos would have appeared as heretical to the eastern Church as he did in the Rome of his day. Simeon's strict prescription runs as follows:

The method by which he who wishes it may raise himself from off the earth and rise to heaven is as follows; first, he must wrestle with his mind and tame his passions; second, he must practise psalmody, that is, pray with the lips, for, when passions are subdued, prayer quite naturally brings sweetness and enjoyment even to the tongue and is accepted by God as pleasing to Him; third, he must pray mentally; fourth, he must rise to contemplation. The first is appropriate to beginners; the second, to those who have already achieved some measure of success; the third to those drawing nigh to the last rungs of achievement, and the fourth – to the perfect.

Thus the only possible beginning is the diminishing and taming of passions. This can only be achieved in the soul by guarding the heart and by attention, for, as the Lord says, out of the heart proceed evil thoughts which defile a man. So it is there that attention and guarding are needful. When, through the heart's opposition to them, passions are completely subdued, the mind begins to long for God . . .

(Philokalia)

Here the 'guarding of the heart' seems to be presented as a preliminary to any kind of prayer. It is only when 'all passions are completely subdued' that the process of purification can begin. The gospel says that the kingdom of heaven can be taken by force. But whence can the monk draw the force to subdue the passions except by taking the prayer into the heart? For the lower energy that feeds the passions has to be transmuted into that higher energy which kindles the fire in the heart.

In alchemical language, base metal must be changed into gold. Simeon has spoken of the refining fire some pages earlier:

'Can a man take fire in his bosom, and his clothes not be burned?' says the wise Solomon [Proverbs 6:27]. And I say: can he who has in his divine fire of the Holy Spirit burning naked, not be set on fire, not shine and glitter and not take on the radiance of the Deity in the degree of his purification and penetration by fire? For penetration by fire follows upon purification of the heart, and again purification of heart follows upon penetration by fire, that is, inasmuch as the heart is purified, so it receives divine grace, and again inasmuch as it receives grace, so is it purified. When this is completed (that is, purification of heart and acquisitions of grace have attained their fullness and perfection), through grace a man becomes wholly a god.   *(Philokalia)*

Thus in the end grace kindles the consuming fire. The old man is burnt to ash from which he is reborn like the phoenix. But throughout the *Philokalia*, the collection of writings in which we find St Simeon's 'Practical and Theological Precepts', there is none of the joy that informs the writings of Eckhart, even sometimes of Suso. These clinical masters of self-torture seem seldom to have received the grace for which they so violently struggled, and which was simply granted to the questioning Jew in the following brief Hassidic story:

A disciple asked Rabbi Shmelke: 'We are commanded to love our neighbour as ourself. How can I do this if my neighbour has wronged me?'

The rabbi answered: 'You must understand these words aright. Love your neighbour like something which you yourself are. For all souls are one. Each is a spark from the original soul, and this soul is wholly inherent in all souls, just as your soul is in all the members of your body. It may come to pass that your hand makes a mistake and strikes you. But would you then take a stick and chastise your hand, because it lacked understanding, and so increase your pain? It is the same if your neighbour, who is of one soul with you, wrongs you for lack of understanding. If you punish him, you only hurt yourself.'

The disciple went on asking: 'But if I see a man who is wicked before God, how can I love him?'

'Don't you know,' said Rabbi Shmelke, 'that the original soul came out of the essence of God, and that every human soul is a part of God? And will you have no mercy on him, when you see that one of his holy sparks has been lost in a maze, and is almost stifled?'

(*Tales of the Hassidim*)

Thus the Buddhist 'friendliness' towards an enemy is enjoined by the simplest exposition. Between the seventeenth-century Jewish sect and the Zen masters there are pleasing resemblances. Both were struck by the same lightning flashes of understanding. Anywhere, regardless of faith and culture, the lightning flash may strike at the heart without warning. Often the preliminary state may suggest the 'dark night' of John of the Cross, but today it will be thought of more as a mood of depression, a negative state, perhaps indicating the need for psychological treatment. It did not seem so, however, to the narrator of the following story:

Towards the end of the 1950's, the various negative aspects of my life had made me into a neurotic, incapable of loving, inhibited, apprehensive and with a gloomy cast of mind which sometimes impelled me to long for death as the only way out of an unendurable existence . . .

At this time, my husband and I met the man who was to become the dearest friend of both of us. For me it was the closest relationship of mind and spirit, frequently telepathic, that I have ever known or expect to know: one which I could never have dared to hope for, or believe possible.

[Then] he died suddenly. One had known that his life would not be long, as his health had always been wretched, but nevertheless the shock and desolation were crushing. I remember thinking: 'At a time like this, a belief in the soul's immortality must be the most tremendous support.' But I could not pretend to share it, and indeed did not try to.

On the following Sunday my husband and I were driving along a country road . . . We were talking sorrowfully of our dear friend, when suddenly I knew that his spirit lived and was as close to me that moment as it had ever been in life. When I say I knew, words are inadequate to convey the experience. This was 'knowing' more vivid and real than anything I have ever experienced in the literal sense. It was as if for a moment one had known reality and in comparison the world of the senses was the dream. I was filled with an unutterable joy, which I shall never be able to describe. I seemed to apprehend, in a measure, the inexhaustible love of God for us, which envelops the universe and everything in it. Above all, I understood beyond all questioning that nothing in life, however seemingly insignificant, is ever lost or purposeless, but all tends towards the fulfilment of a design which one day will be made clear to us . . .

From the day of what I can only consider my rebirth, my neurotic difficulties disappeared and have never since returned.   (RERU 809)

What is most remarkable about this experience is its permanent effect. It had the nature of a conversion. Yet at the same time it was many-sided. The presence of the dead friend was felt, there was an assurance of immortality and the experiencer received both a vivid 'knowledge' of reality and very great joy. One is reminded of the assurance of Julian of Norwich that 'all shall be well' . . . Yet this experience arose out of grievous loss, out of the sense that all was not well. Underlying the loss, however, was a shared love. The experience was born in the heart and illumined the whole mind.

The opening of the heart does not often take place with such total effect as in this case. It may seem a purely emotional experience; as in instances previously quoted, the emotion may seem to be no more than a shift in consciousness. A heightened sense of reality may not be accompanied by an infusion of true and lasting knowledge concerning the reality behind the veil of appearances. For a moment the experiencer may think in other categories, yet after a short while nothing will be left that can be put into words. Soon, indeed, the whole experience may fade. In the last case quoted, however, and in the one that follows, it did not do so. Indeed, it remained for the experient 'always below the surface':

On January 23rd, 1961, I came home after an evening lecture at the house of some friends. It was a freezing night . . . I had absolutely no premonitions of anything unusual, but suddenly, I don't know exactly what happened, but it was a bit like a long electric shock. Of course this was quite different, it wasn't mechanical, it was a person; I could have no doubt about this at all. There was a feeling of heat and light rushing through my bloodstream, sweeping over me and paralysing me almost, as if some person outside were blowing something in me to white heat, and I was sobbing tears of love and gratitude. I was longing for it to go on and for some time it kept returning more and more strongly, leaving me weak and shivering in between. There were no visions or voices, but the person communicated with words, or rather ideas, or certainties, with a sort of close intimacy, much more closely than into my ear or imagination . . .

For more than a week I went about as if I were drunk; I could think of nothing else and spent a lot of time waiting and praying and hoping for more of this sensation for the sheer happiness of it. But it was always below the surface, like an electric heater unexpectedly being switched on at the most unlikely moments – such as driving on busy roads, in supermarkets, or walking about, gardening or doing housework.

(RERU 1057)

A special feature of this experience is the presence of physical heat, the fire in the heart so often referred to by Richard Rolle. Indeed, it is perhaps more common in such circumstances to note physical manifestations than to observe any infusion of knowledge. The heightening of consciousness is seen in terms of more acute vision, sharper hearing, greater awareness of the surroundings. This is certainly true of the two brief flashes that follow below. The first is almost pure sensation, an awareness of beauty that leads to a sudden separation between reality and illusion:

I was at work, busy on my job, when suddenly this sensation of peace and compassion 'descended' around me, accompanied by the feeling of glorious *beauty*, as if all the beauty in the world would only be one tiny fraction of this beauty. It only lasted a few minutes. There was nothing to see, hear, touch, taste, or smell.

The experience was strongly reminiscent of a passage in the *Mandukya Upanishad*:

like two birds of golden plumage, inseparable companions, the individual self and the immortal self are perched on the same tree. The former tastes of the sweet and bitter fruits of the tree; the latter, tasting of neither, calmly observes.

(RERU 1817)

In the second, a young woman tells succinctly and in the most authentic language of a vivid experience apparently self-induced: no more than a picking up of sixpence, perhaps, but of a very bright sixpence. Although she mentions Brother Lawrence, who has already been quoted, she gives no hint of her method:

When I was in my mid-teens, I read Brother Lawrence's *Practice of the Presence of God* and it profoundly moved me. I re-read it in my early twenties and decided to try and capture the divine presence within myself once, for one instant, every day. After several quite abortive efforts I was on the point of abandoning the whole exercise, when suddenly in the middle of one day, I touched some hitherto hidden button within me, and a little packet or quantum of warmth, light, love (call it what you will) flipped into the middle of me and then spread outwards, irradiating my whole being. The experience was the most exciting I ever had. It was piercingly pleasurable.

(RERU 1528)

Are these experiences, one may ask, to be compared to those of the professed religious, of those who have passed many years in meditation and have followed strict disciplines? The heightened awareness that has overtaken these contemporaries has generally had no prelude. They do not count themselves followers of a faith. Yet not only have they evidently received that grace which many have spent their lives praying for, but in two of the cases just quoted the experience has worked a permanent change. Is it possible to gain the reward unearned?

If the answer is no, there must still be some qualifications. But indeed, unless one accepts the doctrine of many lives one cannot understand the inequality between people. To some, the idea of immaterial existence is incomprehensible – they have no invisible means of support. To others, it is a nagging possibility which they try to ignore, since it makes their materialist stupor uncomfortable. They do not want to wake up. To yet others, it is a vital reality – present, as it was to Wordsworth, in childhood – and a living component of their adult lives.

Apparently spontaneous experiences come to members of the last two classes. For some, it takes the form of conversion. They are swept away by a sudden reversal of the values to which they had clung. The walls of Jericho are thrown down by a single trumpet blast. But, as we have seen from many experiences quoted, the walls may be speedily rebuilt. The trumpet blast remains no more than a faint echo. To the third and last class the experience is a revelation of what they have always known. It is blinding but not unfamiliar. It confirms what was always subconsciously latent. And in some cases, as in the two just quoted, it leaves a lasting change.

But is the experience of the woman travelling in a car with her husband the same in kind and value as that of Henry Suso when he fell in unconscious rapture on the altar steps? Who can judge this? Only one who can assess the effect of that moment on the experiencer's subsequent life. To Suso and his kind, such a rapture is no more than a confirmation that his feet are on the path, which he has been pursuing since boyhood and which he will pursue till death. But to many of our contemporaries it may be no more than a confirmation of the path's existence. It owes its vividness to the contrast between it and the general level of consciousness of the day before. People following a discipline of prayer or meditation may, at the outset at least, receive a few of these flashes of insight. The reason is that since their level of consciousness is steadily rising, the peaks hardly stand out from the ascending ridge. The way seems almost flat and uneventful.

We can only account for the vast inequalities of spiritual experience by reincarnation. By the law of *karma*, which connects action with result, deed with merit and demerit, both in a single life and from life to life, the point at which we enter the way is determined at birth. It is said that good or bad *karma* may lie dormant for many years, or for many lives, until the moment appropriate for its working out. In these revelations, seemingly great or seemingly small, comes an infused knowledge of order – a sense that the universe is an ordered reality from which the self is not separate. One receives a 'quantum of warmth, light, love', which is also understanding but which, when the experience passes, may leave no intellectual trace. It is the fire spoken of in the *Katha Upanishad*:

Count the links of the chain: worship the triple fire: knowledge, meditation, practice; the triple process: evidence, inference, experience; the triple duty: study, concentration, renunciation; understand that everything comes from Spirit, that Spirit alone is sought and found; attain everlasting peace; mount beyond birth and death.

When a man understands himself, understands universal Self, the union of the two kindles the triple fire, offers the sacrifice; then shall he, though still on earth, break the bonds of death, beyond sorrow, [and] mount into heaven.

(The Ten Principal Upanishads)

The Upanishad points beyond the stage of love, charity and compassion to realms where self and non-self are one. Although hints of this ultimate unity may be implicit in many chance experiences, the return to duality is immediate and the knowledge brought back can only be explained in the language of duality, or perhaps in parable. For the deepest truths can be expounded in our world of duality – of body and spirit, here and there, this and that – only in parable or paradox. Hence Chuang Tzu's well-known tale of the butterfly:

Once upon a time, I Chuang Tzu, dreamt I was a butterfly, fluttering hither and thither, to all intents and purposes a butterfly. I was conscious only of following my fancies as a butterfly, and was unconscious of my individuality as a man. Suddenly I awaked, and there I lay, myself again. Now I do not know whether I was then a man dreaming I was a butterfly, or whether I am now a butterfly dreaming I am a man. Between a man and a butterfly there is necessarily a barrier. The transition is called metempsychosis (the transmigration of souls).

(Musings of a Chinese Mystic)

Hence also the paradoxical discovery of an anonymous musician that, although he is treading the path, there is in fact no path:

As a violinist, early on in life when playing I at times fell into a dream-like state – I hesitate to use the word trance – in which I seemed to penetrate to the very centre of my tone. An inner non-physical silence seemed to descend upon me. This was accompanied by a change of rhythm in breathing, which became slow and deep. The tone underwent a metaphysical change. Later in life I had the same experience conducting orchestras. Now I am able to tune in to this all-embracing silence in the open country and particularly in woods, where I find myself in union with the trees. It is a powerful experience.

After years of intensive study and meditation it has become clear to me that in the intuitional sphere there is no path, no seeker, no method and no enlightenment. I am relieved from the weight of intellectual effort in this direction, which is unavoidably a state of barking up the wrong tree.

(RERU 1223)

'I am relieved from the weight of intellectual effort', he writes. And there is no doubt that what holds many people back from the way is the effort expended in trying to find it. Most of our contemporary hucksters at the path's entrance proclaim the uselessness of intellectual effort, the need to be as a little child. But the efforts demanded in order to regain this lost simplicity are frequently considerable. 'There is no System', they announce, only to elaborate a formidable one, acceptance of which is desirable, if not obligatory, if one is to attain advanced states of meditation. Sometimes a pseudo-scientific mish-mash is promulgated in the name of the spirit, and subscription to its tenets is set up as a means-test of understanding.

The contemporary Indian teacher, Dr R. P. Kaushik, has an approach similar in several respects to that of Krishnamurti, both of whom, like the violinist, would claim that there is in fact no path, no seeker, no method, no enlightenment at some future point in time:

A mind which is seeking something in particular is incapable of looking, incapable of seeing. The very search creates a blindness. If you are looking for a spiritual state of mind, a better state of mind where there is clarity of sensitivity or perception, who is looking for this state but the thinker, the very mind which is confused? It is looking through its confusion. Whether you are looking for love, or God, or clarity of mind, it is the same movement – you are looking out of frustration and confusion, looking for something in the future. And therefore you deny the possibility of it being in the present – you imply that clarity does not exist now.

(*Light of Exploration*)

Sometimes it is only when the intellectual effort of studying a system has been abandoned that the revelation comes. Flashes of compassion and insight frequently arrive at the moment when one has ceased to beat one's head against an impenetrable wall of thoughts which cut off the light of reality.

But what if the 'spark of friendliness' refuses to kindle? One of Ouspensky's followers once complained to him that he felt no love for anyone. How could he begin? 'Begin with the dog', Ouspensky advised him. But as we have seen, the Buddhist's advice would be: 'Begin with yourself.' No one is capable of proceeding to further stages of enlightenment who has not accepted himself for what he is, who still hates himself for his sins; for sins thrive on our obsession with them. Obsession with sin is like Suso's hair shirt. The nails are forever pricking the flesh, giving one no peace, no time for silence:

The pupils of the Tendai school used to study meditation before Zen entered Japan. Four of them, who were intimate friends, promised one another to observe seven days of silence.

On the first day all were silent. Their meditation had begun auspiciously, but when night came and the oil lamps were growing dim, one of the pupils could not help exclaiming to a servant: 'Fix those lamps.'

The second pupil was surprised to hear the first one talk. 'We are not supposed to say a word,' he remarked.

'You two are stupid. Why did you talk?' asked the third.

'I am the only one who has not talked,' concluded the fourth pupil.

(*Zen Flesh, Zen Bones*)

Perhaps our inability to be silent is our principal 'sin', the single greatest obstacle on the way to enlightenment.

4 Enlightenment

Enlightenment is not a single process, nor in its early stages is it permanent. The experience is generally brief and the experients may report it so differently that one might suppose that they were reporting quite different happenings. But one characteristic is common to all flashes of enlightenment: there is always an extension of consciousness, a temporary dissolution of the confines of the self, an infusion of something variously named nature, timelessness, divinity, knowledge, joy, harmony, light, creativity.

One description, a woman's memory of a childhood experience, states that what the child 'knew' in the brief seconds of her ecstasy was no more than that she was on the *verge* of something:

When I was about eleven years old I spent part of a summer holiday in the Wye Valley. Waking up early one bright morning, before any of the household was about, I left my bed and went to kneel on the windowseat, to look out over the curve which the river took just below the house. The trees between the house and the river – I was on a level with their topmost branches – were either poplars or silver birch, and green fields stretched away beyond the river to the far distance. The morning sunlight shimmered on the leaves of the trees and on the rippling surface of the river. The scene was very beautiful, and quite suddenly I felt myself on the verge of a great revelation. It was as if I had stumbled unwittingly on a place where I was not expected, and was about to be initiated into some wonderful mystery, something of indescribable significance. Then, just as suddenly, the feeling faded. But for the brief seconds while it lasted I had known that in some strange way, I, the essential 'me', was a part of the trees, of the sunshine, and the river; that we all belonged to some great unity. I was left filled with exhilaration and exultation of spirit.

(quoted in E. Robinson, *The Original Vision*)

Another example shows a great expansion of consciousness also arising from a heightened perception of nature:

One afternoon I was lying down resting after a long walk on the Plain . . . The grass was hot and I was on an eye level with insects moving about. Everything was warm, busy and occupied with living. I was relaxed but extraneous to the scene.

Then it happened: a sensation of bliss. No loss of consciousness, but increased consciousness . . . I could feel the earth under me right down to the centre of the earth, and I belonged to it and it belonged to me. I also felt that the insects were my brothers and sisters, and all that was alive was related to me, because we were all living matter that died to make way for the next generation . . . And I felt and experienced everything that existed, even sounds and colours and tastes, all at once, and it was all blissful . . . I had a conviction that a most important truth had been enunciated: that we are all related – animal, vegetable and mineral – so no one is alone. I have never forgotten this experience.

(RERU 822)

Most English people who have recorded such experiences resort to the poets, and especially to Wordsworth, when seeking a comparison for their momentary visions. It is probably the influence of that great poet that makes so many associate these childhood or adolescent intimations of nature with a sense of loss. Wordsworth looked back on a pre-natal unity with nature:

> There was a time when meadow, grove, and stream,
> The earth, and every common sight,
>   To me did seem
>   Apparelled in celestial light,
> The glory and the freshness of a dream.
> It is not now as it hath been of yore;
>   Turn wheresoe'er I may,
>   By night or day,
> The things which I have seen I now can see no more.

(*Intimations of Immortality*)

Wordsworth's life perhaps marked a decline from pure to clouded vision. In one sense he was a refugee from the spread of industrialism: from being a nature mystic he deteriorated into a stuffy Anglican who lived in a remote and quiet corner of England where nature had not yet been desecrated with mills and mines. But despite his loss of immediate vision, Wordsworth was still able to sense an underlying 'presence' both in nature and in the minds of men.

Yet his was always a backward look. An earlier poet, whom he deeply admired, looked by contrast outside time into the eternal nature of his early experience. Although he was remembering it from childhood, Thomas Traherne's vision was actual when he described it in the best known of his *Centuries of Meditation*:

The Corn was Orient and Immortal Wheat, which never should be reaped, nor was ever sown. I thought it had stood from everlasting to everlasting. The Dust and Stones of the Street were as Precious as GOLD. The Gates were at first the end of the World, the Green Trees when I saw them first through one of the Gates Transported and Ravished me; their Sweetness and unusual Beauty made my Heart to leap, and almost mad with Extasie, they were such strange and Wonderfull Things; The Men! O what Venerable and Reverend Creatures did the Aged seem! Immortal Cherubims! And Young Men glittering and Sparkling Angels and Maids strange Seraphick Pieces of Life and Beauty! Boys and Girls Tumbling in the Street, and Playing, were moving Jewels. I knew not that they were Born or should Die. But all things abided Eternally as they were in their Proper Places. Eternity was Manifest in the Light of the Day, and something infinite Behind every thing appeared: which talked with my Expectation and moved my Desire. The Citie seemed to stand in Eden, or to be Built in Heaven. The Streets were mine, the Temple was mine, the People were mine, their Clothes and Gold and Silver was mine, as much as their Sparkling Eyes Fair Skins and ruddy faces. The Skies were mine, and so were the Sun and Moon and Stars, and all the World was mine, and I the only Spectator and Enjoyer of it. I knew no Churlish Proprieties, nor Bounds nor Divisions: but all Proprieties and Divisions were mine: all Treasures and the Possessors of them. So that with much adoe I was corrupted; and made to learn the Dirty Devices of this World. Which now I unlearn, and become as it were a little Child again, that I may enter into the kingdom of GOD.

(Centuries of Meditation)

However familiar this passage, to read it afresh in the present context is perhaps to read it differently. Traherne, like Wordsworth, is conscious of the fall from purity of vision into the corruption of worldly life. He states, however, that thanks to this vision at the gates of the city (which was probably Hereford) it was only 'with great ado' that he came to 'learn the dirty devices of the world'. Yearning is absent. Wordsworth, by contrast, falls into regret that 'The things which I have seen I now can see no more'. Peculiar to Traherne's vision is the apprehension that all things were at that moment his. In this claim, however, there is no hint of possession. There was for him no distinction on that day between the seer and what he saw. Traherne's experience passes perhaps beyond identity with nature to a more profound unity. It is not far from this to a passage from Eckhart's sermons: 'This is the now of eternity, when the soul knows all things in God, as new and fresh and lovely, as I find them now at present.'

But it is not far either from the quite unembellished experience of a bored and lonely mother pushing her pram in Scotland during a bleak moment of the First World War:

In 1916 I was walking along the shore road westward out of Culross wheeling a pram which contained one child recumbent and one doing everything but lie down. There were three other young children running round me, getting under my feet and asking the silliest questions . . . The sun was not shining. I looked across the waters of the Firth of Forth over to the hills hiding the town of Linlithgow, studying their outline against the watery sky, and out of the utter boredom and empty meaninglessness of that afternoon came a stab of knowledge. I *knew* and have known ever since that there *is* some Reason, some Plan, some Cause, some Soul – call it what you will – which can be relied upon . . . For a split second, there upon the shores of the Firth, I *understood*. What I understood I don't know. I don't know now, but I *know* I understood then and I have remained firm and calm and unshaken upon that rock – i.e., that once I understood – ever since.

(quoted in M. Laski, *Ecstasy*)

Here, unexpectedly, and apparently without any religious context, came a moment of deep understanding which had lasting results for the experiencer. Perhaps it was the external landscape, or some inner effect of 'self-remembering' that elicited this sudden change of consciousness.

By contrast, there can be no doubt of the influence of the

Palestinian night on the writer and archaeologist, Jacquetta Hawkes, whose account in her autobiography of an extended experience of this kind is carefully detailed and conveys an unexaggerated and undistorted description of the event as it occurred:

One night when the land was still fresh from the rain, I was wandering near our camp enjoying the moonlight when an immense exaltation took possession of me. It was as though the White Goddess of the moon had thrown some bewitching power into her rays. It seemed to me that our arid satellite was itself a living presence bounding in the sky . . . Indeed, the whole night was dancing about me.

It appeared that the moonlight had ceased to be a physical thing and now represented a state of illumination in my own mind. As here in the night landscape the steady white light threw every olive leaf and pebble into sharp relief, so it seemed that my thoughts and feelings had been given an extraordinary clarity and truth.

So powerfully was I moved by this sense of possession that I climbed up onto a high outcrop of rock against the mouth of the wadi and knelt down there. The moonlight swam round, and in, my head as I knelt looking across the plain to the shining silver bar of the Mediterranean.

From far behind me, still muffled in the folds of the mountain, I heard the bronze sound of camel-bells. To my sharpened but converging senses they seemed like a row of brown flowers blooming in the moonlight. In truth the sound of bells came from nothing more remarkable than a caravan, perhaps twenty camels with packs and riders, coming down the wadi on its way northward to Haifa. But even now I cannot recognize that caravan in such everyday terms; my memory of it is dreamlike, yet embodies one of the most intense sensuous and emotional experiences of my life. For those minutes, and I have no notion how many they were, I had the heightened sensibility of one passionately in love and with it the power to transmute all that the senses perceived into symbols of burning significance. This surely is one of the best rewards of humanity . . .

The bells came nearer and another sound mingled with theirs; a low, monotonous chanting. I looked behind me for a moment and saw the dark procession swaying out from behind the last bend in the wadi, then I turned back so that the column should pass me and enter my world of vision from behind. I found myself comprehending every physical fact of their passage as though it were a part of my own existence. I knew how the big soft feet of the camels pressed down upon and embraced the rough stones of the path; I knew the warm depth of their fur and the friction upon it of leather harness and the legs of the riders; I knew the blood flowing through the bodies of men and beasts and thought of it as echoing the life of the anemones which now showed black among the rocks around me. The sound of bells and the chanting seemed rich and glowing as the stuff of the caravan itself . . .

As the moon leapt and bounded in the sky, I took full possession of a love and confidence that have not yet forsaken me.

(Man on Earth)

Common to all these sudden moments of vision is a vivid sharpening of the senses. Here, despite the use of the word 'trance' by Tennyson and his contemporaries, there is no clouding of the senses. The girl's vision of the garden from her window seat and Jacquetta Hawkes' apprehension of the Palestinian night are all much more acute than in ordinary life. Indeed, in the latter case, the experiencer hears, sees and feels with preternatural acuteness. To those who practise meditation, this simultaneous extension of inner and outer consciousness will not be surprising. There is usually more light in the room after a session of meditation.

Instances of such experiences in the countryside could be greatly multiplied. Some people find themselves more liable to such transports in the mountains. Here is the discovery of 'Phaedrus', the philosophical *alter ego* of the motorcyclist in Robert M. Pirsig's book *Zen and the Art of Motorcycle Maintenance*, as he rides towards the summit of a pass over the Rockies:

Phaedrus felt that at the moment of pure Quality-perception, or not even perception, at the moment of pure Quality, there is no subject and there is no object. There is only a sense of Quality that produces a later awareness of subjects and objects. At the moment of pure Quality, subject and object are identical. This is the *tat tyam asi* truth of the Upanishads, but it's also reflected in modern street argot: 'getting with it', 'digging it', 'grooving on it', are all slang reflections of this identity.

In this book the Zen quality of immediacy only slowly reveals itself. The narrator's vision is seldom pure and often wholly masked. He is perhaps typical of contemporary technique-obsessed man, who, approaching the babble at the entrance to the way, shies off and decides desperately to be his own guide. In the end, however, the motorcyclist's private version of Zen does seem to work.

Even a city is not an impossible place for such an experience:

One day as I was walking along Marylebone Road I was suddenly seized with an extraordinary sense of great joy and exaltation as though a marvellous beam of spiritual power had shot through me linking me in rapture with the world, the universe, life with a capital L, and all the beings around me. All delight and power, all things living, all time fused in a brief second.

(RERU 58)

The boy of the Ipswich barber's shop recalls as a middle-aged man being suddenly overwhelmed by such a change of consciousness in one of the back streets of Reading. He made for the nearest church and sat down to meditate. It was an ordinary meditation and when it was over the event had passed.

Is it possible, one may ask, to induce such experiences? The same witness remembers one such attempt during the time when he was a follower of an Ouspensky succession group. It was during a walk in Kensington Gardens. His self-devised method was to lengthen and regularize his pace, also his breathing, and to direct his gaze far ahead. As a result, when he paused at the head of the Serpentine, his view down the water was particularly bright and his mood very calm. But many such attempts during those years produced only this single 'sixpence'. One could not call it a good investment. Ouspensky himself, attempting a similar exercise, had far more impressive results:

I remember once sitting on a sofa smoking and looking at an ashtray. It was an ordinary copper ashtray. Suddenly I felt that I was beginning to understand what the ashtray was, and at the same time, with a certain wonder and almost with fear, I felt that I had never understood it before and that we do not understand the simplest things around us.

The ashtray roused a whirlwind of thoughts and images. It contained such an infinite number of facts, of events; it was linked with such an immense number of things. First of all, with everything connected with smoking and tobacco. This at once roused thousands of images, pictures, memories.

I remember writing a few words on a piece of paper in order to retain something of these thoughts on the following day. And next day I read: 'A man can go mad from one ashtray.'

The meaning of all that I felt was that in one ashtray it was possible to know *all*. By invisible threads the ashtray was connected with everything in the world, not only with the present, but with all the past and with all the future.

'Everything is alive', I said to myself in the midst of these observations; 'there is nothing dead, it is only we who are dead. If we become alive for a moment, we shall feel that everything is alive, that all things live, think, feel and can speak to us.'

(*A New Model of the Universe*)

It is likely that Ouspensky modelled his experiment on the first phase of Jakob Boehme's illumination which occurred in 1600, when he twenty-five and working as a shoemaker in Goerlitz:

'Sitting one day in his room, his eyes fell upon a burnished pewter dish, which reflected the sunshine with such marvellous splendour that he fell into an inward ecstasy, and it seemed to him as if he could now look into the principles and deepest foundations of things. He believed that it was only a fancy, and in order to banish it from his mind he went out upon the green. But here he remarked that he gazed into the very heart of things, the very herbs and grass, and that actual nature harmonized with what he had inwardly seen. He said nothing of this to anyone, but praised and thanked God in silence.'

(quoted in William James, *The Varieties of Religious Experience*)

As a result of this experience, Boehme 'learned to know the innermost foundation of nature, and acquire the capacity to see henceforth with the eyes of the soul into the heart of all things, a faculty which remained with him even in his normal condition'. So wrote Boehme's biographer, who continues with an account of the second phase of this first illumination, which also occurred in 1600:

'In the twenty-fifth year of his age, he was again surrounded by the divine light and replenished with the heavenly knowledge; insomuch as going abroad in the fields to a green before Neys Gate, at Goerlitz, he there sat down and, viewing the herbs and grass of the field in his inward light, he saw into their essences, use and properties, which were discovered to him by their lineaments, figures and signatures. In like manner he beheld the whole creation, and from that foundation he afterwards wrote his book, *De signatura Rerum*. In the unfolding of those mysteries before his understanding he had a great measure of joy, yet returned home and took care of his family and lived in great peace and silence, scarce intimating to any these wonderful things that had befallen him, and in the year 1610, being again taken into this light, lest the mysteries revealed to him should pass through him as a stream, and rather for a memorial than intending any publication, he wrote his first book, called *Aurora*, or the *Morning Redness*.'

(quoted in *The Varieties of Religious Experience*)

Many of the experiences already quoted bear some resemblance to this last experience of Boehme's outside the gates of his town. One thinks immediately of Traherne's vision outside the gates of Hereford later in the same century. One profound difference, however, separates Boehme's illumination from these others, for though some claimed a permanent change, none retained the original vision as he did. For many the experience passed rapidly and remained only as a memory.

Illumination of this kind may lead to scientific discovery, or even, in the case of Descartes, to theories which would change the whole course of western thought. His theory of a rational universe depended on a sudden illumination, a lightning flash which struck him, alone in Amsterdam, on the night of 10 November 1619. Hitherto Descartes had always been seeking for a key to the world's mystery, to find an entirely new system by which all questions could be solved. He read the Catalan mystic Ramon Lull, but it was not a mystical apprehension that he sought. To him mechanics and geometry seemed to offer models to which a new universal science must conform. Then on the night of his illumination, he reached the triple certainty that all knowledge was one, that it was the work of a single mind, and that it took the form of a poetic intuition. Descartes devoted himself to the ·

pursuit of this universal science which would enable man to subdue nature, to lengthen his own life, and to know the relations and proportions that bound one object to another. He had found a rational God, had deified the rational quality in man and in nature, and now sought to demonstrate the truths of meta-physics in the same manner as a geometrical theorem.

For almost two centuries, the theories of Descartes separated science from religion. Recent theorists, however, have tended to reconcile them by relating an increasingly irrational science with an increasingly undogmatic religion. Among the anti-cartesians of our own time, the American physicist, Fritjof Capra, draws together the essential thought-patterns of Taoist mysticism and sub-atomic physics. His insights began, like those of Descartes, with an illumination, described in the preface to his book *The Tao of Physics*:

Five years ago, I had a beautiful experience which set me on a road that has led to the writing of this book. I was sitting by the ocean one late summer afternoon, watching the waves rolling in and feeling the rhythm of my breathing, when I suddenly became aware of my whole environment as being engaged in a gigantic cosmic dance. Being a physicist, I knew that the sand, rocks, water and air around me were made of vibrating molecules and atoms, and that these consisted of particles which interacted with one another by creating and destroying other particles. I knew also that the earth's atmosphere was continually bombarded by showers of 'cosmic rays', particles of high energy undergoing multiple collisions as they penetrated the air. All this was familiar to me from my research in high-energy physics, but until that moment I had only experienced it through graphs, diagrams and mathematical theories. As I sat on that beach my former experiences came to life; I 'saw' cascades of energy coming down from outer space, in which particles were created and destroyed in rhythmic pulses; I 'saw' the atoms of the elements and those of my body par-ticipating in this cosmic dance of energy; I felt its rhythm and I 'heard' its sound, and at that moment I *knew* that this was the Dance of Shiva, the Lord of dancers worshipped by the Hindus.

(*The Tao of Physics*)

Here Capra's training in the sciences no doubt dictated the nature of his vision. Boehme's cosmological imagery derives from the semi-scientific nature of his preoccupation with the theory of alchemy and, like Capra's, led to the writing of books which set out to describe the universe in terms of his illumination. The alchemical imagery makes these difficult in a way that Capra's book is not, at least for those with an up-to-date scientific training. Moments of enlightenment frequently come today in scientific disguise.

A follower of transcendental meditation over many years, who is no scientist, gives the following account of what would appear to be a symbolic vision:

One morning when I was dozing in bed I had a very vivid experience. I seemed to see hundreds of tiny dark specks moving very fast on a light background, like so many ants rushing about endlessly and to no purpose. This brought a feeling of agitation and meaninglessness. Then I saw one speck which was just like all the others except that it stood quite still. Awareness of this motionless speck brought with it a very strong sense of happiness and reassurance. Though it was so small its presence entirely overcame the fearful feelings produced by the hectic and random movements of all the other specks and made sense of the total picture.

(S.J.C.)

This can perhaps be interpreted as an assurance that amid the ever-changing phenomena of life there exists one stable point, which is a permanent self. To be assured in this way of its existence brought the experient great happiness. This particular person – a social worker in his mid-forties – is primarily religious, and his experience, despite its scientific symbolism, may count as such.

Illumination may also arise from the contemplation of a work of art. The great American art critic and historian, Bernard Berenson, attributes the deepening of his insights to the effect of a carving, which by itself was probably no more remarkable than many others that he had seen on his Italian journey:

Then, one morning as I was gazing at the leafy scrolls carved on the door jambs of S. Pietro outside Spoleto, suddenly stem, tendril and

D

foliage became alive and, in becoming alive, made me feel as if I had emerged into the light after long groping in the darkness of an initiation. I felt as one illumined, and beheld a world where every outline, every edge, and every surface was in a living relation to me and not as hitherto, in a merely cognitive one. Since that morning, nothing visible has been indifferent or even dull. Everywhere I feel the ideated pulsation of vitality, I mean energy and radiance, as if it all served to enhance my own functioning.

(*Aesthetics and History*)

This may appear to be a more profound version of the experience already quoted of the man in the National Gallery who was drawn into the picture by Gerard David. Berenson himself may have thought of it as an aesthetic experience; certainly it had no specific religious overtones. It can be considered perhaps to be an example of what the Austrian poet Rilke described as *einfühlung*, or empathy: it is clear that the quality of the carving contributed to Berenson's experience. A religious person moved to illumination by a statue or painting would certainly be moved more by the work's subject than by its execution.

This was certainly true of the painting of Christ which sometimes seemed to come alive for Santa Teresa of Avila:

At times it certainly seemed to me as if I were looking at a painting, but on many other occasions it appeared to be no painting but Christ Himself, such was the clarity with which He was pleased to appear to me. Yet there were times when the vision was so indistinct that I did think it was a painting, though it bore no resemblance even to the most perfect of earthly pictures, and I have seen some good ones. No, it would be absurd to speak of any resemblance; the vision was no more like a painting than a portrait is like a living man. However well a portrait is painted, it can never look completely natural, for it is plainly a dead thing.

(*The Life of Saint Teresa*)

Teresa's argument is meticulous. She has been asked to give an account of her spiritual life to her superiors, whose knowledge of such high matters was no more than theoretical. She is careful not to claim too much; for her, a probably mediocre work of art has been transformed into what it represents. As Teresa was by then far advanced along the way, one cannot describe this experience as a sudden illumination, but rather as a progressive series of contemplations.

A very different religious illumination, which led to a lifetime of preaching and persecutions and also to the foundation of the Quaker movement, is described by George Fox in his *Journal*. Prior to this moment he had cut off communication with his family, with the priests, with the Puritan sects and with almost all men. Fox was wandering from town to town, racked by temptations and utterly confused:

> Now was I come up in spirit, through the flaming sword, into the paradise of God. All things were new, and all the creation gave another smell unto me than before, beyond what words can utter. I knew nothing but pureness, innocency, and righteousness, being renewed up into the image of God by Christ Jesus, so that I was come up into the state of Adam, which he was in before he fell.
>
> (quoted in Ronald Knox, *Enthusiasm*)

Fox felt himself called upon to preach peace and sobriety throughout this country and the American colonies. Yet he preached in the most violent way, denouncing all other Christian sects and even resorting to street brawling. His denunciation of the 'bloody city of Lichfield' is in the vein of the Old Testament prophets. In fact, Fox's illumination has many parallel features with the cases of conversion recorded by William James, although some of the sudden converts quoted by James soon relapsed into their old sinful ways, which was not the case with Fox.

Fox's illumination, compared with those of Boehme, was only partial. It gave him an access of emotional energy sufficient to sustain him through a storm-tossed life. But it gave him no extension of knowledge. He did not see more deeply into the nature of the universe, only into some of its delusions. He was unaware that among those priests whom he so vociferously denounced, were Platonists as peaceful and clear-sighted as Traherne, and among the hated Roman Catholics, men of the highest quality like Brother Lawrence and Molinos. Nevertheless, he had a more vital experience than many directors of conscience in the Church who laboured to keep those of greater experience on the rails of orthodoxy.

The fourteenth-century Dutch mystic, John of Ruysbroeck, offers a rough-and-ready method of distinguishing an enlightened man from one who merely discourses learnedly on the subject of holiness:

Whereas the enlightened man, by virtue of the divine light, is simple and stable and free from curious considerations, these others are manifold and restless and full of subtle reasonings and reflections; and they do not taste inward unity, nor the satisfaction which is without images. And by this they may know themselves.

(John of Ruysbroeck)

A similar test of one who claims enlightenment is given in the *Diamond Sutra*:

'What think you Subhuti? Suppose a disciple has attained the degree of *arahat* (full enlightenment), could he entertain within his mind any such arbitrary conception as "I have become a fully enlightened one?"'

'No, honoured of the worlds! Because speaking truly, there is no such thing as a fully enlightened one. Should a disciple who has attained such a degree of enlightenment cherish within his mind such an arbitrary conception as "I have become an *arahat*", he would soon be grasping after such things as his own selfhood, other selves, living beings and a universal self.'

(*Diamond Sutra*)

In another eastern scripture the portrait is drawn of a man on the verge of enlightenment, who views all the signs of the new state as symptoms of disease; in this state the Taoist master to whom he goes for a cure is powerless to help him:

'You are the master of cunning arts. I have a disease. Can you cure it, sir?'

'So far', replied Wen Chih, 'you have only acquainted me with your desire. Please let me know first the symptoms of your disease.'

'I hold it no honour', said Lung Shu, 'to be praised in my native village, nor do I consider it a disgrace to be decried in my native state. Gain excites in me no joy, and loss no sorrow. I look upon life in the same light as death, upon riches in the same light as poverty, upon my fellow men as so many swine, and upon myself as I look upon my fellow men. I dwell in my home as though it were a caravanserai and regard my native district with no more feeling than I would a barbarian state. Afflicted as I am in these various ways, honours and rewards fail to rouse me, pains and penalties to overawe me, good or bad fortune to influence me, joy or grief to move me. Thus I am incapable of serving my sovereign, of associating with my friends and kinsmen, of directing my wife and children, or of controlling my servants and retainers. What disease is this and what remedy is there that will cure it?'

Wen Chih replied by asking Lung Shu to stand with his back to the light, while he himself faced the light and looked at him intently. 'Ah!' said he after a while, 'I see that a good square inch of your heart is hollow. You are within an ace of being a true sage. Six of the orifices in your heart are open and clear, and only the seventh is blocked up. This however is doubtless due to the fact that you are mistaking for a disease that which is really divine enlightenment. It is a case in which my shallow art is of no avail.'

(Musings of a Chinese Mystic)

This story is particularly relevant today. Lack of relish for the common joys of the world is frequently considered a morbid state, to be cured by drugs or psychological treatment. Instead, it can be viewed as the Taoist master saw it, or in Christian terms as a version of the 'dark night' in which the common lights have gone out and the new illumination has not yet struck the sufferer. Of those milling around the stalls at the entrance to the way, sampling the goods on one then on another, perhaps the majority are 'within an ace of becoming true sages', were it not that 'a good square inch of their hearts is hollow'. But few of the 'masters of the cunning arts' who offer their nostrums today will admit with the Taoist teacher that against this their arts are of no avail. Only when the person has worked out his own *karma* (the outcome of his past actions) is the blockage dissolved.

The wake of Gurdjieff and many other teachers is strewn with damaged souls, for whom their 'treatment' was either premature or unsuitable. Those who accept the doctrine of rebirth will understand that the absence of illumination in this life is not a final deprivation. The cloud of bad *karma* may take long to disperse and may persist until death. But in the end those who seek will find.

Illumination is not a single and uniform state. It has several degrees, which we, the unilluminated writers, can only tentatively distinguish. The first has been called 'cosmic consciousness', a term invented in the nineteenth century by the American investigator of such states, R. M. Bucke, a doctor, who wrote a book with that title. His classic description of this expanded form of consciousness is based on an experience of his own:

It was in the early spring, at the beginning of his thirty-sixth year. He and two friends had spent the evening reading Wordsworth, Shelley, Keats, Browning, and especially Whitman. They parted at midnight and he had a long drive in a hansom (it was an English city). His mind, deeply under the influence of the ideas, images and emotions called up by the reading and talk of the evening, was calm and peaceful. He was in a state of quiet, almost passive enjoyment. All at once, without warning of any kind, he found himself wrapped around as it were by a flame-coloured cloud. For an instant he thought of fire, some sudden conflagration in the great city; the next he knew the light was in himself. Directly afterwards came upon him a sense of exultation, of immense joyousness accompanied or immediately followed by an intellectual illumination quite impossible to describe. Into his brain streamed one momentary lightning-flash of the Brahmic splendour which has ever since lightened his life; upon his heart fell one drop of Brahmic bliss, leaving thenceforward for always an aftertaste of heaven. Among other things . . . he saw and knew that the cosmos is not dead matter but a living Presence, that the soul of man is immortal, that the universe is so built and ordered that without peradventure all things work together for the good of each and all, that the foundation principle of the world is what we call love and that the happiness of everyone in the long run is absolutely certain. He claims he learned more within the few seconds during which the illumination lasted than in previous months or even years of study and that he learned much that no study could ever have taught.

(*Cosmic Consciousness*)

It would be hard to exaggerate the comprehensiveness of this brief experience. It affirmed the rightness of the universe, as it had been affirmed by Julian of Norwich – that the universe was a living thing and that life was eternal, as was known to Boehme. And it went beyond the Christian promise of eternal life in the future, to see eternity as a present reality – and here Dr Bucke was at one with William Blake. There was in it joy and exaltation, and also that indescribable intellectual revelation that turned cartesian dualism and materialism upside down. 'The principle of the world', he learnt, 'is love.'

From the moment of Bucke's envelopment in what he calls fire (which other experiencers think of as light), to that in which he found himself still trotting on through the city in the hansom cab, the temporal span was a few seconds. But twenty-five years later, when he wrote this account, he was still living in the light of this revelation, which had seen him through spells of depression. As far as one knows, there was no preparation by Bucke for this experience. A member of Walt Whitman's circle, he was used to thinking in poetic and unmaterialistic terms. Thomas Aquinas said of his own experience that it contained more truth than he had been able to put in all his books: 'Such things have been revealed to me that now all I have written appears in my eyes as of no greater value than straw.' Julian of Norwich and Boehme underwent a progressive series of revelations. Bucke had, as far as we know, only one access of what he called cosmic consciousness.

An instance of cosmic consciousness deliberately induced in a disciple by his teacher is given in the autobiography of the Yogi Paramhansa Yogananda. The young man was distractedly meditating, when his master called him:

'Poor boy, the mountains couldn't give you what you wanted.' Master spoke caressingly, comfortingly. His calm gaze was unfathomable. 'Your heart's desire shall be fulfilled.'

Sri Yukteswar seldom indulged in riddles; I was bewildered. He struck gently on my chest above the heart. My body became immovably rooted; breath was drawn out of my lungs as if by some huge magnet. Soul and mind instantly lost their physical bondage and streamed out like a fluid piercing light from my every pore. The flesh was as though dead, yet in my intense awareness I knew that never before had I been fully alive. My sense of identity was no longer narrowly confined to a body, but embraced the circumambient atoms. People on distant streets seemed to be moving gently over my own remote periphery. The roots of plants and trees appeared through a dim transparency of the soil; I discerned the inward flow of their sap.

The whole vicinity lay bare before me. My ordinary frontal vision was now changed to a vast spherical sight, simultaneously all-perceptive. Through the back of my head I saw men strolling down Rai Ghat Lane, and noticed also a white cow who was leisurely approaching. When she reached the space in front of the open ashram gate, I observed her as though with my physical eyes. As she passed by, behind the brick wall I saw her clearly still.

All objects within my panoramic gaze trembled and vibrated like quick motion pictures. My body, Master's, the pillared courtyard, the furniture and floor, the trees and sunshine, occasionally became violently agitated, until all melted into a luminescent sea; even as sugar crystals, thrown into a glass of water, dissolve after being shaken. The unifying light alternated with materializations of form, the metamorphoses revealing the law of cause and effect in creation.

An oceanic joy broke upon calm endless shores of my soul. The Spirit of God, I realized, is exhaustless bliss; His body is countless tissues of light. A swelling glory within me began to envelop towns, continents, the earth, solar and stellar systems, tenuous nebulae, and floating universes. The entire cosmos, gently luminous, like a city seen afar at night, glimmered within the infinitude of my being. The dazzling light beyond the sharply etched global outlines faded somewhat at the farthest edges; there I could see a mellow radiance, ever-undiminished. It was indescribably subtle; the planetary pictures were formed of a grosser light.

The divine dispersion of rays poured from an eternal source, blazing into galaxies, transfigured with ineffable auras. Again and again, I saw the creative beams condense into constellations, then resolve into sheets of transparent flame . . .

Suddenly the breath returned to my lungs. With a disappointment almost unbearable, I realized that my infinite immensity was lost. Once more I was limited to the humiliating cage of a body, not easily accommodative to the Spirit. Like a prodigal child, I had run away from my macrocosmic home and imprisoned myself in a paltry microcosm.

(*Autobiography of a Yogi*)

The vision may have been no more intense than Bucke's, but the change in the apparent constitution of matter was greater. Everything seemed to be in vibrant motion and things could be seen from more than one viewpoint simultaneously. Yogananda was conscious of people in distant streets, of the roots of plants in the soil and of immense bliss. His description of this release from gross materiality is reminiscent of Bucke's experience and of Aldous Huxley's drug-induced vision.

Yogananda was recalled to the cage of his body. His intense introduction into cosmic consciousness became a memory and he proceeded to the teaching of yoga in California, Britain and India. We can presume that his way of perception was altered by this vision, and it is likely that he remained for the rest of his life in a state of cosmic consciousness, in a permanent but far less intense enjoyment of this blissful state.

Bucke's choice of the term cosmic consciousness is a good one and has stuck. For in this first phase of enlightenment, a person becomes conscious of his relationship to the universe. At later stages he will learn to live on the level of gods and angels – divine consciousness – and to live in unity with the universal spirit, no longer a separate ego, but both all and nothing (unity and Nirvana). These are, as seen from the relative plane on which we live, three separate levels of enlightenment, in which the distinction between the light and the being which it illuminates becomes progressively smaller.

A person living in cosmic consciousness is simultaneously aware of himself as doer and of the objective world in which the deed is performed. But at this level the doer is less deluded with the idea of his own individuality than in the world of illusion in which most of our lives are led. He is not attached to objects or to the results of his actions, be they what they may. He is detached, though not inactive, fighting the battle like Arjuna, or performing a servant's job in the kitchen like Brother Lawrence. Brother Lawrence and his fellow Christians attained this state of detachment by dedicating each action to the glory of God. Hindus and Buddhists see detachment in purely human terms as a necessary hygiene. In the instructions to Buddhist monks on the practice of mindfulness, full attention is recommended to each action:

> Mindful he breathes in, mindful he breathes out. Whether he is
> breathing in a long or a short breath, he comprehends that he is
> breathing in a long or a short breath. Similarly when he is breathing
> out. He trains himself, thinking: 'I shall breathe in, I shall breathe out,
> clearly perceiving the whole body.'   (*Some Sayings of the Buddha*)

Detachment, or 'not grasping', and attention to each action are
complementary features of this exercise in mindfulness. It is
reminiscent of Gurdjieff's 'self-remembering', although in
Buddhist belief there is no *self* to be remembered, only a transient
body subject to continuous change and decay. 'Self-remembering'
postulates a true self concealed behind the shifting veils of
personality.

How is it that despite the emphasis placed on 'self-remembering', Ouspensky's followers so far failed to put these principles
into practice that his final conclusion, already quoted, was that
the nearest we come to 'self-remembering' is when we remember
that we do not remember ourselves? The reason is simple. His
precepts for mindfulness are practicable only for those who, like
Buddha's followers, have combined mindfulness, meditation and
the practice of right thought and right action. Ouspensky was
gambling on the possibility that by imitating the supposed
behaviour of men who lived in cosmic consciousness, he and his
followers could attain that state. If he reached it himself – and it is
likely that he did – it was probably only through the shipwreck
of the system, the lightning-flash of simplicity.

Contemporary with Ouspensky's meetings in London, a
series of colloquies took place over the years at the ashram of
Ramana Maharshi, an Indian sage who attracted devotees from
east and west. The following dialogue took place between an
elderly Indian, a civil servant trained in philosophy, and the
Swami, who, being under a vow of silence at the time, wrote
his answers on a slate:

Q. How are we to realize the real?
A. When the things seen disappear the true nature of the seer or
subject appears.

Q. Is it not possible to realize that while still seeing external things?

A. No, because the seer and the seen are like the rope and the appearance of a serpent therein. Until you get rid of the appearance of a serpent you cannot see that what exists is only the rope.

Q. When will external objects vanish?

A. If the mind, which is the cause of all thoughts and activities, vanishes, external objects will also vanish.

Q. What is the nature of the mind?

A. The mind is only thoughts. It is a form of energy. It manifests itself as the world. When the mind sinks into the Self then the Self is realized; when the mind issues forth the world appears and the Self is not realized.

Q. How will the mind vanish?

A. Only through the enquiry 'Who am I?' Though this enquiry also is a mental operation, it destroys all mental operations, including itself, just as the stick with which the funeral pyre is stirred is itself reduced to ashes after the pyre and corpses have been burnt. Only then comes realization of the Self. The I-thought is destroyed, breath and other signs of vitality subside. The ego and the *prana* (breath or vital force) have a common source. Whatever you do, do without egoism, that is without the feeling 'I am doing this'. When a man reaches that state even his own wife will appear to him as the universal mother. True Bhakti (devotion) is surrender of the ego to the Self.

(*Ramana Maharshi and the Path of Self-Knowledge*)

At first, Ramana Maharshi seems to be describing a process that can only take place in deep meditation (*samadhi*). Only by sinking below the level of thought, it seems, can the 'appearance of the serpent' vanish. But he soon leads us to the point of application in common activity – and the relinquishing of the I-consciousness – and this he advocates as a daily practice. In another dialogue he quite specifically states that this practice can be followed in the everyday world. Here is his answer on this point, given to the English writer Paul Brunton:

Q. How is it possible to become selfless while leading a life of worldly activity?

A. There is no conflict between work and wisdom.

Q. Do you mean that one can continue all the old activities, in one's profession, for instance, and at the same time get enlightenment?

A. Why not? But in that case one will not think that it is the old personality which is doing the work because one's consciousness will gradually become transformed until it enters in That which is beyond the little self.

TM

This is the 'householder's' way, which Maharishi Mahesh Yogi claimed to have rediscovered, together with his master Guru Dev, when he first introduced 'TM' (Transcendental Meditation) in 1959–60. The difficulty for a devotee of Ramana Maharshi was that, unless he was able to visit the master frequently, the impetus of his teaching was likely to die down. Gurdjieff and Ouspensky kept their followers within reach, detaching them from their former friends and gradually persuading them to centre their lives on the Work and its activities. TM and other such movements have also developed multiple activities and built up formidable organizations with which to mould their followers' beliefs to accord with a simple, pseudo-scientific world picture. But to learn one must find an individual teacher, and no amount of meetings or videotape will form a substitute. The most reliable guides are not to be found on the largest stalls.

It is not rare to meet people who appear to have attained, or to have been born with, cosmic consciousness. Of one thing one may be certain: that they will not claim any special qualities, nor in any way call attention to themselves. One will observe a certain detachment, which may at first glance seem cold, but will be found to conceal a true concern for others; an absence of 'grasping'; a scrupulous attention to any task in hand; a capacity for listening, and a talent for answering sensibly and objectively; a liking for silence, the countryside, mountains, solitude; and above all, an absolute reliability, a consistency from day to day which is lacking in people at large, who are swayed by a succession of moods and desires. This person may be of one religion or another, or none, but will be plainly recognizable by anyone with clear eyes; which is probably equivalent to saying by anyone already on the way to the same level of consciousness.

The relation between cosmic consciousness and artistic creation is close. Few artists have attained the permanent level, as their lives clearly show. But in a work of art, outside reality is seen as inner idea, and the inner landscape is projected as an outward vision – or, in T. S. Eliot's phrase, as an objective co-relative. This two-way traffic is clearly described by Plotinus writing 'On Intellectual Beauty':

> To those that do not see entire, the immediate impression is alone taken into account; but those drunken with this wine, filled with the nectar, all their soul penetrated by this beauty, cannot remain mere gazers: no longer is there a spectator outside gazing on an outside spectacle; the clear-eyed hold the vision within themselves, though for the most part, they have no idea that it is within but look towards it as to something beyond them and see it as an object of vision caught by a direction of the will.
>
> All that one sees as a spectacle is still external; one must bring the vision within and see no longer in that mode of separation but as we know ourselves; thus a man filled with a god – possessed by Apollo or by one of the Muses – need no longer look outside for his vision of the divine being; it is but finding the strength to see divinity within.
>
> (Plotinus)

The person who has attained this level of being acts without acting, and consequently no longer incurs bad *karma* as the result of his deeds or thoughts. Incurring no new debts, he has only to pay off what remains of the old. He is at one with his surroundings, accepting and increasingly understanding the laws of the universe. His knowledge expands, not in breadth but in depth of insight. Should he need to acquire some new aptitude, he will do so more easily than of old because the psychological impediments to learning are dissolved. But he has still further to go.

The level of divine consciousness can scarcely be defined by the unenlightened. Here the person's will is completely at one with the divine or evolutionary purpose. His understanding is still further deepened, since his mind moves on the level of essences or platonic ideas. In Vedantist thought, this is called 'god-consciousness', since the gods of the Hindu pantheon represent these same essences, which are of course not abstractions but living beings or aspects of the Godhead. In Buddhist thought they are the various Buddhas represented with different imagery as incarnations of particular qualities of the Buddha or perfected man – such as wisdom, compassion and peace. Plotinus sees this level at which knowledge of a thing is the same as actually being that thing: there is no division between the knower and the known. Sister Katrei, Meister Eckhart's disciple, realized the same level of divine apprehension (the dialogue is between Eckhart as confessor and the nun):

The confessor visits his daughter frequently, inquiring 'Tell, me, how goes it with thee?' 'Ill', she replies. 'Heaven and earth are too confined for me.' He entreats her to tell him something. She says, 'I have nothing whatever to tell.' 'Just a word, for God's sake', he pleads, and wins it for the asking. She proceeds to reveal to him such profound and marvellous things concerning the pure perception of divine truth that he exclaims, 'Thou knowest this is not common knowledge, and were I not among those priests who have read it in theology, I had not known it either.' 'Much good it is to you', she said. 'I would you had a lively sense of it.' Said he, 'I am this much alive to it, I feel as certain of it as of my having said the mass today. Natheless, this lack of actual experience does trouble me.'

With the words, 'Pray God for me', the daughter returns into her solitude to enjoy God's society. Ere long she appears at the door again, demanding her confessor, to whom she says, 'Sir, rejoice with me, I am God.' 'Glory be to God!' he cries. 'Retire again into thy solitude; all joy be thine an thou remainest God.'

Obedient to her confessor, she goes into the chapel, into a secluded corner. There oblivion descended upon her, and she forgot everything named and was so far withdrawn from self and everything created that she had to be carried from the church and lay till the third day, surely accounted for dead. 'I misdoubt she is dead', quoth her confessor. Know, had there been no confessor they would have buried her. They essayed by all manner of means, but whether her soul was in her body they could not discover. They said, 'For sure she is dead.' 'For sure she is not', said her confessor. On the third day the daughter returned. 'Alas, me miserable, I am back!' she cried. Her confessor, who was already there, addressed her saying, 'Permit me to taste divine truth in the revelation of thy experience'. She said, 'God knows, I cannot. My experience is ineffable.' 'Hast got now all thou wilt?' he asked. She answered, 'Aye. I am confirmed.'

(*Eckhart, I*)

Julian of Norwich is perhaps saying the same thing as Sister Katrei, but in far less shocking language:

Highly ought we to rejoice that God dwelleth in our soul, and much more highly ought we to rejoice that our soul dwelleth in God. Our soul is *made* to be God's dwelling place; and the dwelling place of the soul is God, which is *unmade*. And high understanding it is, inwardly to see and know that God, which is our maker, dwelleth in our soul; and an higher understanding it is inwardly to see and to know that our soul, that is made, dwelleth in God's substance: of which substance God, we are that we are.

(Revelations of Divine Love)

A similar statement formulated by Plotinus raises no difficulties at all:

Then the soul neither sees, nor distinguishes by seeing, nor imagines that there are two things . . . It belongs to God and is one with Him . . . in this conjunction with Deity there were not two things, but the perceiver was one with the thing perceived.

(Plotinus)

The German nun, even before going into *samadhi*, makes the astounding statement that she *is* God – words that might not seem strange from a Sufi ecstatic with God-intoxication, but which sound strange in a Christian context. Sister Katrei has become one with divine consciousness and Eckhart joyfully acknowledges that her level is higher than his own. To be one with God, to be infused with the divine consciousness, is a state never described by Christians without due accent on the gulf which even then separates the creature from the creator.

In itself, the claim amply justifies the charges of heresy levelled against Eckhart. But the history of this passage is obscure. Recent scholars do not include it among those works that are certainly Eckhart's. It could have emanated from the heretical circle of the Friends of God. But if it is not Eckhart's, then among that circle there must have been a man with vision as profound as Eckhart's. In a sermon which does not depart an inch from orthodoxy, Eckhart is in effect saying the same thing:

I was wondering lately whether I am willing to ask or to accept anything from God. I must take earnest counsel with myself, for by accepting anything from God I make myself inferior to God, like a servant to his master, in respect of giving. That is not the case with us in eternal life.

I once said here, and it is very true: When a man goes out of himself to find or fetch God, he is wrong. I do not find God outside myself nor conceive him excepting as my own and in me. A man ought not to work for any why, not for God nor for his glory nor for anything at all that is outside him, but only for that which is his being, his very life within him.

Some simple folk fondly imagine they are going to see God as it were standing there and they here. Not so. God and I are one in knowing. When I take God into me in loving I am going into God. Some say that happiness does not lie in knowledge but in will alone. They are wrong; if it were merely a matter of will it would not be one. Working and becoming are the same. When the carpenter stops working the house will stop becoming. Still the axe and stop the growth. God and I are one in operation: he works and I become. Fire changes to itself the fuel cast upon it, which is converted to its nature. The wood does not assimilate the fire, the fire assimilates the wood. 'We shall be changed into God so that we shall know him as he is', says St Paul. And the manner of our knowing shall be this, I him as he me, not more or less: just the same.
(*Eckhart, I*)

It would seem that, irrespective of dogma, it is possible for a saint to experience a momentary or even sustained identification with God, a dissolution of the individual self. The meditator deep in *samadhi* experiences but does not *know* this condition. On his return to the level of thought and explanation, he will no doubt account for the experience to himself and others in terms of the theology he accepts. If the church to which he belongs is a jealous church, he will be careful, like Santa Teresa, to translate his apprehensions into acceptable language. Sister Katrei, however, was unconscious of the censors, and Eckhart it seems (for we do not accept the theory of Eckhart's double) was so moved that he repeated her words unchanged.

To find similar ecstatic language, we must turn to the Sufis and, as an example, to a parable by the Persian poet Attar:

I went from God to God, until they cried from me in me, saying, 'O thou I!' for I have reached annihilation in God.

For thirty years God most high was my mirror, now I am my own mirror, and that which I was I am no more, for 'I', and 'God' represent a denial of his unity. Since I am no more, God most high is his own mirror. Behold, now I say that God is the mirror of myself, for with my tongue he speaks and I have passed away. (*Attar*)

In these last quotations we have perhaps passed from the stage of divine consciousness to that of unity. For here the Sufi proclaims with Sister Katrei that he is identical with God. But in speaking of the unitive state, Christian mystics still insist on the continuing division between man and God: for them, only one man was one with God. For the eastern faiths, however, no man is born so but all men may become so.

The God-conscious man has power to perform the divine will. He may have other powers also – the supernormal *siddhis*, to be considered later – that enable him to transcend what are currently regarded as the natural laws. The God-conscious man may heal the sick, may know and influence the minds of others, may foresee the future, or be aware of events at a distance. But these powers are seldom witnessed and can never be used in the interests of his own development. Their possession in fact is no more than a testimony or byproduct of his state. The person who is united with the divine requires no powers and no testimony; the will is at one with the divine and one cannot act from any independent volition. Plotinus very briefly describes the nature of living there, at that level:

In our realm all is part rising from part and nothing can be more than partial; but There each being is an eternal product of a whole and is at once a whole and an individual manifesting as part but, to the keen vision There, known for the whole it is.

There is little that can be usefully said by commentators concerning the unitive state. A number of quotations on this state must speak for themselves. In another sermon, Meister Eckhart describes unity in a very homely way, taking care to warn his listeners against heretical interpretations:

. . . our Lord declares, 'Where I am there shall also my servant be', so thoroughly does the soul become the same being that God is, no less, and this is as true as God is God. Dear children I beseech you realize what this means. I pray you for God's sake do it in love's name and carefully preserve this frame of mind. All such are in unity, as I have said, for they are free from form, and we durst not think that there is in form less chance of their departing from the unity. To do so would be wrong and might even be called heresy, for you must know that there, in the unity, there is no Conrad nor yet Henry. I will tell you how I think of people. I try to forget myself and everyone and merge myself for them in unity. May we abide in unity, so help us God.

(*Eckhart, I*)

For Ruysbroeck there is certainly no Conrad, nor Henry, and this is how he sees the unified state:

The third and highest unity is above the comprehension of our reason, and yet essentially within us. We possess it in a supernatural way when in all our works of virtue we have in mind the praise and glory of God, and above all aims, above ourselves, and above all things would rest only in Him. This is that unity wherein, according to our being, we are at home.   (*The Spiritual Marriage*)

Rumi also uses homely language to describe the ecstatic experience:

When the rose is dead and the garden ravaged, where shall we find the perfume of the rose? In rose-water.

Inasmuch as God comes not into sight, the prophets are His vicars. Do not mistake me! Tis wrong to think that the vicar and He whom the vicar represents are two.

To the form-worshipper they are two; when you have escaped from consciousness of form, they are one.

Whilst you regard the form, you are seeing double: Look not at the eyes but at the light which flows from them.

You cannot distinguish the lights of ten lamps burning together, so long as your face is set towards this light alone.

In things spiritual there is no partition, no number, no individuals. How sweet is the oneness of the Friend with his friends! Catch the spirit and clasp it to your bosom.

Mortify rebellious form till it melts away: unearth the treasure of unity!

Simple were we and all one essence; we were knotless and pure as water.

When that goodly light took shape, it became many, like shadows cast by a battlement.

Demolish the dark battlement, and all difference will vanish from amidst this multitude.

(Rumi)

Union can only be described in parable or by analogy. Indeed much Christian writing on the subject is so technical that it can hardly be understood except by practitioners of inner prayer. In any case, what can the distinctions between the three stages of enlightenment mean to the beginner on the way, who has perhaps occasionally 'picked up sixpence' but is too grateful to enquire to which currency it belongs?

The realized man, says Chuang Tzu, is a drunkard, but not with wine:

A drunken man who falls out of a cart, though he may suffer, does not die. His bones are the same as other people's; but he meets his accident in a different way. His spirit is in a condition of security. He is not conscious of riding in the cart; neither is he conscious of falling out of it. Ideas of life, death, fear, etc., cannot penetrate his breast; and so he does not suffer from contact with objective existences. And if such security is to be got from wine, how much more is it to be got from God? It is in God that the sage seeks his refuge, and so he is free from harm.

(*Musings of a Chinese Mystic*)

The Buddhist *Sutra of the Sixth Patriarch* tells how, among all the sages in the monastery, it was an illiterate fool, a kitchen servant like Brother Lawrence, who secretly received enlightenment and was appointed patriarch. Various monks have written gnomic verses on the walls, each hoping to be nominated the fifth patriarch's successor, believing that his verses will show that he has attained enlightenment. The kitchen-boy persuades a petty official to read the verses already written and then to write up his own. He tells the rest of the story himself:

'Please recite your stanza', said he, 'I will write it down for you, but if you should succeed in getting the Dharma [true teaching], do not forget to deliver me.'

My stanza read as follows:

> By no means is Bodhi a kind of tree,
> Nor is the bright reflecting mind a case of mirrors,
> Since mind is emptiness,
> Where can dust collect?

Later on, seeing that a crowd was collecting, the patriarch came out and erased the stanza with his shoe lest jealous ones should do me injury. Judging by this, the crowd took it for granted that the author of it had not yet realized mind-essence.

Next day the patriarch came secretly to the room where the rice was being hulled and seeing me at work with the stone pestle, said, 'A seeker of the path risks his life for the Dharma. Should he do so?'

Then he asked, 'Is the rice ready?' 'Ready long ago,' I replied, 'only waiting for the sieve.' He knocked the mortar thrice with his stick and went away.

Knowing what his signal meant, in the third watch of the night, I went to his room. Using his robe as a screen so that no one would see us, he expounded the Diamond Sutra to me. When he came to the sentence, 'One should use one's mind in such a way that it will be free from any attachment', I suddenly became thoroughly enlightened and realized that all things in the universe are mind-essence itself.

I said to the patriarch, 'Who could have conceived that mind-essence is intrinsically pure! Who could have conceived that mind-essence is intrinsically free from becoming and annihilation! That mind-essence is intrinsically self-sufficient and free from change! Who could have conceived that all things are manifestations of mind-essence!'

Thus at midnight, to the knowledge of no one, was the Dharma transmitted to me.

(Sutra of the Sixth Patriarch)

The Buddha became enlightened while meditating beneath a bodhi tree, but *bodhi* also signifies enlightenment, a *bodhisattva* being an enlightened person. Buddhism, however, does not greatly concern itself with *stages* of enlightenment, so it is impossible to say whether the sixth patriarch attained divine consciousness or union, to use Christian terms. Having realized that all things are the creation of mind and have no separate existence, he was immediately enjoined to set out and preach the *dharma*, or way of truth, so as to deliver as many beings as possible, which, for the Buddhist, is the ultimate aim of all enlightenment.

The Vedantist, however, sees enlightenment as a process of two stages: *samadhi* (deep meditation) may be 'with seed' or 'without seed'. Patanjali, the prime theorist of yoga, explains:

These forms of samadhi are conscious and are described as 'meditation with seed'.

In this high state of conscious samadhi there is complete absorption and contentment.

At this stage knowledge is gained by intuition and is completely reliable. The intuitive method is one of direct cognition, and is superior to that of inference and testimony.

In this state of consciousness all ideas are gradually generalized into one, which is as a stationary spectacle before the spectator.

When the stationary spectacle is also removed, unconscious samadhi or meditation without seed is attained.

(quoted in G. Costa, *Yoga and Western Psychology*)

This distinction between two levels of *samadhi* was not unknown to Christian mystics. The following passage from Richard Rolle, for example, seems to define the difference, although in much less definite language than Patanjali's:

But as it is shown ravishing is understood in two ways. One manner forsooth is when some man is ravished out of fleshly feeling, so that in the time of his ravishing he plainly feels nought in the flesh, nor what is done concerning his flesh; and yet he is not dead but quick, for the soul yet gives life to the body. And in this manner saints are sometimes ravished to their profit and other men's learning; as Paul was ravished to the third heaven. And in this manner also sinners are ravished sometimes in a vision, that they may see the joys of the saints and the pains of the demand for their own and others' correction; as we read of many.

Another manner of ravishing there is, that is the lifting of the mind into God by contemplation. And this manner of ravishing is in all that are perfect lovers of God, and in none but in them that love God. And this is well called a ravishing, as the other, for it is done with a violence and as it were against nature . . .

(*The Fire of Love*)

al Ghazali, anatomizing the two stages of the Sufi's experience, makes a similar distinction:

With this first stage of the 'way' there begin the revelations and visions. The mystics in their waking state now behold angels and the spirits of the prophets; they hear these speaking to them and are instructed by them. Later, a higher state is reached; instead of beholding forms and figures, they come to stages in the 'way' which it is hard to describe in language; if a man attempts to express these, his words inevitably contain what is clearly erroneous.

In general what they manage to achieve is nearness to God; some, however, would conceive of this as 'inherence', some as 'union' and some as 'connection'. All that is erroneous ... He who has attained the mystic 'state' need do no more than say:

> Of the things I do not remember, what was, was;
> Think it good; do not ask an account of it.
>
> (*Confessions of al Ghazali*)

We shall now pass on to Teresa's fourth and highest stage of prayer:

I am now speaking of that rain that comes down abundantly from heaven to soak and saturate the whole garden. If the Lord never ceased to send it whenever it was needed, the gardener would certainly have leisure; and if there were no winter but always a temperate climate, there would never be a shortage of fruit and flowers, and the gardener would clearly be delighted. But this is impossible while we live, for we must always be looking out for one water when another fails. The heavenly rain very often comes down when the gardener least expects it. Yet it is true that at the beginning it almost always comes after long mental prayer. Then, as one stage succeeds another, the Lord takes up this small bird and puts it into the nest where it may be quiet. He has watched it fluttering for a long time, trying with its understanding and its will and all its strength to find God and please Him; and now He is pleased to give it its reward in this life.

> (*The Life of St Teresa*)

Teresa confesses her inability to explain this state of union which has visited her sometimes and which she feels it would be impossible to hold. 'If there is really a union of all the faculties,' she writes, 'then the soul cannot make it known, even if it wants to.' Of course it is explained in works of theoretical mysticism, which make distinctions between 'mind', 'soul' and 'spirit', but they all seem one to her. It is beyond understanding, and in this state of union the soul can do nothing. Everything has dissolved except the experience itself. Only consciousness persists in this state of '*samadhi* without seed'.

The meditative discipline which culminates in these supreme experiences of union made up only a half of Teresa's life. Her activities as reformer of her Carmelite order and in the foundation of new convents was prodigious. She travelled around Spain, begging money from the wealthy, supervising alterations and extensions to buildings which were to house her new convents, recruiting novices and training her 'girls' in prayer and hard work. When she joined the order its convents had degenerated into hospices for old ladies. Her reformed order – the discalced, or barefoot Carmelites (the original went shod) – was devoted to prayer and works. Their endowment was scanty and life for her 'girls' was hard. Moreover, she was a hard mistress and a great scourge to false virtue:

When I see people very anxious to know what sort of prayer they practise, covering their faces and afraid to move or think, lest they should lose any slight tenderness and devotion they feel, I know how little they understand how to obtain union with God since they think it consists in such things as these.

No, sisters, no; our Lord expects *works* from us. If you see a sick sister whom you can relieve, never fear losing your devotion: treat her with compassion; if she is in pain, feel for it as if it were your own, and when there is need, fast so that she may eat. This is the true union of our will with the will of God. If someone else is well spoken of, be more pleased than if it were yourself; this is easy enough, for if you were humble it would vex you to be praised. It is a great good to rejoice in your sister's virtues being known and to feel as sorry for the fault you see in her as if it were yours, hiding it from the sight of others.   (*The Life of St Teresa*)

With Teresa, meditation and right action went hand in hand. Reading her life we meet a very determined woman, who would argue her case with the king yet was compliant towards her spiritual directors, even when she knew they were ignorant. However, with increasing age she learnt to choose directors who were themselves experienced in interior prayer.

The parallel between Christian mystical theory and that of Patanjali and the Hindu tradition is clear. The difference lies in the Christian insistence on the Church as mediator. St Peter, once entrusted with the keys, insisted that it lay with him to open or close the gates of enlightenment – whence the holocaust of Albigensians, Friends of God, early Protestants and lapsed Jews, all of whom believed the way to be open to all who could find it.

The Buddhist understanding of enlightenment is simpler than the Christian or the Hindu. Although modern Buddhists like Lama Govinda quote Patanjali, Buddhism as a whole does not categorize, for Buddhist enlightenment is a single state achieved by the practice of meditation, right action and compassion. Some Vedantists claim that because Buddhists do not categorize, the Buddha preached only one level of enlightenment – the lowest, or cosmic consciousness. A study of Buddhist enlightenment is inextricably bound up with compassion. The Buddhist desires to escape from the wheel of recurrent birth and death. Yet by his vow of compassion he dedicates his own merits, gained by meditation and right action, to the benefit of all beings. None shall escape in advance of the rest.

5 *The Void*

The way to enlightenment charted by Santa Teresa may be thought of as a positive way: the water rises with greater and greater ease and the flowers blossom in the garden of the soul. But there is another way – the way of emptiness. Although this alternative and featureless path is most generally associated with Buddhism, it was also known and followed by many of the medieval mystics. While Ruysbroeck proclaimed the positive goal of the spiritual espousal – the union of the soul with the heavenly bridegroom – he at the same time visualized the emptiness of concept in which it would take place:

> At times, the inward man performs his introspection simply, according to the fruitive tendency, above all activity and above all virtues, through a simple inward gazing in the fruition of love. And here he meets God without intermediary. And from out of the Divine Unity, there shines into him a simple light; and this light shows him darkness and nakedness and nothingness.
>
> (John of Ruysbroeck, *The Spiritual Marriage*)

Ruysbroeck speaks of the complete cessation of mental activity as a condition for entering the way of emptiness. The author of *The Cloud of Unknowing* makes the same point when he explains the need to forsake even the most spiritual thought, since it stands between the contemplative and God:

> For though it sometimes helps to think of particular creatures, what they are and do, in this case it is virtually useless. For the act of remembrance or thinking about what a thing is or does has a spiritual effect. Your soul's eye concentrates upon it, just as the marksman fixes his eye on the target. Let me say this: everything you think about, all the time

you think about it, is 'above' you, between you and God. And you are that much farther from God if anything but God is in your mind.

(*The Cloud of Unknowing*)

The author advocates that we shall have no thought but God – about whom it is impossible to think – since any act of thinking comes between you and Him. This is in absolute contrast to the practice of such a mystic as Julian of Norwich, who in her prayer directs attention to some incident of the passion, which brings her into a recollected state.

The *Tao Te Ching* defines the way in terms of pure emptiness:

> The way is like an empty vessel
> That yet may be drawn from
> Without ever needing to be filled.
> It is boundless; the very progenitor of all things in the world.
> In it all sharpness is blunted,
> All tangles united,
> All glare tempered,
> All dust smoothed.
> It is like a deep pool that never dries.
> Was it too the child of something else? We cannot tell.
> But as a substanceless image it existed before the ancestor.

(*Tao Te Ching*)

Nothing – an empty cup; a substanceless image. And for the Sufis too, a cup – the cup of annihilation. All the Sufis, except perhaps al Ghazali, call for the renunciation of thought. The adept must clothe himself in the garment of nothingness if he hopes to become altogether lost to self:

Whoever leaves the world behind him passes away from mortality, and when he has passed away from mortality, then he attains to immortality. If thou findest thyself bewildered, o heart, pass over the bridge (which is thinner than a hair, sharper than a knife-edge) that spans the burning fires of hell. Grieve not, for the flames from the oil in the lamp give forth smoke black as an old crow, but when the oil has been consumed by the flame, it has ceased to exist as oil. If thou do.t desire to reach the abode of immortality, and to attain to this exalted station, divest thyself first of self, then summon to thyself a winged steed out of nothingness to bear thee aloft. Clothe thyself in the garment of nothingness and drink the cup of self-annihilation. Cover thy breast with nothingness, and draw over thy head the robe of non-existence. Set thy foot in the stirrup of complete renunciation and, looking straight before thee, ride the steed of non-being to the place where nothing is. Thou wilt be lost again and again. Yet go on thy way in tranquillity, until at last thou shalt reach the world where thou art lost altogether to Self.   (*Attar*)

The wine in Attar's cup of self-annihilation breathes an intoxication utterly foreign to the scholarly Dominican, Eckhart, who, two centuries later, preached the same cancellation of all thought and image:

God is such that we apprehend him better by negation than by affirmation. Hence the dictum of one master that to argue about God from likeness is to argue falsely about him, but to argue by denials is to argue correctly. Dionysius says, writing about God, He is super-essential, he is super-luminous; he attributes to him neither this nor that. For whatever he conceives, God far transcends it. There is no knowing him by likeness. Rather by attributing unlikeness may we make some approach to understanding him. Take an illustration. Supposing I describe a ship to someone who has never seen one, then on looking at a stone he will plainly see that it is not a ship. And the plainer he sees that it is not ship-like, the more he will know about a ship. It is the same with God.   (*Eckhart, I*)

As usual when he is preaching to his simple nuns, Eckhart resorts to a plain analogy. He has cited all the philosophers and concludes that God can only be defined by what he is not. Paul, he says, was lifted up into the third heaven and saw unspeakable things. He saw, but was unable to express them.

In ordinary meditation a person will not see unspeakable things. Indeed John of the Cross recommends an emptiness of all images during recollection, not because it will lead to a great elevation of the spirit, but because most thoughts contribute to the increase of vanity:

While the soul is self-recollected and forgetful of all things, it is prepared for the inflowing and teaching of the Holy Spirit, who will withdraw himself from thoughts that lack understanding. Even if we

were to derive no greater benefit from this forgetfulness and emptiness
of the memory than deliverance from disturbance and pain, that of
itself is a great gain and blessing, because the pain and disturbance
occasioned by this life's reverses bring no relief, but rather aggravate
these reverses in general and harm the soul ... Even if the whole
world were thrown into confusion and all things with it, disquietude
on that account is vanity, for it harms us more than it relieves us. To
endure all things with an equable and peaceful mind not only brings
many blessings to the soul; but it also enables us, amid difficulties, to
have a clear judgement and remedy them in the most fitting way.

(John of the Cross, *The Dark Night*)

John's attitude seems extremely cold-blooded. It displays a
Buddhist detachment without the accompanying compassion.
Does he mean that all life's reverses should be dismissed from the
mind, even when not ourselves but others are the victims?

An experienced meditator may not aim at this degree of
detachment from the adversities of the world. Indeed part of his
practice will no doubt be devoted to the growth of compassion.
Nor will he expect the lightning flash that struck Paul. But he too,
in the practice of quiet or *samadhi*, will follow the way of emptiness; and what strikes his inner eye, what occupies his attending
mind, will also in some fashion, as Eckhart stated, be ineffable,
whatever words may afterwards be used to describe it. Thought
will have disappeared, perhaps unbidden; and any mantra,
mandala or image that may have been used at the beginning will
have faded, once it has led along the fine edge of attention to
nothing.

The purpose of meditation is to engage the mind with a single
thought in order to empty it of all thought. This cannot be done
by expelling thoughts as they arise. They will resist and the mind
will become a wrestling ground. Intruding thoughts must be
allowed to fade, which they will do if attention is gently turned
away from them, back to mantra, breath, or whatever else is
being used. Attention even to these must be allowed to fade,
until they are filmy as the images that swim between sleep and
waking. Then, facing oneself, one begins to experience the
positive power of nothingness, *sunyata*. But it is only with the

realization of one's own utter nothingness that the experience of the true void may begin.

The concept of the void is explained at great depth in one of the principal sutras of the Zen Buddhists:

All things here are characterized with emptiness: they are not born, they are not annihilated; they are not tainted, they are not immaculate; they do not increase, they do not decrease. Therefore, O Sariputra, in emptiness there is no form, no sensation, no thought, no confection, no consciousness; no eye, ear, nose, tongue, body, mind; no form, sound, colour, taste, touch, objects; no element of vision, till we come to no element of consciousness; there is no knowledge, no ignorance, till we come to where there is no old age and death, no extinction of old age and death; there is no suffering, no accumulation, no annihilation, no path; there is no knowledge, no attainment, and no realization, because there is no attainment. In the mind of the Bodhisattva who dwells depending on deep meditation there are no obstacles; and, going beyond the perverted views, he reaches final Nirvana. All the Buddhas of the past, present and future, depending on the deep meditation used, attain to the highest perfect enlightenment.

(quoted in Suzuki, *Manual of Zen Buddhism*)

In his meditation, the *bodhisattva* learns that Nirvana or total enlightenment lies beyond distinction of forms, sensations or consciousness. The idea of emptiness is based on perception, and, although definable only in negative terms, it is in fact the absolute, beyond creation and dissolution. It is primarily an experience. But between Eckhart and the sutra there is one vital difference: in the sutra there is no mention of God. It goes straight to the formless absolute, which for Eckhart was Godhead:

While I subsisted in the ground, in the bottom, in the river and fount of Godhead, no one asked me where I was going or what I was doing: there was no one to ask me. When I was flowing all creatures spake God. If I am asked, Brother Eckhart, when went ye out of your house? Then I must have been in. Even so do all creatures speak God. And why do they not speak the Godhead? Everything in the Godhead is one, and of that there is nothing to be said. God works, the Godhead does no work, there is nothing to do . . .

(*Eckhart, I*)

Eckhart's perception of the Godhead is much more than philosophical. The ground or bottom of the river is perceived in the
depth of meditation, but once the river begins to flow, we are
back in the region of forms and distinctions. Godhead is empty
of these; it is *sunyata*. We have already referred to the contemporary teacher's remark that Eckhart knew Vedanta. A
Buddhist might say likewise: 'That man knew Mahayana.'
On the ground of the riverbed, all experience is the same. When
emerging into the flux of forms and distinctions, all those who
have dived will speak alike of an experience for which there are
no words.

A Zen parable points at the same truth:

Two monks were arguing about a flag. One said: 'The flag is
moving.'
The other said: 'The wind is moving.'
The sixth patriarch happened to be passing by. He told them: 'Not
the wind, not the flag; mind is moving.'
Mumon's comment: The sixth patriarch said: 'The wind is not
moving, the flag is not moving. Mind is moving.' What did he mean?
If you understand this intimately, you will see the two monks were
trying to buy iron and gaining gold. The sixth patriarch could not bear
to see those two dull heads, so he made such a bargain.

> Wind, flag, mind moves.
> The same understanding.
> When the mouth opens
> All are wrong.

(*Zen Flesh, Zen Bones*)

The tale has a *koan*, an inner riddle: 'trying to buy iron and
gaining gold'. The questions were naive; the answer was profound.
All material reality is the product of the restless mind. When the
mind ceases to move, there is no longer distinction of forms. Man
is indifferent both to the wind and the flag. He has attained
even-mindedness; his face is turned to the void; he is himself
the void, since in the deepest meditation – *samadhi* 'without seed'
– the percipient is one with what is perceived, and Nirvana is
attained.

Nirvana, like *sunyata*, is a term of apparently negative meaning which nevertheless connotes a positive state. It is the double minus that becomes a plus. It is the state of the enlightened person, differing only from the Christian state of union in that the individual is completely merged in the absolute. There is no longer a distinction between man and God, as Sister Katrei knew. Thus a second coming of the Buddha Gautama is inconceivable. But his successor, the Maitreya Buddha, will at some time in the future repeat his function; and a succession of *bodhisattvas*, achieving full enlightenment, will in turn follow him.

It is important that the Buddha was not born fully enlightened, but was finally precipitated into enlightenment by his experience of this world of change, suffering and decay. He was born the son of a prince and destined to succeed his father. But, aroused by pity for the condition of man, he retired to become a hermit. Having achieved enlightenment sitting beneath a tree, he set out as a wandering preacher, gathering around him a band of followers, male and female. To these he preached the Fire Sermon, perhaps the greatest manifesto of human freedom ever proclaimed:

All things are on fire. And what are all things which are on fire?

The eye is on fire; forms are on fire; eye-consciousness is on fire; impressions received by the eye are on fire; and whatever sensation, pleasant or unpleasant, or indifferent, originates in dependence on impressions received by the fire, that also is on fire.

And with what are these on fire?

With the fire of passion, say I, with the fire of hatred, with the fire of infatuation; with birth, old age, death, sorrow, lamentation, misery, grief, and despair are they on fire.

The ear is on fire; sounds are on fire; the nose is on fire; odours are on fire; the tongue is on fire; tastes are on fire; the body is on fire; things tangible are on fire; the mind is on fire; ideas are on fire; mind-consciousness is on fire; impressions received by the mind are on fire; and whatever sensation, pleasant or unpleasant, or indifferent, originates in dependence on impressions received by the mind, that also is on fire.

And with what are these on fire?

With the fire of passion say I, with the fire of hatred, with the fire of infatuation; with birth, old age, death, sorrow, lamentation, misery, grief, and despair are they on fire.

Perceiving this, the learned and noble disciple conceives an aversion for the eye, conceives an aversion for forms, conceives an aversion for eye-consciousness, conceives an aversion for impressions received by the eye; and whatever sensation, pleasant or unpleasant, or indifferent, originates in dependence on impressions received by the eye, for that also he conceives an aversion. Conceives an aversion for the ear, conceives an aversion for sounds, conceives an aversion for the nose, conceives an aversion for odours, conceives an aversion for the tongue, conceives an aversion for tastes, conceives an aversion for the body, conceives an aversion for things tangible, conceives an aversion for the mind, conceives an aversion for ideas, conceives an aversion for mind-consciousness, conceives an aversion for the impressions received by the mind; and whatever sensation, pleasant or unpleasant, or indifferent, originates in dependence on impressions received by the mind, for this also he conceives an aversion. And in conceiving this aversion he becomes divested of passion, and by the absence of passion he becomes free, and when he is free, he becomes aware that he is free; and he knows that rebirth is exhausted, that he has lived the holy life, that he has done what it behooved him to do, and that he is no more for this world.   (*The Buddha's Fire Sermon*)

There is no promise of immortality for the disciple who, escaping from the fire, achieves Buddhahood. Rather there is a promise of extinction, albeit in a positive not a negative sense – there will be no need to return to the wheel of lives. But here there is no vision of heaven. Nirvana is not a state of enjoyment of a future existence at the right hand of God. There are heavens in the Buddhist cosmology, but these are states where the results of merit may be enjoyed, perhaps for an age. Then, when merit – good *karma* – is exhausted, there is a return to earthly life. For only on earth can new merit be gained. The life of an angel – *deva* – is unproductive. Buddhahood is to be gained only in the fire of human experience. The greatest boon to be prayed for is to be reborn with a human body in a land where the *dharma* – religious truth – is preached.

Nirvana is freedom from the illusion of the world. In another of the fundamental sermons of the Buddha, finding his disciples ready to comprehend his whole teaching, he set out the truth of Nirvana, not in a parable but in a statement as direct and essential as the Sermon on the Mount. The Buddha had said: 'Rooted in

Nirvana, the holy life is lived. Nirvana is the end.' Now he proceeded to invent a conception, necessarily compounded of negatives, with a positive quality. Nirvana is freedom from the fetters of those illusions to which we most passionately cling:

There is a condition wherein there is neither earth, nor water, nor fire, nor air, nor the sphere of infinite space, nor the sphere of infinite consciousness, nor the sphere of the void, nor the sphere of neither perception nor non-perception: where there is no 'this world' and no 'world beyond': where there is no moon and no sun. That condition do I call neither a coming nor a going nor a standing still nor a falling away nor a rising up: but it is without fixity, without mobility, without basis. THAT IS THE END OF WOE.

(Some Sayings of the Buddha)

It is interesting that the Buddha proclaims Nirvana to lie beyond all spheres, even that of *sunyata* or the void, which to the unenlightened seems to be the nearest approximation to it. To face the void in meditation is, beyond any possible chance experience, any casual 'sixpence', a person's most certain pointer towards an ultimate Nirvana.

Turning to the west, one finds in Eckhart's Sister Katrei treatise the clearest definition of Nirvana in Christian terms:

The theologians say: God is by nature bound to draw his likes out of their selfhood into himself, as the sun will draw up moisture. Then the soul, merged in the naked Godhead, is no more to be found than a wine-drop in mid-ocean . . . The man is said to be conformed to God. God is his active principle. He has real perception. Things are to him without image, for he is one with God, in whom are all things.

(Eckhart, I)

Perhaps, as Eckhart sees it, the merging with the Godhead is less complete than the Buddhist Nirvana. Eckhart is speaking of a person living in a state of unity. But Nirvana is the supreme paradox, in which being bewilderingly merges with non-being. The truth, one must suppose, is so dazzling that even the passionless mind, all dualisms resolved, cannot contemplate it without 'bewilderment'. One is reminded of the ecstatic bride at Ruysbroeck's spiritual marriage:

E

And the coming of the Bridegroom is so swift that He is perpetually coming, and yet dwelling within with unfathomable riches; and ever coming anew, in His Person, without interruption, with such new brightness that it seems as though he had never come before. For His coming consists, beyond time, in an eternal NOW, which is ever received with new longings and new joy.

(John of Ruysbroeck, *The Spiritual Marriage*)

The Sufis describe the same bewilderment or intoxication, as in Attar's fable of the moth and the candle:

One night, the moths gathered together, tormented by the desire to unite themselves with the candle. All of them said: 'We must find one who can give us some news of that for which we seek so earnestly'.

One of the moths went to a castle afar off, and saw within the light of a candle. He came back and told the others what he had seen, and began to describe the candle as intelligently as he was able to do. But the wise moth, who was chief of their assembly, observed: 'He has no real information to give us of the candle'.

Another moth visited the candle; he passed close to the light and drew near to it. With his wings, he touched the flames of that which he desired: the heat of the candle drove him back and he was vanquished. He also returned, and revealed something of the mystery, in explaining a little of what union with the candle meant, but the wise moth said to him: 'Thine explanation is of no more real worth than that of thy comrade.'

A third moth rose up, intoxicated with love, to hurl himself violently into the flame of the candle. He threw himself forward and stretched out his antennae towards the flame. As he entered completely into its embrace, his members became red like the flame itself. When the wise moth saw from afar that the candle had identified the moth with itself, and had given to it its own light, he said: 'This moth has accomplished his desire; but he alone comprehends that to which he has attained. None other knows it, and that is all.'   (*Attar*)

Nowhere in Buddhist writings do we find such ecstatic descriptions of the spirit's absorption into Nirvana, but there are some lyrical passages:

To those who in mid-stream stay in great peril of the flood; for those who are engaged in living and dying, I proclaim the Island. There is nothing where nought is grasped. This is the Island of No-beyond. I call it Nirvana: the utter extinction of living and dying.

(Lankavatara Sutra)

This promise is surely addressed not to dedicated monks but to sufferers at large.

What relation do we find between Nirvana and the heaven described by Christian mystics? Almost always, Christian imagery conveys a sense of a place created by the same God who created earth. Even Ruysbroeck draws a heaven that can be represented by the imagination, a 'dwelling place' for God and his saints:

God has created the highest heaven, a pure and simple radiance which rings and encloses all the heavens and all bodily and material things that God has ever created; for it is an outward dwelling place and a kingdom of God and his saints, full of glory and eternal joy. Now since this heaven is an unimagined radiance, there is here neither time nor space, nor movement, nor any change; for it is immovable and unchangeable above all things.

(The Spiritual Marriage)

But having defined this heaven, in these last phrases in negative terms, Ruysbroeck proceeds to elaborate a cosmogony of Aristotelean spheres, to speak of the power of God as the prime mover. For all the ecstatic strength of his experience he must to some degree count among the philosophers.

The philosophers have on the whole dominated Christian thought on the subject of heaven. That the Kingdom is within has deteriorated into a platitude. Heaven became very early in Christian history a state or region into which admission had to be purchased by deeds conforming to the rules and injunctions of Holy Church. Non-Christians were by definition excluded, except those few whose entry was purchased by Christ's descent into hell after his death. Thus those Greek and Hebrew worthies on whose teaching Christianity was built received posthumous entry into heaven by virtue of a redemption that was for them made retroactive. Plato, Aristotle, Moses and Jeremiah gained heaven, but Plotinus, who rejected Christianity, must languish among the damned.

The doctrine of purgatory, whereby the dead atone for their

sins for an indeterminate period, which may be shortened by the prayers of the living, and the theory of the Last Judgement, which will follow the Second Coming, are, compared with the teachings of Mahayana, extremely vague. Hell, the region to which sinners and heathens are automatically condemned, is, in traditional theology, a place of perpetual torture from which those condemned may never be released.

Such are the penalties of the early surrender of Christian thought to dualism: sinner or saint, Christian or pagan, saved or damned. Thus they have concretized in perpetuity states that are in reality for ever changing. True, there is a judgement at death, but heaven, hell and purgatory are transient experiences. Christian philosophers have transformed them into rigid permanencies, enduring in a time that is a vast extension of the time recorded in life by our own senses – 'for ever and ever, Amen'.

These philosopher-theologians have imprisoned themselves in a replica of the time and space world, in the illusion of materiality. Even the spheres of Dante's hell, purgatory and paradise are conceived as material and permanent. Once the experiencer begins to hew down the imaginary walls that form his prison, to see them as illusory – 'not a stone' – he finds himself facing the emptiness within him, which is Christ's Kingdom.

Of this kingdom the fourteenth-century Dominican, John Tauler, speaks in terms of a descent by the Godhead into the soul made ready for his coming. For this, many exercises must be performed. But even so, he will not, like Sister Katrei, see himself as God when his senses and reason are gathered up into what other mystics would call the cloud of darkness. More modestly, Tauler says that he will merely 'fancy himself God' – an ecstatic illusion:

This Kingdom is seated properly in the inmost recesses of the spirit. When, through all manner of exercises, the outward man has been converted into the inward, reasonable man, and thus the two, that is to say, the powers of the senses and the powers of reason, are gathered up into the very centre of the man's being – the unseen depths of his spirit, wherein lies the image of God – and thus he flings himself into the divine abyss, in which he dwelt eternally before he was created; then when God finds the man thus simply and nakedly turned towards

Him, the Godhead bends down and descends into the depths of the pure, waiting soul, and transforms the created soul, drawing it up into the uncreated essence, so that the Spirit becomes one with Him. Could such a man behold himself, he would see himself so noble that he would fancy himself God, and see himself a thousand times nobler than he is himself, and would perceive all the thoughts and purposes, words and works, and have all the knowledge of all men that ever were.

Now thou shouldst look into the bottom of thy heart, and see whether thou wouldst fain enter into this Kingdom and partake of this high dignity. Then were all thy cares over and gone for ever! This is the Kingdom which we are told to seek first.   (Tauler, *Sermons*)

Tauler was a favourite authority of Martin Luther, who saw in him a critic both of scholastic learning and of mystical quietism. He was also, as this sermon shows, simpler in his approach than Eckhart or Suso. He preached in German and preferred humble topics to abstruse ones. Referring to Eckhart, whom he claimed as one of his masters, Tauler observed: 'About the mystic union a beloved master has written and spoken to you, but you have not understood.' He did not wish to dwell on such exalted subjects.

Tauler spoke little of his own experience, which was probably not as profound as Eckhart's. His more modest range may have accounted for his greater popularity. When the Lutherans began to claim him as a forerunner, much contention arose as to the authenticity of various works which bore his name.

No doubt the theologians or philosophers helped to build the prison that walled in the humble man. Theology had made the way to God appear forbiddingly difficult. But, even among the learned, there were men who recognized that the kingdom was for the unlearned also. One final passage from the very learned Meister Eckhart will complete the proof that he possessed this insight:

Now when the soul has lost herself in every way ... she finds herself to be the very thing she vainly sought. Herself the soul finds in the supernal image wherein God really is in all his Godhead, where he is the kingdom himself. There the soul recognizes her own beauty. There she must go out to get into her own and realize that she and God are one felicity; the kingdom which, without seeking, she has found.

(*Eckhart, I*)

In Eckhart, as in Christian thought as a whole, the absolute carries a plus sign, even though for those of deepest experience it can only be defined by negatives. Eckhart whittles away the concept of soul until it becomes little more than a receiving set for the radiations of Godhead. Still it is not, as it was for those 'heathen philosophers', the Greeks, *purely* a spark of the Godhead – this would be the heresy of pantheism. For if man were indeed centred on a divine spark, what need would he have of a redeemer? He would have only to turn inward, to find the way and follow it, throw off the fetters of self-will – the 'self-cherishing' of the Buddhists – and all would be well with him. If the kingdom of heaven is truly within, there is no need of St Peter or his Church to turn the key. As Socrates said in the dialogue *Phaedrus*, the soul has nothing to learn: she has only to remember what she already knows, for all inquiry and learning is 'remembering':

Since the soul, then, is immortal, and has often been incarnate, and has seen both the things here and the things in Hades, and all things, there is nothing which she has not learnt. No wonder then, that she is able, of herself, to recall to memory what she formerly knew about Virtue or anything else; for, as Nature is all of one common stock and kind, and the soul has learnt all things, there is no reason why, starting from her recollection of but one thing (this is what is called 'learning'), a man should not, of himself, discover all other things, if only he have good courage, and shirk not inquiry – for, according to this account, all inquiry and learning is 'remembering'.   (Plato, *Phaedrus*)

Only one of Plato's dialogues, the cosmological *Timaeus*, was known in the Middle Ages. But Plato's thought came down to Eckhart through a variety of channels. It is understandable that he was thought of as 'a soul Christian by nature' – a sure candidate for release when Christ descended into hell – for some aspects of his writing run parallel to Christian thought. In the following passage, from the *Phaedrus*, one finds, along with the cardinal platonic theme of 'remembrance', a suggestion of the 'fall from innocence' and of course of the beatific vision, 'that image of another world whereby men are rapt in amazement':

Every soul of man has in the way of nature looked on true being: this was the condition of her passing into the form of man. But all souls do not easily recall the things of the other world; they may have seen them for a short time only, or they may have been unfortunate in their earthly lot, and, having had their hearts turned to unrighteousness through some corrupting influence, they may have lost the memory of the holy things which once they saw. Few only retain an adequate remembrance of them; and they, when they see here any image of that other world, are rapt in amazement: but they are ignorant of what this rapture means, because they do not clearly perceive. For there is no light of Justice or Temperance or any of the other jewels of the soul in their earthly copies; they are seen through a glass dimly; and there are a few who, going to the images, behold in them the realities, and these only with difficulty. (*Phaedrus*)

This extract concludes with an exposition of Plato's doctrine of ideas or forms, which is closer to Mahayana than to Christian thought. The 'lights' of justice, temperance and those other jewels of the soul which man in his earthly existence only perceives 'through a glass dimly', are none other than the aspects of the Buddha, who is the incarnation of compassion, wisdom and the other cardinal qualities to which humanity aspires. Again, Plato is closer to Buddhism than to Christianity in his assumption that man has many lives and is born with much experience that he must seek to remember. Buddhism, however, carries the argument further.

The soul, which is ultimately a void, being an indissoluble part of the great void, which is the absolute, has a relative being and a path of progress. Jakob Boehme sees the soul living a double life. One part lives in God, but the other part does not know it. In the first sentence of the next quotation he clearly states the human predicament in an age of materialism. Boehme, an unorthodox Protestant as unpopular with his church as his Catholic predecessors were with theirs, is the first modern guide to the mystic path:

Thus now I live in God, and my self-hood does not know, for it lives not in God, but in itself. God is indeed in it, but it does not apprehend him, and hides the pearl which I am in Christ . . .
I am known to myself, but not in my self-hood, but in his mirror

which of grace he has put into me, thereby to allure my self-hood to him ... and so likewise, dear brethren, it shall again be represented to you out of his glass, which he has set forth through my capacity in him as his instrument.

(The Signature of All Things)

Boehme uses an alchemical or theosophical language in which to point a Christian truth. Thus the 'signature' which gives its name to the book from which this extract is taken, stands for what might be called a decoding device. 'If the spirit is open to a man', says Boehme, 'then he understands the speech.' So in the blind selfhood is hidden this potential instrument for receiving the divine message. But also there is set in man a mirror capable of reflecting God and thereby attracting the 'selfhood' to him. Boehme sets out the 'great mystery of all beings' whereby they are capable of an alchemical transformation; the base metal of their common being can be transformed into spiritual gold.

We have already quoted the account of how this transformation occurred in Boehme himself and also part of his dialogue between a master and his disciple. Boehme's teaching, however, set forward in a number of books, is generally obscure, since once theological language is abandoned, any would-be scientific exposition of the way to self-realization becomes hermetic. Yet his picture of the universe as a mechanism of harmonious parts in all of which the spirit dwells according to its nature, has a beauty that looks back to Plotinus (whom Boehme had not read) and forward to Pascal and beyond:

Thus each thing goes into its harmony, and is driven by the only spirit, which is in each thing according to the property of the thing; and thus the clock of the great mystery of eternity in each principle according to the property of the principle, and then according to the minute form of the composed instrument.

(The Signature of All Things)

The lines which follow this are cryptic. But Boehme seems to imply that not only is the great clock or mechanism made up of all creatures, animate and inanimate, but that each is there according to its principle or signature. This may seem a very abstruse method of affirming a belief in the absolute rightness of all things. Perhaps Julian of Norwich put it more succinctly. Yet the rightness of the machine had to be affirmed afresh for an age that was becoming increasingly concerned with machines.

Pascal, whose great visionary affirmation follows, was professionally engaged in devising machines that were forerunners of our modern calculators. The vision, which came to him after a long period of sickness and religious turmoil, was recorded by him in a 'memorial', perhaps written shortly after the event, which lasted for two hours. The memorial has a double rhythm of affirmation: joy and certainty permeate both mind and heart. But it is plain that Pascal is not trying to record the happening as it occurred. From the initial dismissal of 'philosophers and savants', to the final gratitude to 'my director', Pascal is using the experience as a peg on which to hang an affirmation of Catholic loyalty:

The year of grace, 1654

Monday, 23rd November, Feast of St Clement, Pope and Martyr, and
  of others in the Martyrology
Vigil of St Chrysogonus, Martyr, and others,
From about half past ten in the evening until half past twelve

FIRE

God of Abraham, God of Isaac, God of Jacob, not of the philosophers
  and savants
Certitude. Certitude. Feeling. Joy. Peace.
God of Jesus Christ.
My God and thy God
'Thy God shall be my God'
Forgetfulness of the world and of everything except God
He is to be found only in the ways taught in the Gospel
Grandeur of the human soul
Righteous Father, the world hath not known Thee, but I have known
  Thee
Joy, joy, joy, tears of joy
I have fallen from Him
'They have forsaken Me, the fountain of living waters'
'My God, wilt Thou forsake me?'
May I not fall from Him for ever

This is life eternal, that they might know Thee, the only true God,
and Jesus Christ whom Thou hast sent
Jesus Christ
Jesus Christ
I have fallen away: I have fled from Him, denied Him, crucified Him
May I not fall from Him for ever
We hold Him only by the ways taught in the Gospel
Renunciation total and sweet
Total submission to Jesus Christ and to my director
Eternally in joy for a day's exercise on earth
I will not forget Thy word. Amen.

(Pensées)

Despite the many interpolations of scripture and dogma, the
traces of the experience are plainly conveyed. It begins, like Dr
Bucke's and others already quoted, with the perception of fire,
from which springs 'certitude, feeling, joy and peace'. Forgetfulness of the world and of everything except God, which follows,
is again familiar, and so is the release of tears. But interspersed
with references to the vision are some over-determined doctrinal
affirmations that give evidence of Pascal's all-pervading anxiety:
'May I not fall from him for ever' is a wish for something of which
in the experience itself he felt assured. Those practised in meditation will recognize in Pascal's memorial not only the double
strand of certainty that swept over him in the two hours of that
night, but the sense of loss that followed and that he tried to
obliterate by affirmations of faith which have nothing to do with
the joy that was granted him. 'This is life eternal, that they might
know thee' is a statement on an entirely different level from the
conclusion: 'we hold him only by the ways taught in the gospel'.

The nature of Pascal's actual vision can be guessed from the awe
pervading those passages in the *Pensées* in which he confronts the
void of infinite space, when he contemplates the infinities of
greatness and smallness in the discoveries of the 'philosophers and
savants' whom he disowned in his memorial, and yet of whom he
was one.

The following short account suggests, as its narrator has observed, some parallels with Pascal. Her emptiness prior to that

moment was seemingly caused not by religious doubt – she insists on her lack of concern for religion – but by a severe emotional shock:

> The following occurred at a time when I had no feeling for religion. It was not the result of religious ecstasy or a joyous heightening of the spirit. A certain event had hurt and humiliated me. I rushed to my room in a state of despair, feeling as worthless as an empty shell. From this point of utter emptiness it was as though I were caught up in another dimension. My separate self ceased to exist and for a fraction of time I seemed part of a timeless immensity of power and joy and light. Something beyond this domain of life and death. My subjective and painful feelings vanished.
>
> The intensity of the vision faded, but it has remained as a vivid memory ever since. Years later I read of Pascal's moment of illumination and was amazed at the similarity to mine.
>
> (RERU 1146)

Pascal's fire is reduced in this case to a mere mention of light. But the words 'Caught up in another dimension', while recalling the ecstasy of the mystics, also have a Pascalian ring, not linked with any passage from the memorial, but rather with the *pensée*: 'It is not in space that I must seek my dignity, but by the control of my thoughts ... In space the universe encompasses me and swallows me like a dot; in thought I encompass the universe.'

But in thought or meditation, Pascal is confronted with an existential fear. Compared with sub-atomic particles, man is a colossus; compared with the vastness of the universe, he is a dot:

> A man who considers himself in this light will be frightened for himself; seeing himself suspended in the material body that nature has given him, between the two abysses of infinity and nothingness, he will tremble at the sight of these marvels. And I believe that as his curiosity turns to awe, he will be more inclined to contemplate than presumptuously to examine them.
>
> (*Pensées*)

Feeling himself lost in the universe and fearing the void that he met in meditation, Pascal took refuge in religious dogma. Making his famous wager, he staked his faith on religion rather than on freedom of perception, which might have confronted him with an absolute that had no godlike face and that seemed to him in his deep anxiety to bear a minus rather than a plus sign. The vision of fire gave him certitude for a while only, but at the cost of renouncing his freedom of philosophical inquiry. He demanded permanence, and ruthless inquiry along his own scientific track would have brought him a picture of the world in continuous change, as Heraclitus saw it in the early decades of Greek inquiry into the nature of the universe:

All mortals, being in the process of coming-to-be and passing away, appear as phantoms and uncertain apparitions of themselves. No one can step twice into the same stream, nor touch a living object twice in the same condition. In swift and repeated change, things disperse and gather again; not in temporal succession, but in substance only they come together and flow away, approach and depart. So it is that becoming never ends in being.

(Heraclitus)

Across the void, which is a mirror, images pass and change and pass again. There is no permanence, nor is there the certitude that Pascal and Dr Bucke found in the fire. But the infinitudes great and small that awed Pascal are the creations of the human mind – man's interpretations of a reality that he cannot truly apprehend. For, as Heraclitus stated in a gnomic fragment from his lost writings, 'the way up is the way down; they are the same'. For every direction in space and time is a figment of the mind, which, as the Buddha taught, is the creator of all things. When mind ceases its working, there is true emptiness: 'In the midmost depths of the ocean, no wave arises. All is still. So let the monk be still. May no movement, no wave of thought, stir in his mind.'

6 The Light

The enlightened are bathed in light. Likewise they irradiate light, which is represented by the aura that surrounds the heads of saints and *bodhisattvas* in Christian and Buddhist art. There is a subtle form of light that strikes the inward eye and suffuses the body. Enlightenment is no metaphorical term; nor is the opening of the third eye mere anatomical fiction. With the third eye, William Blake saw angels and godlike beings whom he did not claim to have seen with the eyes of the flesh:

... Blake was talking to a little group gathered round him, within hearing of a lady whose children had just come home from boarding school for the holidays. 'The other evening', said Blake in his usual quiet way, 'taking a walk, I came to a meadow, and at the farther corner of it I saw a fold of lambs. Coming nearer, the ground blushed with flowers; and the wattled cote and its woolly tenants were of an exquisite pastoral beauty. But I looked again, and it proved to be no living flock, but beautiful sculpture.' The lady, thinking this a capital holiday-show for her children eagerly interposed, 'I beg pardon, Mr Blake, but *may* I ask *where* you saw this?' 'Here, madam', answered Blake, touching his forehead.

(Gilchrist, *The Life of William Blake*)

Whether the third eye is or is not related to the pineal gland as theosophical theory asserts, it is capable of receiving subtle forms of radiance, which the percipient claims to have *seen*, but which are invisible to other eyes. The following experience, which befell a child alone on a moor, was not only an experience of light. It conveys much more. Yet in memory it carried with it a whole landscape which was 'lit with a kind of inner shining beauty':

I was twelve years old at the time and it was September, the end of the summer holidays. I was out for a walk alone, up at the top of my favourite hill from which one could see a panoramic view of the north Staffordshire countryside, right away towards the Peak District. It was getting towards evening and I had climbed over a wall and was standing on a piece of rough ground covered with heather, bracken and brambles, looking for blackberries – when suddenly I stood quite still and began to think deeply, as an indescribable peace, which I have since tried to describe as a 'diamond moment of reality', came flowing into (or indeed, waking up within) me, and I realized that all around me everything was lit with a kind of inner shining beauty – the rocks, bracken, bramble bushes, view, sky and even blackberries – and also myself . . . And in that moment, sweeping in on that tide of light, there came also knowledge. The knowledge that though disaster was moving slowly and seemingly unavoidably towards me (and this I had known subconsciously for some time) yet in the end 'All would be well . . . All manner of things would be well'. At that time I had never heard of Julian of Norwich, but that timeless, and even now clearly remembered moment I think probably did much to help me over the following bitterly difficult years . . .

(RERU 1520)

The moment, 'sweeping in on that tide of light', brought a foretaste of what has earlier been referred to as cosmic consciousness. There was unity with nature, peace and assurance.

The next experience, of a mature man and clearly a seeker for the path, begins with a vision of light which suffuses not the outward world but the experiencer himself; and with it comes a great expansion of consciousness which lasted for six days. Its duration, contrasting so signally with the transience of most happenings of this kind, was perhaps due to the narrator's previous seeking; it was no 'quantum' or fragment of vision, but an event which brought a lasting calm and peace:

During the early hours of the morning, and for six successive mornings altogether, I found myself awake and conscious of being suffused with a sort of warm light and a feeling of great expansion into it. And simultaneously I was aware of a strong current of 'something' which filled me with power and changed my breathing from shallow to great deep, rhythmical and strong inhalations and exhalations. I felt immersed and integrated into a great sea of light and power, expansion and joy . . .

As never before I was conscious of the reality of power which transcended that of the physical world. Overwhelmed, astonished, and not a little awed (but not in the least frightened) by it, and at the same time deeply thankful and comforted, I realized I should never feel 'alone' again . . .

The impact of this terrific vision was so deep and sacred that I could not bring myself to disclose it to anyone, not even my wife, for three days. I felt virtually stunned and during this period acted out my part in Caesar's world as in a wonderful dream – I felt transmuted into a state of heavenly glory – a kind of intoxication; my body felt lighter and I was more conscious of all things, both animate and inanimate, on the earth and throughout all creation everywhere.

I felt the truth of Walt Whitman's words: 'A vast similitude interlocks us all'. If I lived a thousand years I could ask no greater joy and blessing than to have this ineffable experience again.

As so often happens in my experience, when I have arrived at a certain stage of development I come across an article, book or poem which epitomizes my recent experience. On this occasion, I shortly after came across this verse from the *Oxyrhynchus Papyrus*:

> Jesus saith, Let not him who seeks,
> Cease until he finds;
> And when he finds, he shall be astonished;
> Astonished he shall reach the Kingdom,
> And having reached the Kingdom, he shall rest.

I had sought the Kingdom of Heaven – I had found it within, as I was told I would years ago – I *was* utterly astonished, and I have certainly come to a state of spiritual calm and peace. Religious problems no longer bother me – a new vast tolerance accepts the thread of gold and truth in all of them.

(RERU 1052)

Another experience of light, also apprehended as an external phenomenon, comes from the autobiography of G. R. Levy:

The cataclysm of my father's sudden death forced me out of absorption in my own search and purpose, to a greater sharing in the lives of those around me, while it removed for ever the dreaded pressure of social obligations.

It was during this period of conclusive loss and partial submersion in the family circle, that I received at the age of twenty-two my first direct intimation (apart from aesthetic visualization) of other-world existence.

Entering a small room into which I had moved to be near my mother and sister, I one day found it dominated by a white light of intense brilliance, alive and concentrated to a vaguely spherical form. It appeared once only, but left a sense of positive energy at hand as a support through the years that immediately followed.

(The Phoenix' Nest)

Miss Levy was at that time torn between her academic concern with the classics and a desire to paint. Both ambitions conflicted with her widowed mother's desire that she should make a conventional marriage. The experience undoubtedly sprang from these tensions, which were only resolved many years later when she became the artist to an archaeological expedition in Iraq. Deepening experiences continued throughout her life.

The appearance of light in an empty room is not rare, although most commonly the opening of the inner eye takes place behind closed lids. Many meditators find their vision flooded with intense light – white, blue or violet, at the deepest point of their meditation. This light is unrelated to the refraction of actual light that appears shortly after the eyes are closed. It is clear, and usually spherical, and its coming is accompanied by great calm. Some Hindu forms of meditation stimulate it by concentrating the gaze on a candle flame before the eyes are closed. Buddhist methods include deliberate visualizations in great detail of Buddha figures, which may well dissolve into pure light. The colour of the light is interpreted in Tantric theory, each colour being associated with the *chakra* or psychic centre that is stimulated. Blue light, for example, belongs to the heart, and its appearance is accompanied by the dissolving of hatred. White light is of course the purest and accompanies a total enlightenment.

This illumination was known to the Christian mystics. The

light of reason, whereby the meditator partially 'sees' God, is not a chance metaphor of Walter Hilton's:

He openeth the inner eyes of the soul when He lighteneth the reason through touching and shining of His blessed light, for to see Him and know Him; not all fully at once, but little and little by divers times, as the soul may suffer him. He seeth Him not what He is, for that may no creature do in heaven or in earth; nor he seeth Him not as He is, for that sight is only in the bliss of heaven. But he seeth Him that He is: an unchangeable being, a sovereign might, sovereign soothfastness, sovereign goodness, a blessed life, an endless bliss.

(*The Scale of Perfection*)

Ruysbroeck also speaks of the light that lies beyond the 'divine dark':

When love has carried us above and beyond all things, above the light, into the Divine Dark, there we are wrought and transformed by the Eternal Word who is the image of the Father; and as the air is penetrated by the sun, thus we receive in idleness of spirit the Incomprehensible Light, enfolding us and penetrating us. And this Light is nothing else but an infinite gazing and seeing. We behold that which we are, and we are that which we behold; because our thought, life and being are uplifted in simplicity and made one with the Truth which is God.

(*The Spiritual Marriage*)

Comparing this with the vision of light on six successive mornings in the RERU account (No. 1052), one is struck by some parallels: the 'uplifting' of Ruysbroeck corresponds, for instance, to the other man's feeling of bodily lightness. Ruysbroeck's experience goes further, however, in the direction of unity, since in this light he sees what he is and is what he sees. Visionary and vision are one.

The opening of the inner eye seems to be a double happening. The light may appear to be within or without. In fact the illumination may have an outward aspect whereby natural objects are bathed in a preternatural light. But this is always accompanied by an inward effulgence, which the experiencer may interpret as love, peace or assurance that 'all manner of things shall be well'. As we have said before, it is a common experience in meditation that on opening the eyes afterwards, the objects in the room appear brighter. One may have closed one's lids on an overcast day; the room is gloomy. On opening them one is frequently struck by an apparent change in the weather. But on going to the window one finds that the clouds are as thick as before. There is no more light in the room; only in the inner space of the meditator's head. The inner eye has slightly opened.

It is often difficult to distinguish inner from outer light. Bucke, riding in his hansom cab, at first thought that there was an immense conflagration somewhere in the city. A few seconds later he realized that the fire was within him. A practitioner of TM, and friend of one of the authors, felt himself prompted by a voice, when meditating, to open the door of the closet in the room, but only a very little or he would be dazzled. He was suffused by a blinding white light, which remained for a while, then gradually faded. He continued to meditate. In fact, he opened neither his eyes nor the closet door. The experience was of inner light alone.

Another experience of G. R. Levy took place in the old Queen's Hall in London during the playing of music from *Götterdämmerung*:

> ... the spectator was in a concert hall, seated behind the orchestra, and thus facing the dimly seen auditorium. As the music rose to a climax this became an amphitheatre blazing with sunshine, in which the single figure was noticeable of a woman in her early thirties, the motionless white folds of her dress, her white shoulder and the gold ornaments above it, all burning in the intense light. The heavy waves of her red-brown hair were confined in a golden net; the dark eye that was visible stared unseeing towards the stage. She looked proud and therefore aloof, but the spectator was now feeling with the strange woman's heart and mind, which was wholly imprisoned in a tumult of horror and fear. This, the watcher knew, concerned the actions of a boy of about sixteen, on whose shoulder her hand was resting, seen from behind and clothed in a chlamys [mantle] of shimmering sea-coloured material, over which his light hair hung down in formal curls.
>
> The participant tried to force her gaze round the corner, as it were, to see the boy's face, but with the effort, the blue dimness of a London afternoon became once more apparent in the auditorium, rocked with the tremendous harmonies of Götterdämmerung.

(*The Phoenix' Nest*)

The incident began with a vision 'blazing with sunshine'. As Miss Levy herself notes, the woman who appeared in that light was at first an objective figure seen by the spectator, who then began to be identified with the woman, to feel her emotions. The vision was instantaneous, composed like a painting, we are told, and although it pertained to some past drama, lived by other people, it was also relevant to the spectator's own life. She went on to say that 'the unwinding of that particular moment of shock and tension continued through many later reveries, till the whole story became not only coherent but relevant to the present day'.

Although she believed in reincarnation, Rachel Levy related these dramatic episodes firmly to her present life; and the figures from them were certainly her familiars through long periods of 'unwinding'. Her life, very active in archaeology and classical scholarship, was, like Blake's, never strictly divided from the world of vision. But, except in her brief autobiography and in occasional conversation, she did not refer to her visionary experiences and only described them briefly and reluctantly in her book, because she felt it needful to assure others that human life was not inevitably bounded by the material world.

The next experience to be noted, described by the journalist Warner Allen in his book *The Timeless Moment*, also occurred in the Queen's Hall and is much more strictly a coming of the light:

When the writer was on the threshold of fifty, it occurred to him, as it must have occurred to many another ordinary journalist, no less hostile to the apparent sloppiness of fashionable mysticism than he was, that he had lived for nearly half a century without discerning in life any pattern or rational purpose. His views on the matter might have been roughly summed up in a vague notion that the meaning of the universe was shrouded in impenetrable darkness by the Powers of Life and Death, for fear that life should lose its savour as a brave adventure, if the mystery of death and suffering was solved and uncertainty was exchanged for the assurance of future beatitude. A curiously vivid dream shook his faith in this tentative explanation of human ignorance, though he could not possibly have said what the appearance in his sleep of a light brighter than the sun had to do with the matter. Almost before he knew it, he found himself involved in the task of recalling everything he could remember of his past life in the hope of tracing some pattern or design that underlay its outward incoherence and fitting the disjointed episodes of his thoughts, feelings and actions into the unity of a rational purpose. This quest of truth led through paths of unforeseen darkness and danger, but within a year of clock-time an answer came.

It flashed up lightning-wise during a performance of Beethoven's Seventh Symphony at the Queen's Hall, in that triumphant fast movement when 'the morning stars sang together and all the sons of God shouted for joy'. The swiftly flowing continuity of the music was not interrupted, so that what T. S. Eliot calls 'the intersection of the timeless moment' must have slipped into the interval between two demi-semi-quavers.

                                        (*The Timeless Moment*)

In contrast to Rachel Levy's Queen's Hall drama, this seemed to arise from the music. Warner Allen's attention is directed not only to the music, but to the spaces between the notes. This is not so much an aesthetic experience as a 'timeless moment' – the book's title is very apt. All such things take place in an altered time scale and Allen is particularly aware of the fact. His vision occurs in the intervals between what we usually accept as the fixed scale of time. Just as a dream or day-dream will pass in the infinitesimal moment between sleep and waking, so all this took place between one note and another of Beethoven's Seventh Symphony.

The boy of the Ipswich barber's shop remembers a similar but less dramatic happening in a suburban cinema. Suddenly the film appeared to stop and the same frame to remain on the screen for an appreciable moment. This was not due to any fault in the projector, for his sons, who were with him, noticed nothing. This was at a time when he was much moved emotionally by P. D. Ouspensky's last meetings.

Warner Allen's experience aroused in an agnostic working journalist a metaphysical concern that remained with him throughout his subsequent life. The universe assumed a new aspect for him. For Martin Israel, a Jewish schoolboy in South Africa at the time, a similar experience transformed the whole pattern of his existence:

. . . I returned home that day in a rather dispirited state of mind, and after supper repaired to bed. There I listened to my radio. (I was aged sixteen at the time.)

The overture to Weber's opera *Oberon* was announced, and I listened in pleasant anticipation, for although it was not a special favourite of mine I knew and liked the music very much. After a minute or so I suddenly became aware of an alteration in my perception. The music became blurred and indistinct, and at the same time the bedroom was bathed in a light of iridescent radiance so that its outlines and furniture could no longer be delineated. I was filled with a menacing fear that lasted for a mere instant, but then, as soon as I submitted to the experience, the fear disappeared and its place was taken by a sense of uplift and peace that I had never previously known . . .

I was no longer in the universe at all, but in the realm of eternal life which is neither past nor future but only the ever-living present. I had been lifted to a height above all measurable heights. I was able, in this situation, to perceive the entire created world, for I was outside it. I 'saw' and 'heard' with the 'eyes' and 'ears' of the soul which also 'felt' the loving impact of the supreme power that embraced and raised me. In the language of science the nearest description would be one of sensing with an inner, hidden organ of perception that included all five senses, each and all functioning in a magnified, transformed awareness. Furthermore, the information obtained was integrated by an inner organ of intelligence into a coherent system of supersensual purpose and meaning . . .

The entire created universe was shown to me symbolically as a gigantic sphere whose movement was discernible as a minute turn of a wheel, but this movement encompassed countless generations of human beings over a vast time-scale.

As these spiritual truths were being revealed to me, I suddenly was aware that my own personality had been transformed. I was no longer a separate, isolated unit. Although I had not lost my identity – indeed, for the first time in my life I had really experienced the identity of a whole person – I was in union with all creation and my identity was added to it, giving of its essence to the created whole. In this state of expanded consciousness, I had transcended private existence. But at the moment of bliss, when union was realized, I felt myself being gradually, but decisively lowered. As this occurred, my personality became dominant once more and rebelled against this descent from the realm of eternal life. Indeed, it tried to raise itself up again to this life, but in vain . . .

The silent music of eternity gave way to the strains of the *Oberon* overture. I could establish, through my knowledge of the music, that the entire episode had lasted about three minutes.

(*Precarious Living*)

It is interesting that in addition to its greater intensity than most others we have noted, Martin Israel's experience was longer in duration. In that time he perceived 'the entire created world'. How could it be that a rather bored and apparently unprepared schoolboy could be granted a vision on a scale comparable with those of Eckhart and Julian of Norwich? Placing beside it an account by the anchorite of her raptures and subsequent lapses into suffering, one cannot fail to see that the young South African and the medieval nun shared a similar revelation:

And after this he shewed a sovereign ghostly pleasance in my soul. I was fulfilled with the everlasting sureness, mightily sustained without any painful dread. This feeling was so glad and so ghostly that I was in all peace and in rest, that there was nothing in earth that should have grieved me.

This lasted but a while, and I was turned and left to myself in heaviness, and weariness of my life, and irksomeness of myself, that scarcely I could have patience to live. There was no comfort nor none ease to me but faith, hope and charity; and these I had in truth, but little in feeling.

And anon after this our blessed Lord gave me again the comfort and rest in soul, in satisfying and sureness so blissful and so mighty that no dread, no sorrow, no pain bodily that might be suffered should have distressed me. And then the pain shewed again to my feeling, and then the joy and the pleasing, and now that one, and now that other, divers times – I suppose about twenty times . . .

(*Revelations of Divine Love*)

The effects of these two experiences, however, were entirely different. Julian remained on her switchback of exaltation and patient suffering, sustained by the divine comfort that ultimately 'all shall be well'. Martin Israel, on the other hand, embarked on a career that was to make him a lecturer in pathology, an Anglican priest and an active participant in Christian healing.

Warner Allen's experience began with the appearance of a light 'brighter than the sun' which afterwards assumed the shape of a sphere. His attention remained alive to his surroundings; he did not miss a bar of the music. But Dr Israel's attention was lifted; his 'sense became dark' to him and the room faded, as did the Queen's Hall for Miss Levy, during her vision of the Greek woman and boy. For, she says, when it was over, not only the music but the 'dimness of a London afternoon in the auditorium' re-engaged her senses.

It would seem that the appearance of the light and the opening of the inner eye are a prelude to experiences of more than one kind. It may be a prelude to an expansion or to a deflection of consciousness. But such distinctions may in fact be unreal. If it is possible to judge the value of an ecstatic experience, it can only be by assessing the effect on the experiencer's subsequent life. But even so, any positive attempt at assessment would be presumptuous.

Some superficial resemblance to Warner Allen's experience appears in that of a girl student, described below. Here the ostensible impulse for the occurrence is not aesthetic – it is a philosophical question, to which the seconds that follow seem to provide an answer:

[Two undergraduates were discussing the life force. One asked: 'But where is it? and what is it?']

In between her question and the uncontrollable tears which started to filter down my face, was a timeless moment. Then I experienced great fear; something invisible, yet momentous, was happening in the room . . . [which] all of a sudden seemed to be filled with light, a whitish, yet warm, light. It seemed to be both in the room and within me. Although 'it' was obviously outside me, it was also part of me; yet a part with no physical location. It was united completely with a region of my mind. The curious thing is that I *felt* the light. Although my eyes were open, the perception of the light was an interior perception. I continued to see everything in the room quite clearly, but all the objects were lit up by this interior light.

As soon as I perceived this light I felt great joy and peace. I wanted to worship the force which was manifesting itself in such an inexpressible way . . .

Sometimes during the experience I had a thought, which (like the light) I 'felt' or perceived inwardly: 'thirty, forty, seventy years are nothing. Only when you are united with this force does life really begin . . .'

The outstanding feature was the change in perception. My eyes felt as though they were open very wide. Everything in the room was shining. I was seeing things – ordinary objects like a kettle, spoon, cigarette-end – in a transcended form, on a totally different plane of perception. It was as though a dimension had been added – timelessness. Each object was perfect in itself and perfect in its relation to everything else in the room. It simply *was*, and that was sufficient. I felt that I was completely 'outside' time – nothing from my temporal existence mattered. Colours were intensified and seemed to burn towards me in their brightness . . .

It ended with an indescribable feeling of strength, certainty and great serenity.

(RERU 1519)

The sense of timelessness and of peace are common to many experiences and the emotional release of joy with tears is not rare. The desire for worship in a girl apparently not religious was directed to the light or force itself, which a mystic would have identified with the divine. But, as she observes, there was 'an outstanding feature' in this experience – a change of perception. Colours became brighter, common objects appeared to have 'an added dimension', an extra-temporal being. This strongly recalls Aldous Huxley's description of the way things look under the effects of mescalin.

Another experience seems fittingly to continue our sequence. Standing in a village church during the singing of the *Te Deum*, the writer, W. L. Wilmhurst, records the emergence of light, in the first instance apparently from between the flags of the floor. From this developed a vision which in its conclusion hints at the presence of a 'single coherent organism of angelic nature, filling space and time':

I caught sight, in the aisle at my side, of what resembled bluish smoke issuing from the chinks of the stone floor. Looking more intently, I saw it was not smoke, but something finer, more tenuous – a soft, impalpable, self-luminous haze of violet colour, unlike any physical vapour. Thinking I experienced some momentary optical defect or delusion, I turned my gaze farther along the aisle, but there too the same delicate haze was present. I perceived the wonderful fact that it extended farther than the walls and roof of the building and was not confined by them. Through these I now could look and could see the landscape beyond ... I saw from all parts of my being simultaneously, not from my eyes only. Yet for all this intensified perceptive power there was as yet no loss of touch with my physical surroundings, no suspension of my faculties of sense ...

I felt happiness and peace – beyond words. Upon the instant the luminous blue haze engulfing me and all around me became transformed into golden glory, into light untellable ... The golden light of which violet light seemed now to have been as the veil or outer fringe, welled forth from a central immense globe of brilliancy ... But the most wonderful thing was that these shafts and waves of light, that vast expanse of photosphere, and even the great central globe itself, were crowded to solidarity with the forms of living creatures ... a single coherent organism filling all space and place, yet composed of an infinitude of individual existences ... I saw moreover that these things were present in teeming myriads in the church I stood in; that they were intermingled with and were passing unobstructedly through both myself and all my fellow-worshippers ... The heavenly hosts drifted through the human congregation as wind passes through a grove of trees.

(W. H. Wilmhurst, *Contemplations*)

Singular in this account is the curious extension of vision enjoyed by Wilmhurst: standing in his pew, he was able to see both inside and outside the church. Of this we have had few instances so far – that of the young Yogananda in meditation, for example. The vision of light, generally noted as white, is here differentiated stage by stage, from blue, to violet, to gold, to a 'central immense globe of brilliancy'. The colours, as has already been observed, are related in the theories of Buddhist Tantricism to the arousal of the various *chakras* or nervous centres lying along the spinal column, the complete arousal of which leads to the Kundalini experience of total awareness.

The examples already quoted in this section show that the phenomenon of light is not uncommon among both the religious and those outside traditional church structures. Many extracts from the RERU records contain references to the light as at least a constituent in the experience described, and more instances could be quoted from the Unit's archives.

Wilmhurst's vision is in the manner of the Christian mystics. But in Christian mysticism in general, the coming of the light is merely described as an illumination and the manner of its appearance hardly dwelt on. The monks of the Sinai desert, however, are more exact in references to illumination. The life of St Simeon the New Theologian is specific in its description of the phenomenon:

> One night when he was at prayer and his purified mind was joined with the primal Mind, he saw a light in the sky, which suddenly threw its beams down on him, a great pure light which illumined all things and cast a splendour as bright as day. It illumined him also, and he felt as if the whole building, with the cell in which he was, had vanished and passed in the wink of an eye into nothingness, that he himself had been snatched into the air and entirely forgotten in his body.
>
> (quoted in M. Eliade, *The Two and the One*)

A second experience of the same monk is recorded with equally precise detail:

> A light like that of dawn began to shine from above . . . It gradually grew, making the air brighter and brighter, and he felt as if he and his whole body had quitted the things of this world. As the light continued to shine with ever increasing brightness and became like a midday sun shining in splendour above him, he saw that he was himself the centre of the light and the sweetness invading his whole body from so near filled him with joy and tears. He saw the light unbelievably uniting with his flesh and gradually pervading his limbs. He saw this light finally pervading his body, his heart, and his bowels, the whole light invading his whole body, and turning him completely to fire and light; and as just before it had destroyed the outlines of the house, so now it destroyed for him all awareness of the shape, position, bulk and appearance of his body.
>
> (Eliade)

These experiences of the light by the desert fathers and the monks of Sinai who succeeded them were far from subjective. When at prayer, they were seen by others 'to radiate light'. Abba Arsenius, glimpsed by a visitor through the window of his cell, 'was like a fire'; while another, also at prayer, resembled 'a pillar of light'. It is noticed, indeed, in the case of some Indian yogins, that their faces or their eyes shine with a preternatural brightness. The frequent references to light in the scriptures are not figurative. In the *Pistis Sophia*, Jesus is shown as teaching 'the mysteries of light':

I am saved out of the chaos and loosed from the bonds of darkness. I am come unto thee, O Light! For thou wert light on all sides of me, saving me and helping me. By the light, wisdom is purged of self-will and released from chaos.   (*Pistis Sophia*)

In Gnosticism, and especially in this Egyptian scripture, light-power expresses the spiritual element in man. It is impossible to disentangle the various strands of Gnosticism from the earliest forms of Christianity. The Gnostics considered themselves Christians and interpreted the gospel story in their own way. Alleging the authority of the disciple James, they quote Jesus as saying to his followers: 'If ye go into the cities, or kingdoms or countries, proclaim first unto them, saying "Search ever and cease not till ye find the mysteries of the Light, which will lead you into the Light-kingdom".'

This same light, seen by so many in the context of joy, spiritual ecstasy, peace and revelation, may well clarify many otherwise mysterious occurrences recorded from sources as various as the gospels and the seance rooms. If the spirit of man is a 'light-power' capable of detection by the inner eye and sometimes by the outward senses, does it not suggest the manner in which the disciples saw the risen Jesus, as well as the nature of apparitions and 'ghosts'? Certainly the Gnostics would not have made Jesus insist on his corporeality, making Thomas thrust his fingers into his wound. But Gnosticism was proclaimed heretical at a series of Church Councils and 'I am the Light of the world' became for the orthodox a mere metaphor.

In *Heaven and Hell*, Emanuel Swedenborg observes in his scientific manner that there are two forms of light – that of the world and that of heaven – and that the latter can be seen equally well by night as by day:

People who think only from nature cannot comprehend that there is light in the heavens. Yet, such is the light in the heavens that it exceeds by many degrees the noonday light of the world. I have often seen that light even during the evening and night. At first, I marvelled when I heard angels saying that the light of the world is little more than a shadow in comparison with the light of heaven, but, having seen it, I can testify that it is so. The brightness and splendour are such as cannot be described. The things that I have seen in the heavens have been seen in that light, thus more clearly and distinctly than things in this world.

(*Heaven and Hell*)

It was in the light of heaven that Swedenborg saw the denizens of heaven and hell; and it is not clear that he realized how rare his type of vision is. He was not prone to state, like Blake, who also possessed this second type of vision, that he did not see his visions with the corporeal eye. His inhabitants of heaven and hell appear to be wraiths or astral bodies of commonplace eighteenth-century persons, while Blake's are incarnations of poetic ideas.

It was not Swedenborg who was the 'Samson shorn by the Churches', as Blake put it, but rather the churches that were shorn by that scientific method which he attempted to apply to the visionary world. Henceforth the light of vision became a subject for poets, occultists, spiritualists, and finally for technicians of psychical research armed with encephalograms and other subtle measuring devices. The churches became suspicious of all psychic phenomena. For them the light of vision was a weary metaphor. Not so for the Sufis:

. . . glance within. As a lover now, in contemplation of the Beloved, be unveiled within, and behold the essence. Form is a veil to thee and thy heart is a veil. When the veil vanishes, thou shalt become all Light.

Tear aside the veils of all thou seest in this world and thou wilt find thyself apart in solitude with God. If thou dost draw aside the veils of the stars and the spheres, thou wilt see all to be one with the essence of thine own pure soul. If thou wilt tear aside the veil, thou shalt become pure, as He is pure. Cast aside the veil from existence and non-existence and thou shalt see forthwith the true meaning of God's purpose. When thou hast cast aside the veil, thou wilt see the essence, and all things will be shown forth within the essence. If thou dost draw aside the veil from the face of the Beloved, all that is hidden will be made manifest, and thou wilt become God, for then wilt thou be the very essence of the Divine.

Here the essence is the inner light, Eckhart's spark and the divine light lie outside. The way to it is by self-knowledge, the tearing off of the veils. But as the veils of illusion are cast aside, the veils fall also from the face of the Beloved, who is God. Then essence and light become interchangeable terms and 'all that is hidden will be made manifest'; the 'Most Secret' name of the God of the Old Testament will be known by name.

So also for the Sufis, who understood that to be one with the divine light, one must become 'all light'. Rumi sees mankind as 'children of the light' and contrasts the world, which is subject to the visible stars and their conjunctions, which govern men's fate, with that more radiant heaven whose other stars derive their light directly from the divine light: 'Whoso hath his fortune from these stars, his soul . . . consumes the unbelievers'. The phrase appears strange to the mystical tradition. Its meaning is that, as in Mahayana Buddhism, his merit redeems those beings who are still immersed in unreality. The Sufi also devotes himself to this highest charity:

'Beyond the stars are Stars in which there is no combust [extinction by the sun's light] nor sinister aspect,
Stars moving in other heavens, not the seven heavens known to all,
Stars immanent in the radiance of the Light of God, neither joined to each other nor separate.
Whoso hath his fortune from these stars, his soul drives off and consumes the unbelievers.
God sprinkled His Light over all spirits, but only the blest held up their skirts to receive it;
And, having gained the largesse of light, they turned their faces away from all but God.

That which is of the sea is going to the sea; it is going to the place whence it came –
From the mountain the swift-rushing torrent, and from our body the soul whose motion is inspired by love.'

(Rumi)

Those 'who hold up their skirts . . . to receive the largesse of light may not know that they are doing so. All that our next writer claims to know is that 'beyond the stars' are 'stars moving in other heavens':

When I was sixteen I had an experience which I can only describe as mystical . . . Something happened suddenly and quite out of the blue . . . the sheer wonder and ecstasy of it have never left me over the years . . . The feeling was that I suddenly, that very moment, became aware of the answer to the mystery of life and the knowledge of it made me want to shout with joy. It seemed at that moment so simple – I wondered why one didn't see it and feel it and be bursting with joy! As if I had been dead before that moment, and suddenly I was alive. Of course the actual experience didn't last long; I could not have borne to live at that intensity for too long, I imagine, but the memory of it has *never* faded, and it completely changed my life. From time to time I have again experienced these wonderful ecstasies, always at completely unexpected times, sometimes while washing-up and doing daily chores about the house. Always this same feeling, leaving me weeping with a great joy and feeling of deep reverence and feeling of worship and love, I think best described as a sort of homesickness, a nostalgia for some-other-where, almost as if I had known an existence of such great beauty and indescribable happiness and am yearning and homesick for it again . . .

I don't know who coined the phrase nostalgia for some-other-where but whoever it was, he or she *knew* this thing, this certainty, and was able perfectly to express it in those words.

(RERU 975)

This person's access of joy at a sudden revelation of the answer to the mystery of life, the sudden change in her life from that moment, the feeling of worship and love for an unspecified God – all these resemble the ecstasies of the Sufi. Had she attempted to write down the knowledge she had received, she might well have found herself scrawling Ouspensky's gnomic injunction 'think in new categories'. But she found no need for an intellectual explanation. All was well as it was.

The light does not occur frequently in Sufi literature. More is to be learnt of it from the far east, where it is thought of as a subtle radiation which can be made to work for man's benefit. The Taoist *Secret of the Golden Flower* is a treatise on 'the circulation of the light', a form of directed meditation. The definition from which this text begins has a gnostic echo: here we have the mystery of the light translated into a practice. The commentary explains the principle by which the thoughts are brought to one-pointedness:

The work on the circulation of the light depends entirely on the backward-flowing movement, so that the thoughts (the place of heavenly consciousness, the heavenly heart) are gathered together. The heavenly heart lies between sun and moon (i.e., between the two eyes).

The *Book of the Yellow Castle* says: 'In the square-inch field of the square-foot house, life can be regulated.' The square-foot house is the face. The square-inch field in the face: what could that be other than the heavenly heart? In the middle of the square inch dwells the splendour. In the purple hall of the city of jade dwells the God of Utmost Emptiness and Life. The Confucians call it the centre of emptiness; the Buddhists, the terrace of living; the Taoists, the ancestral land, or the yellow castle, or the dark pass, or the space of former heaven. The heavenly heart is like the dwelling place, the light is the master.

Therefore when the light circulates, the energies of the whole body appear before its throne, as, when a holy king has established the capital and laid down the fundamental rules of order, all the states approach with tribute; or as, when the master is quiet and calm, men-servants and maids obey his orders of their own accord, and each does his work.

Therefore you only have to make the light circulate: that is the deepest and most wonderful secret. The light is easy to move, but difficult to fix. If it is made to circulate long enough, then it crystallizes itself; that is the natural spirit-body. This crystallized spirit is formed beyond the nine heavens. It is the condition of which it is said in the *Book of the Seal of the Heart*: 'Silently thou fliest upward in the morning'.

(*The Secret of the Golden Flower*)

'The heavenly heart is like the dwelling place; the light is the master.' The purpose of the exercise is to put the mind, the dwelling place, in such order that the spirit may dwell there. The practice begins with a synchronization of the breath with the movements of the heart – possibly the heart-beat – and unites the 'circulation of the light' with both. The light is seen as twofold: a light of the eye and a light of the ear, which have the same origin, says the commentary, and are different only in name. One may interpret the light of the eye as that which may appear in meditation. That of the ear is the light of understanding.

The aim of the process is to activate the various centres of the brain. This is also the ultimate aim of Kundalini Yoga, which, by awakening the various *chakras*, calls to life those centres in the brain which correspond to them. Thus *The Secret of the Golden Flower* is in the essence a Tantric treatise, and the opening of the flower itself is the same as the opening of the lotus associated in Tantric Yoga with the *chakra* at the solar plexus.

The final object of these practices is not just to circulate the light – which, according to the commentary, is easy – but rather to fix it, which is to attain permanent enlightenment.

There is a Mahayana meditation technique which follows a roughly parallel course. It begins with the visualization of a Buddha figure above the head, and a stream of light or nectar flowing down from him through the suture of the skull to each of the *chakras* of the head, throat, heart, solar plexus and genitals to the base of the spine. Thence it is sent out for the enlightenment of all other beings. This is an exercise for the opening of the heart, but not for personal enlightenment. Its effect is to stimulate a glow in the heart commonly perceptible as physical heat.

Warmth in the heart may appear in much mystical writing as no more than metaphorical. Only Richard Rolle writes of it with an accent that suggests a physical experience of a Tantric nature:

Truly the lover of Almighty God is not raised in mind to see into high things withouten skill, and to sing the song of love that springs up in the soul, the which is ardently and openly burnt with the fire of love, and spread out in sweet devotion, abiding in songs that yield honey from our fairest Mediator. Therefore the singer is led into all mirth, and, the well of endless heat breaking forth in mirth, he is received into halsing and singular solace, and the lover is arrayed with the might of the most lovely passage and refreshed in sweet heat.

(*The Fire of Love*)

Rolle's association between fire and song is in the spirit of the Upanishads. If any Christian writer could have celebrated the unity of all creation – earth, water, fire, wind, sun, moon, lightning, thunder and all mankind, and the Self that permeates them all – it would have been Rolle of Hampole, or perhaps Francis of Assisi. But such a paean to the presence of God in all things, as one finds in the Upanishad known as the 'Famous Debates in the Forest', would from the Christian standpoint be condemned as pantheistic:

This earth is the honey of all beings; all beings the honey of this earth. The bright eternal Self that is in earth, the bright eternal Self that lives in this body, are one and the same; that is immortality, that is Spirit, that is all.

Water is the honey of all beings; all beings the honey of water. The bright eternal Self that is in water, the bright eternal Self that lives in human seed, are one and the same; that is immortality, that is Spirit, that is all.

Fire is the honey of all beings; all beings the honey of fire. The bright eternal Self that is in fire, the bright eternal Self that lives in speech, are one and the same; that is immortality, that is Spirit, that is all.

Wind is the honey of all beings; all beings the honey of wind. The bright eternal Self that is in wind, the bright eternal Self that lives in breath, are one and the same; that is immortality, that is Spirit, that is all.

The sun is the honey of all beings; all beings the honey of the sun. The bright eternal Self that is in the sun, the bright eternal Self that lives in the eye, are one and the same; that is immortality, that is Spirit, that is all.

The quarters are the honey of all beings; all beings the honey of the quarters. The bright eternal Self that is in the quarters, the bright eternal Self that lives in the ear, are one and the same; that is immortality, that is Spirit, that is all.

F

The moon is the honey of all beings; all beings the honey of the moon. The bright eternal Self that is in the moon, the bright eternal Self that lives in the mind, are one and the same; that is immortality, that is Spirit, that is all.

(The Ten Principal Upanishads)

What more can be said in praise of the omnipresent Self that pervades creation, nourishing it with that *soma* or honey that is said to be the food of the gods?

Self is the honey of all beings; all beings the honey of Self. The bright eternal Self that is everywhere, the bright eternal Self that lives in a man, are one and the same; that is immortality, that is Spirit, that is all.

This joy in the unity of all creation may occur at unexpected times and places. Indeed, this spontaneity is a constituent of most of the moments that we have recorded from the RERU. Here it happens to come at the all-clear after a devastating air-raid in Plymouth in 1941:

When the all-clear went at about midnight some of us went up to the top of the house, which was set on a high hill above the city, and looked down on the terrible scene – buildings that were mere shells, with flames raging inside them . . . I looked down at it all and in my mind registered that this meant that probably hundreds of people had been killed, thousands maimed for life, many homes lost. It seemed to me my heart should have been torn with pity and compassion and yet all I felt was the deepest peace I have ever known – a peace that had nothing whatever to do with my mind or my faculties . . . It flashed through me that those who had so suddenly been flung into eternity that night were rejoicing utterly and were trying to convey to us who were left behind something of what they had found . . .

The veil between this world and the next seemed then to be very thin indeed . . .

(RERU 243)

When one reads of terrible disasters, one can only think of them from the outside. But when one is in them, one can know the peace that passes all understanding.

It is remarkable here that the experiencer, a nun, initially felt this to be the wrong emotion. She would have wished to grieve for the dead and maimed in the bombed city. And yet what came to her was the 'deepest peace I have ever known'. She felt that the dead were 'rejoicing' and wished the survivors to know 'what they had found'. As so often in such narratives, one is again reminded of Julian of Norwich and her assurance that 'all manner of things shall be well'. The nun puts it differently in her last sentence: only when one is in a disaster does one find 'the peace that passes all understanding'. Remaining outside and experiencing the customary emotions of the relative world, one lives in the turmoil and cannot see beyond it.

Poets know the light of another reality. Joy frequently permeates Blake's poetry, although this private mythology of giant spirits with uncouth names contains many 'emanations' of wrath and darkness. The purport of his later work, *The Prophetic Books* and their engraved illustrations, is obscure. Many critics have offered their own interpretations. What is clear, however, is that Blake was familiar with spirits and was unable to explain what he learnt from them in the conventional language of mysticism. He read Boehme and Swedenborg, but the language he chose was not theirs and the abstract forms who people his poems are personal to him. He spoke with angels and from their inspiration come such transparently joyful lines as those of the purified soul in his otherwise forbidding poem, 'The Four Zoas:

'Rise, sluggish soul! Why sitt'st thou here? Why dost thou
                                        sit and weep?
Yon sun shall wax old and decay, but thou shalt ever flourish.
The fruit shall ripen and fall down, and the flowers consume
                                        away,
But thou shalt still survive. Arise! O dry thy dewy tears!'
Ha! shall I still survive? Whence came that sweet and
                                        comforting voice,
And whence that voice of sorrow? O sun! thou art nothing
                                        now to me:
Go on thy course rejoicing, and let us both rejoice together!
I walk among His flocks and hear the bleating of His lambs.
O! that I could behold His face and follow His pure
                                        feet!

I walk by the footsteps of His flocks. Come hither, tender
flocks!
Can you converse with a pure Soul that seeketh for her
maker?
You answer not: then am I set your mistress in this garden.
I'll watch you and attend your footsteps. You are not like the
birds
That sing and fly in the bright air; but you do lick my feet,
And let me touch your woolly backs: follow me as I sing;
For in my bosom a new Song arises to my Lord:
Rise up, O Sun! most glorious minister and light of day!
Flow on, ye gentle airs, and bear the voice of my rejoicing!
Wave freshly, clear waters, flowing around the tender grass;
And thou, sweet-smelling ground, put forth thy life in fruit
and flowers;
Follow me, O my flocks and hear me sing my rapturous
song!
I will cause my voice to be heard on the clouds that glitter in
the sun!
(*The Four Zoas*)

The American poet, Allen Ginsberg, travelling in India in
search of a guru, told some yogin whom he visited about William
Blake. The Indian, perhaps despairing of satisfying such a demanding enquirer, said: 'Let William Blake be your guru!' But
Blake's teaching is far too idiosyncratic for anyone to follow.
Even his poetic style frequently violates the conventions of poetry
and lapses into mere declamation. Yet it is clear, both from his
more familiar brief poems and from the islands of clarity in his
longer works, that he lived at a level of consciousness rare except
among those completely devoted to religion.

The lines from 'The Four Zoas' recall some of the world's
earliest poetry, the Sanskrit hymns of the *Rigveda*. According to
Vedantists, these hymns are incapable of translation, for each
word of the original not only conveys a meaning, but exactly
conforms to the being of that which it signifies. Sanskrit is for
them the primal language of man and every other language is a
deviation from it. In Sanskrit the word for mother, for example,

has the same vibration as the concept mother. The hymns of the *Rigveda* must therefore be sung with the exact intonation that they have borne ever since their composition, around 1500 B.C. According to strict Vedantists, this intonation has never varied and has been preserved by an unbroken line of *pundits* or cantors since their beginnings, which they set back further by many centuries than the date usually ascribed to them by western scholars. For Vedantists, the hymns of the *Rigveda* are not so much poems as spells, operative only when chanted correctly in their primal, unchanged language.

To set some verses from the 'Hymn to the Dawn' beside lines by Blake may seem incongruous to strict Vedantists. In a nineteenth-century English translation they will entirely lose their efficacy. Yet as celebration of the light, both within and without, which brings forth both spiritual and temporal blessings – 'the gift of life and offspring' – these lines deserve their place here, even if the Vedantists' magical claims for them cannot readily be accepted:

> From days eternal hath Dawn shone, the goddess, and shows
>> this light today, endowed with riches.
> So will she shine on days to come; immortal she moves on in
>> her own strength, undecaying.
>
> On the sky's borders hath she shone in splendour: the goddess
>> hath thrown off the veil of darkness.
> Awakening the world with purple horses, on her well-
>> harnessed chariot Dawn approaches.
>
> Bringing all life-sustaining blessings with her, showing
>> herself, she sends forth brilliant lustre.
> Last of the countless mornings that have vanished, first of
>> bright morns to come hath Dawn arisen.
>
> Arise! the breath, the life, again hath reached us: darkness
>> hath passed away, and light approacheth.
> She for the sun hath left a path to travel: we have arrived
>> where men prolong existence.

Singing the praises of refulgent mornings with his hymn's
web, the priest, the poet, rises.
Shine then today, rich maid, on him who lauds thee, shine
down on us the gift of life and offspring.

(Rigveda)

7 *Time and Eternity*

All things, said the Buddha, are created by mind. The concept of time, although it is apparently vouched for by the motion of the earth and the watch-hands on our wrists, is by this rule also a mental creation. In fact the relative nature of time is continually in evidence. Outward events occur according to clock-time so long as they are near us. If they take place in the Antipodes, their hour and day have to be adjusted to our own; and if they take place in a distant galaxy, the adjustment in terms of light years requires more complicated calculation. As for internal events, breath and digestion may be related to temporal biological rhythms, but a dream will undergo a dozen transformations between the moment when the light of day reaches our eyes and our awakening. Dream images pass very rapidly conforming to their own time scale; and so, as we have seen, do those other states of consciousness that occur to those fortunate enough to 'pick up sixpence', in earnest of the greater treasure yet to be discovered.

Few of these experiences can be exactly timed. Only those of Warner Allen and Martin Israel can be precisely related to the watch on the wrist by reference to a musical score. Allen's was incredibly brief; Israel's lasted three minutes, and even in that 'time' there was room not only for the experience but for its translation into words. The experiencer needed at least some 'time' in which to tell himself what was occurring, to find an acceptable simile for an ineffable event. This same act of translation has of course to be performed by a dreamer also – there must be time for him to tell himself what has transpired. The dream's effect passes quickly, whereas that of a deepening of consciousness lasts longer:

I had wonderful experiences which lasted for about ten minutes at a time as a rule. I would be walking along the street when things would suddenly change before my eyes, to become unbelievably beautiful and *real*. Things scientists tell us about light and sound waves, gravity and atoms and so on were clear and understandable. As also passages in the bible that had hitherto eluded me ... Colour was breathtakingly beautiful, everything had significance and *everything and everybody was one*. Not only every other human being, but all animals, plants, stones, everything was one in unity, making nonsense of the view that only human beings have souls. There is no such thing as time as we know it. Everything that is, has been, is and always will be ... And we are *here and now* in eternity.

(RERU 1916)

With great precision and without religious overtones, this person writes of intimations of unity and of the unreality of time: 'we are here and now in eternity'. But we do not know it. Our error lies not so much in our concept of time – a useful if arbitrary measure of events in the relative world – but in our concept of *now*. This is generally seen as an infinitesimal point lying between past and future. But if past and future are nothing but mental concepts, is 'now' also a mental fiction? The last experiencer's answer would be: 'No; it is the point of entrance into eternity.'

Boehme saw this clearly when he wrote of a person's two levels of existence – in time and in eternity – both of which are passing now. The dividing line is not between temporal and eternal experience, but between the two selves, one of which is time-bound and blind to eternity:

Thus now I live in God, and my selfhood does not know, for it lives not in God but in itself (God is indeed in it, but it does not apprehend Him) ... and thus I write of the great mystery of all things, not that I have apprehended it in my selfhood ... I am known to myself, not in my selfhood but in His (Christ's) mirror that in His grace he has put into me.

(*The Signature of All Things*)

The mirror is always there but it is generally clouded by fantasies and projections of the selfhood. Chief among them is our concept of time. Far from living in the 'eternal now', we are for ever regretting the past and anticipating the future. The effect of a sudden unclouding of the mirror is described by another person as being 'like the rotating of a kaleidoscope': the whole vision changes. The young girl knows that she is 'part of eternity':

On the first occasion (aged 8–10) I was in the garden, muddling about alone. A cuckoo flew over, calling. Suddenly, I experienced a sensation I can only describe as an effect that might follow the rotating of a kaleidoscope. It was a feeling of timelessness, not only that time stood still, that duration had ceased, but that I was myself outside time altogether. Somehow I knew that I was part of eternity. And there was also a feeling of spacelessness. I lost all awareness of my surroundings. With this detachment I felt the intensest joy I had ever known, and yet with so great a longing – for what I did not know – that it was scarcely distinguishable from suffering . . .

The second occurred a good while after the first. It was an absolutely still day, flooded with sunshine. In the garden everything was shining, breathless, as if waiting expectant. Quite suddenly I felt convinced of the existence of God; as if I had only to put out my hand to touch Him. And at the same time there came that intensest joy and indescribable longing, as if of an exile, perhaps, for home. It seemed as if my heart were struggling to leap out of my body.

How long I stood, or would have gone on standing, I do not know; the tea-bell rang, shattering the extra dimension into which I had seemed to be caught up. I returned to earth and went obediently in, speaking to no one of these things.

(RERU 1263)

One may, as she does, think of such experiences as primarily religious, confirmation of God's existence. An intense, Wordsworthian apprehension of nature unites this experiencer with many others whom we have quoted. But more important is the sense of timelessness and spacelessness, which amount to 'an extra dimension'. In fact natural objects under these circumstances seem to acquire greater relief. Clouds stand out more boldly from the sky; books on a shelf take on greater depth of colour and contrast. But this is surely the effect not of an added dimension in the object perceived, but in a heightened clarity of vision that accompanies the unclouding of the mirror.

A sudden change of circumstances may induce unexpected

changes in depth of consciousness and understanding. A middle-aged woman leaves her ordinary life to spend a week alone in an isolated seaside cottage:

I spent one week by myself in the cottage when I was fifty ... Then into the quiet consciousness welled up those life-springs of insight, known yet unknown, seen yet unseen. On the rush of the racing sea winds the spirit of truth washed through and beyond me, past all words, all logic, all reason. The world's burden of suffering and my own heartache wept in the wailing cry of the seagulls.

I was alone in retreat for a brief spell, reunited with a nature of searing beauty. In the moment of revelation, there is no past or future, and it seemed my life was welded into one whole present as I reached the top of the hill and leant forward against the salty sea wind.

(RERU 500)

The greater awareness of nature might have been foreseen, but the revelation of timelessness was a surprising 'bonus'. Suddenly the mirror was clean ('the doors of perception were cleansed') and everything was reflected in it as an instantaneous present.

It has become fashionable to speak of time as a fourth dimension, in which an object exists lineally from its birth to its death, its creation to its destruction; and this last narrative would appear to be hinting that eternity is to be understood as a fifth dimension, related to that of time as height is to breadth in the measurement of space. These dimensional speculations, often associated with the name of J. W. Dunne (author of *An Experiment with Time*), ignore the importance of what, to Dunne, is merely a casual point of intersection – the continuous present. But it is precisely here, as William Law observed, that the whole quality of existence may change:

Do but suppose a man to know himself that he comes into this world on no other errand but to rise out of the vanity of time into the riches of eternity; do but suppose him to govern his inward thoughts and outward actions by this view of himself, and then to him every day has lost its evil ... Life and death are equally welcome, because equally parts of his way to eternity ... Heaven is as near to our souls as this world is to our bodies.

(*Selected Mystical Writings of William Law*)

One is once again reminded of Krishnamurti's dictum that 'You have no need to go anywhere. You are already there'. This calls into question the very idea of seeking a goal at some point in future linear time:

Should one seek at all? Seeking is always for something over there on the other bank, in the distance covered by time . . . The seeking and the finding are in the future – over there, just beyond the hill . . .

All life is in the present, not in the shadow of yesterday or in the brightness of tomorrow's hope. To live in the present one has to be free of the past, and of tomorrow. Nothing is found in the tomorrow, for tomorrow is the present, and yesterday is only a remembrance. So the distance between that which is to be found and that which *is*, is made ever wider by the search – however pleasant and comforting that search may be . . .

To live in the present the mind must not be divided by the remembrance of yesterday or the bright hope of tomorrow; it must have no tomorrow and no yesterday . . .

The ending [of the old way of thinking] is the beginning, and the beginning is the first step, and the first step is the only step.

(*The Second Penguin Krishnamurti Reader*)

This was the secret known to the sage in the *Tao Te Ching*:

Without leaving his door
He knows everything under heaven.
Without looking out of his window
He knows all the ways of heaven.
The further one travels
The less one knows.
Therefore the sage arrives without going,
Sees all without looking,
Does nothing, achieves everything.

(*Tao Te Ching*)

So it is that at this motionless moment of now one may 'know everything under heaven' without going anywhere. Although from a still centre all may be known – and concepts of space and time are applied arbitrarily to what is in fact a continuum without limits or dimensional conditions, a unity that only *appears* to be a multiplicity – nevertheless the 'ways of heaven' must be understood. Other images of time may perhaps provide some clues to the understanding of eternity, since today in the west we are strongly conditioned by linear thinking.

Plato thought of time as 'the moving image of eternity'. Time was seen by the early Greek thinkers as a cycle, a snake with its tail in its mouth. In time's course, all will recur; there is nothing new under the sun. But within the Pythagorean doctrine of eternal recurrence lay the saving promise of individual escape. The Greek mysteries aimed to release their followers from time's prison.

A cave is the setting for that allegory which most faithfully transmits the essence of these lost mysteries – Plato's myth from the *Republic*:

And now I said, let me show in a figure how far our nature is enlightened or unenlightened: Behold! human beings living in an underground cave, which has a mouth open towards the light and reaching all along the cave; here they have been from their childhood, and have their legs and necks chained so that they cannot move, and can only see before them, being prevented by the chains from turning round their heads. Above and behind them a fire is blazing at a distance, and between the fire and the prisoners there is a raised way, like the screen which marionette players have in front of them, over which they show the puppets.

I see.

And do you see, I said, men passing along the wall carrying all sorts of vessels, and statues and figures of animals made of wood and stone and various materials, which appear over the wall? Some of them are talking, others silent.

You have shown me a strange image and they are strange prisoners.

Like ourselves, I replied; and they see only their own shadows, or the shadows of one another, which the fire throws on the opposite wall of the cave.   (*Republic*)

All that man sees is shadows of reality. But what will happen if he is released and compelled to see the passing figures as they really are? What follows is perhaps intended as an argument for a gradual instruction in the mysteries, rather than some form of shock-treatment:

And now look again, and see what will naturally follow if the prisoners are released and disabused of their error. At first, when any of them is liberated and compelled suddenly to stand up and turn his neck round and look towards the light, he will suffer sharp pains; the glare will distress him, and he will be unable to see the realities of which in his former state he had seen the shadows; and then conceive someone saying to him, that what he saw before was an illusion, but that now, when he is approaching nearer to being, and his eye is turned towards more real existence, he has a clearer vision – what will be his reply? And you may further imagine that his instructor is pointing to the objects as they pass and requiring him to name them, will he not be perplexed? Will he not fancy that the shadows which he formerly saw are truer than the objects which are now shown to him?

Far truer.

And if he is compelled to look straight at the light, will he not have a pain in his eyes which will make him turn away to take refuge in the objects of vision which he can see, and which he will conceive to be in reality clearer than the things which are now being shown to him?

True, he said.

And suppose once more, that he is reluctantly dragged up a steep and rugged ascent, and held fast until he is forced into the presence of the sun himself, is he not likely to be pained and irritated? When he approaches the light his eyes will be dazzled, and he will not be able to see anything at all of what are now called realities.

(*Republic*)

Gradually the liberated prisoner would get used to looking at things as they are, and finally he would be able to gaze directly on the sun itself. Then he would feel great pity for those still imprisoned in their underground caves. But if he were to try to tell them of the reality he now knew, they would think him mad.

Plato has nothing to say of the descent into the cave, only of the possibility of release and the ridicule that will be poured on the released prisoner by those who are content with the darkness in which they live. What a sudden and unheralded series of escapes from the cave may signify is plain from the cosmic experiences described in the following report:

It was as though my mind broke bounds and went on expanding until it merged with the universe. Mind and universe became *one within the other.* Time ceased to exist. It was all one thing and in a state of infinity. It was as if, willy nilly, I became directly exposed to an entity within myself and nature at large. I seemed to be 'seeing' with another sight in another world . . .

As an atheist and materialist my frame of reference did not provide for an occurrence such as this. I seriously wondered if I had taken leave of my senses. My mind was on fire with feelings, visions, thoughts and ideas, which came with such speed and clarity, but which were so new to me that at first I was bewildered and did not know how best to judge their validity . . .

Although my 'cosmic experience' was irrational in terms of our accustomed view of the world, I am not satisfied that it was simply an illusion, or delusion. It affected me in a very real way, reorientated my outlook and enriched and enlarged my consciousness in many ways. But it did pose a riddle – the kind of riddle one cannot attempt to solve without becoming keenly aware of the ultimate mystery of creation. In this sense, I would call my experience 'religious'.

(RERU 1481)

This moment of expanded consciousness, which began with a form of out-of-the-body experience, seriously perturbed the experient. 'I wondered if I had taken leave of my senses', he writes; and no doubt a behaviourist psychologist might explain these occurrences in some such way. The person concerned was plainly not prepared for these expansions of consciousness, which upset his 'accustomed view of the world'. But at such moments, when one is free from the illusion of the cave, the mind certainly 'breaks bounds', and this inexplicable event can permanently change a person's whole outlook on life and death.

It may be said of the Greeks that their imprisonment in the cave of metaphysical illusion did not impede their very considerable creative powers in poetry, architecture and science. Perhaps their drama and their temples were inspired by the mysteries. Perhaps indeed their great architects, sculptors and poets had attended the mysteries and received enlightenment, although one can adduce no evidence to support this theory. What is clear is that their politicians and soldiers had undergone no such enlightenment. For Greek civilization was ruined by greedy wars between petty states which, having escaped destruction by the Persians and conquered the whole Persian empire under Alexander, succumbed to the efficient ruthlessness of the Romans. But the tradition of a possible liberation from the prison of delusive shadows was passed on to various underground Roman cults, and the mysteries themselves persisted in some form under Roman patronage.

The preaching of Christianity offered an escape from the prison of eternal recurrence. It was, in one respect, a vast popular mystery cult offering universal release. Its secret beginnings are evident to all who walk through the miles of catacombs on the outskirts of Rome. Here was a secret life, hidden from the sun, in which the slave and the petty tradesman were made free by means of an initiatory baptism. Christianity offered the mystery of Orpheus, the singer who descended to the underworld, to Roman and barbarian alike. It was esotericism for all; and as a result, many stumbled and were dazzled, as Plato had prophesied. Christianity offered salvation to all who believed in the sacrifice of the Jewish healer, who was proclaimed, as he never proclaimed himself, the only son of God.

But it was not true freedom that was offered to the Christian adept. Released from one prison, he found himself in another prison of linear time, the great illusion of the west. No longer the prisoner of a deterministic, inevitable recurrence, he was delivered captive to the even more cramping fetters of past, present and future time. Beginning in the mythical Babylonian garden of Eden, human history was now to proceed in a straight line to the second coming of Christ, which might occur in their own lifetime, and which would be followed by the irremediable decisions of the last judgement. But in the view of the earliest Christians, time stood still at the birth of the saviour.

The idea of a timeless moment, a halting of the stream at a central point in history, occurs in the *Protevangelium*, or 'Book of James', an apocryphal gospel. Joseph has found a cave in which the child will be born, and goes out to fetch a midwife:

Now I Joseph was walking, and I walked not. And I looked up to the air and saw the air in amazement. And I looked up unto the pole of the heaven and saw it standing still, and the fowls of the heaven without motion. And I looked upon the earth and saw a dish set, and workmen lying by it, and their hands were in the dish: and they that were chewing chewed not, and they that were lifting the food lifted it not, and they that put it to their mouth put it not thereto, but the faces of all of them were looking upward. And behold there were sheep being driven, and they went not forward but stood still; and the shepherd lifted his hand to smite them with his staff, and his hand remained up. And I looked upon the stream of the river and saw the mouths of the kids upon the water and they drank not. And of a sudden all things moved onward in their course.

(The Apocryphal New Testament)

The 'eternal now' that was the central experience of the old mystery cults was soon covered by the paved Roman road of time. Yet, ironically enough, the main message of that Jewish healer in whose name this religion was preached, had been a proclamation of the eternal now. We find this in the third chapter of John's Gospel, where Jesus is reasoning with Nicodemus – an important person who has come to him, attracted by his miraculous powers. Nicodemus is a very literal person, steeped in the mosaic code; when Jesus postulates a rebirth as the necessary preliminary for entrance into the kingdom of God, he asks humourlessly how an elderly man can be expected to re-enter his mother's womb. Jesus appears surprised that anyone of his standing should be ignorant of these things; he has to explain to him that the postulated rebirth is of water (baptism or initiation) and the spirit, and furthermore to explain that spirit is not of the same materiality as flesh: 'The wind bloweth where it listeth, and thou hearest the sound thereof, but cannot tell whence it cometh, or whither it goes; so is everyone that is born of the Spirit.'

The actions of the enlightened may be seen, but cannot be judged, by those not reborn. Jesus may be telling Nicodemus that the *siddhis* which he exercises are not merely magical powers, but workings of the Spirit. He then goes on to explain that ascent into heaven is only possible for that which has come down from heaven, 'even the Son of man which is in heaven'. This 'Son' of man, who has been reborn from the fleshly man, is surely none other than Eckhart's 'spark', that essence in his soul which is, though unknown to him, divine. For, as the alchemists said, 'you have to have gold to make gold'. Jesus then went on to demand of him belief in 'the Son'; and this came to be interpreted as a prophetic demand for belief in his own future sacrifice upon the cross:

> For God so loved the world, that he gave his only begotten Son, that whosoever believeth in him should not perish, but have everlasting life. For God sent not his Son into the world to condemn the world; but that the world through him might be saved. He that believeth on him is not condemned: but he that believeth not is condemned already, because he hath not believed in the name of the only begotten Son of God. And this is the condemnation, that light is come into the world, and men loved darkness rather than light, because their deeds were evil.
>
> (*John* 3:16–21)

There is no need to impute any prophetic meaning to these words. What Jesus is in fact demanding of those who are to achieve enlightenment is no more – and no less – than that they shall follow God's only-begotten Son, whom he has put in each person's soul. There is no demand for faith in Jesus himself, but instructions for the rebirth that he has postulated for Nicodemus. There is in the whole passage a note of urgency, even of anger. Anyone who does not take advantage of this salvation by believing in the Son will be condemned within his own heart. Jesus identified himself with the light, as the Gnostics remembered. But at the same time his voice, as transmitted by this gospel, carries echoes of the angry Jehovah, as he consigns sinners to the darkness. It is noteworthy that the Buddha, in offering the *dharma*, did not condemn those who were not ready to 'enter the stream'. He had only compassion for them.

This interpretation of Jesus' conversation with Nicodemus might have been acceptable at the time when the gospel was written, perhaps seventy years after Jesus' death. How soon the doctrine of Jesus' unique relationship to God developed cannot be known. The author of *John* appears, if we accept the standard interpretation, to put this claim into Jesus' mouth, although he would have known that a holy man never speaks of his spiritual status or demands belief in himself.

The only contemporary account of Jesus occurs in the Slavonic version of Josephus' *Jewish War*, which contains several pieces that do not occur in other versions. One of these tells the story of Jesus' teaching and execution in a manner credible from its author, a Hellenized Jew:

It was at that time that a man appeared – if 'man' is the right word – who had all the attributes of a man but seemed to be something greater. His actions, certainly, were superhuman, for he worked such wonderful and amazing miracles that I for one cannot regard him as a man; yet in view of his likeness to ourselves I cannot regard him as an angel either. Everything that some hidden power enabled him to do he did by an authoritative word. Some people said that their first Lawgiver had risen from the dead and had effected many marvellous cures; others thought he was a messenger from heaven. However, in many ways he broke the Law – for instance, he did not observe the Sabbath in the traditional manner. At the same time his conduct was above reproach. He did not need to use his hands: a word sufficed to fulfil his every purpose.

Many of the common people flocked after him and followed his teaching. There was a wave of excited expectation that he would enable the Jewish tribes to throw off the Roman yoke. As a rule he was to be found opposite the City on the Mount of Olives, where also he healed the sick. He gathered round him 150 assistants and masses of followers. When they saw his ability to do whatever he wished by a word, they told him that they wanted him to enter the City, destroy the Roman troops, and make himself King; but he took no notice.

When the suggestion came to the ears of the Jewish authorities, they met under the chairmanship of the high priest and exclaimed: 'We are utterly incapable of resisting the Romans; but as the blow is about to fall we'd better go and tell Pilate what we've heard, and steer clear of trouble, in case he gets to know from someone else and confiscates our property, puts us to death, and turns our children adrift.' So they went and told Pilate, who sent troops and butchered many of the common people. He then had the miracle-worker brought before him, held an inquiry, and expressed the opinion that he was a benefactor, not a criminal or agitator or a would-be king. Then he let him go, as he had cured Pilate's wife when she was at the point of death.

Returning to his usual haunts he resumed his normal work. When the crowds grew bigger than ever, he earned by his actions an incomparable reputation. The exponents of the Law were mad with jealousy, and gave Pilate £30,000 to have him executed. Accepting the bribe, he gave them permission to carry out their wishes themselves. So they seized him and crucified him in defiance of all Jewish tradition.

(*The Jewish War*)

Anyone wishing to dismiss this account of Jesus as a forgery, interpolated in a single manuscript from which the Slavonic version was translated, must account for the fact that it could be pleasing neither to Christians nor Jews. A Christian forger would have invented a story closer to that of the gospels, and a Jewish forger would have shown less admiration for Jesus, less belief that, although not an angel, he was something more than an ordinary man. A further passage, moreover, which also appears only in the Slavonic version, speculates about the disappearance of Jesus' body from the tomb and concludes that a miraculous explanation is not unreasonable.

The Jesus of Josephus is a man with supernormal powers, misunderstood by his followers who want to transform him into a political leader. Some considered him the reincarnation of Moses; and the gospels too report him as asking who the people consider him to be. The atmosphere of misunderstanding that surrounds Jesus in the gospels is even more strongly conveyed by the Josephus version. The disciples were for ever failing to understand, and in the end one betrayed him, one denied him and the rest scattered.

But why, if the Slavonic version is genuine, does it not appear in the Greek manuscripts? The explanation of the translator is that in the Roman world of Josephus' day, Christian persecution was at its height and even such temperate praise of Jesus would be tactless. We have therefore to assume that an original manuscript was kept out of circulation and afterwards turned up in Byzantium. From what we know of Josephus' movements, he could have been in Jerusalem at the time of Jesus and would certainly have met people who were there.

Christianity begins in mystery, and from the beginning there are at least two opposing factions – the Jewish Church which remained at home, and the proselytizing missions who were speedily influenced by the Greeks, whose language they used in their preaching and writing.

Jesus convinced and won his following, according to Josephus and the gospels, by his miraculous powers, and we find St Paul, the chief travelling propagandist of Christianity, insisting on the miraculous elements in his master's teaching. In his first epistle to the Christians at Corinth, after insisting that the prime necessity of a Christian community is charity, he passes on to detail the supernormal powers – speaking in strange tongues, prophecies and revelations – and then of the general expectation of a resurrection of the dead, of which Jesus' resurrection was the promise:

> Now if Christ be preached that he rose from the dead, how say some among you that there is no resurrection of the dead? But if there be no resurrection of the dead, then is Christ not risen: and if Christ is not risen, then is our preaching vain, and your faith is also vain.
>
> (*I Cor.* 15:12)

Paul here appears firmly to anchor spiritual reality in time. In earlier verses he adduced the evidence of various witnesses to the fact of the resurrection, finally adding his own testimony, although his belief in that event came of grace and not of knowledge. Christ's resurrection is proof that all shall rise when 'cometh the end, when he shall have delivered up the kingdom to God'. In the end, indeed, the son himself will be gathered back into the father, 'that God may be all in all'. The whole Christian hope was thus fastened on a future event, which would mark the end of the world's history.

Can we still read, here in Paul's writing, an inner meaning whereby the resurrection, guaranteed by Christ's example, is an inner event in each man? Does the 'Son of Man' in a person bring the soul to enlightenment? And is the isolated man finally gathered back by way of unity to a nirvanic re-absorption in the Godhead, which is now 'all in all'? It is possible that this hidden meaning still obtained. But if we judge by the disorderly and excitable conduct of the community at Corinth, each man singing his own psalm and shouting his own revelation, the general expectation was apocalyptic, and the eyes of the faithful were directed towards an event in future time which would gloriously end all time. This event is described in symbolic detail in the *Revelation* of St John (chapters 7–9).

There is a passage on time and eternity in Dostoyevsky's *The Possessed*, where Stavrogin asks Kirilov whether he believes in a future eternal life. Kirilov replies:

'No, not in a future eternal life, but in this present eternal life. There are moments – you can reach moments – when time suddenly stops and becomes eternal.'

'And you hope to reach such a moment?'

'I do.'

'It's hardly likely in our time', Stavrogin said slowly and thoughtfully, also without any irony. 'In the Apocalypse, the angel promises that there'll be no more time.'

'I know. There's a lot of truth in it; it's clear and precise. When man attains bliss, there will be no more time because there will be no need for it. It's a very true thought.'

'Where will they hide time?'

'Nowhere. Time is not a thing, it's an idea. It will vanish from the mind.'

(The Possessed)

The end of the world continued to be expected in the early Christian era and the year 1000 seemed a mathematically suitable date for time to have a stop.

The initial expectation that the second coming was imminent may have been aroused by a misunderstanding of some of Jesus' sayings, such as his answer to Peter after the resurrection: 'If I will that he (the beloved disciple) tarry till I come, what is that to thee?' (*John* 21). Certainly the early Christians lived in daily anticipation of the end of the world, with their minds fixed on an apocalyptic future and a single past drama of the passion and resurrection of the Lord. Thus they were the prisoners of linear time, languishing in Plato's cave, increasingly blind to the eternal now; and thus eventually they gained power in this world to destroy their enemies. The Church became mighty; the message of the Jewish healer was buried beneath a pile of dogma, although it has retained life enough to inspire seekers for the light at intervals throughout history.

Nothing testifies better to the original meaning of Jesus' message concerning the kingdom that is within, whose seed is the 'son of man', than those fragmentary sayings that have been found in the last century on papyrus scraps excavated in Egypt. Here are some examples:

I stood in the midst of the world, and in flesh appeared I unto them, and I found all men drunken, and none did I find thirsting among them, and my soul is afflicted for the sons of men, because they are blind in heart and see not.

Jesus said:
   He who is near me is near the fire,
   and he who is far from me
   is far from the kingdom.

His disciples said to him:
   On what day does the kingdom come?
(Jesus said:)
   It does not come when it is expected.
   They will not say, Lo, here! or Lo, there!
   But the kingdom of the Father
   is spread out upon the earth, and men do not see it.
         (*The Secret Sayings of Jesus According to the Gospel of Thomas*)

Such sayings, many of which duplicate those recorded in the accepted gospels, help to recreate the man who, speaking in the name of the Holy Spirit, performed miracles of healing which gathered an excitable audience, was misrepresented by his followers and was executed by the authorities. That he appeared to them after death seems well testified. It was on that miracle that the expectations of the Church were founded. Through the centuries much was done in his name that was entirely foreign to his spirit. But what he said in the streets of Jerusalem remained on record and has guided many people, in unspiritual times, to the spiritual life.

This guidance has always been in the name of eternity, as a denial of time's dominion. For time, as Krishnamurti shows, is the supreme enemy of true insight:

To meditate is to transcend time. Time is the distance that thought travels in its achievements. The travelling is always along the old path covered over with a new coating, new sights, but always the same road, leading nowhere – except to pain and sorrow.

It is only when the mind transcends time that truth ceases to be an abstraction. Then bliss is not an idea derived from pleasure but an actuality that is not verbal.

The emptying of the mind of time is the silence of truth, and the seeing of this is the doing: so there is no division between the seeing and the doing.

(*The Second Penguin Krishnamurti Reader*)

But Krishnamurti's witness is individual. He does not claim to teach and stands outside all religious frameworks. The true contrast is between Christianity and Buddhism. Compared with Jesus' mission, which ended on the cross and the despairing cry 'Wherefore forsakest thou me?', the Buddha's mission was successful. Having gained enlightenment, he preached, gathered disciples around him, whose understanding deepened with time, and left five hundred enlightened followers and an organic teaching, which has developed, proliferated and, whatever its differences, remained fundamentally one. It has absorbed much from the religions of the countries into which it spread, and has produced heresies which it has never found necessary to eradicate by slaughter. And essentially, despite the vast differences between the Great Vehicle (Mahayana) and the Lesser Vehicle (Hinayana) – the former philosophical and ritualistic, the latter simple and ethical – it has always retained its original purpose: the seeking of enlightenment for the benefit of all creation.

The Buddha's teaching was a reform movement within the Hinduism of the Upanishads. Hinduism placed man in a vast arena of cyclical time. A complete age (*mahayuga*) was said to be made up of four component ages, each with its dawn and twilight. Our own position, according to modern Vedantists, is in the twilight of the final, or *kali yuga*, of the present *mahayuga* – a time of general decline in morals and civilization, but a time of maximum opportunity for the individual seeker.

These vast cyclic panoramas of the Vedas were multiplied to make up a day and a night in the life of the universal spirit (more than twelve million years) and even to a whole lifetime of Brahma. Yet this does not exhaust the multiplication of ages, each of which runs through its own cycle of creation and destruction.

At intervals in this bewildering expanse of cyclical time appear avatars to declare the truth of enlightenment to men. Of these the seventh and last was Gautama, who is acknowledged as the Buddha or 'enlightened one' by Vedantists, even though Buddhism is rejected and has long ago been replaced in India by a revived Hinduism.

Buddha did not combat the cosmology of the Vedas. He may even have passively accepted it. He merely changed the focus of attention of his followers from the vast panorama of ages and gods, to the eternal moment at which it is possible for a person to turn his attention to the underlying reality, which is the void. He did not deny the transmigrating soul, to which the Hindus granted the freedom of all ages in which to die and be reborn. He merely bade his disciples look inwards, to discover that the soul has no permanent being but is itself a succession of thoughts, desires and suffering, not separate from the rest of creation but dependent on its relationship to everything around it. Buddhism speaks of no soul in the Vedic sense.

This world is 'a vale of Soul-making', as Keats, who knew nothing of Vedanta, wrote in a letter at a time when he knew himself to be dying of consumption, with his poetic powers still largely undeveloped. In the previous page of this long letter he had dwelt upon suffering and its inevitability, reaching the conclusion that if there were no suffering and man could achieve perfect happiness, death would be a more terrible end than it seemed to him then. In that part of the letter he rejected the idea of immortality, but in the part which follows he tentatively accepted the idea, although in no Christian sense:

The common cognomen of this world among the misguided and superstitious is 'a vale of tears' from which we are to be redeemed by a certain arbitrary interposition of God and taken to Heaven. What a little circumscribed straitened notion! Call the world if you please 'The vale of Soul-making'. Then you will find out the use of the world (I am now speaking in the highest terms for human nature, admitting it to be immortal, which I will here take for granted for the purpose of showing a thought which has struck me concerning it). I say 'soul-making' – Soul as distinguished from an Intelligence. There may be intelligences or sparks of the divinity in millions, but they are not Souls till they acquire identities, till each one is personally itself. Intelligences are atoms of perception – they know and they see and they are pure; in short, they are God. How then are Souls to be made? How then are these sparks which are God to have identity given them – so as even to possess a bliss peculiar to each one by individual existence? How but by the medium of a world like this? This point I sincerely wish to consider, because I think it a grander system of salvation than the Christian religion – or rather it is a system of Spirit-creation.

(Keats, *Letters*)

Perhaps Keats also attached too much importance to the soul's individuality, thinking of it as essentially different from all other souls. For, just as the spark in each is the same, so souls once created prove to be identical. Individuality is transcended. Perfection bears the negative sign of Nirvana.

Keats was not long dead before materialistic science, taking its inspiration from Darwin's *Origin of Species*, put its full trust in linear time. Unlike the early Christian linearists, however, the scientists saw time leading not to the end of the world but to its perfection. Progress – whether political, scientific, biological, eugenic or intellectual – would lead to a new heaven on earth in which suffering would be minimized, although death itself could probably never be abolished.

Science had not always taken this view. For instance, Paracelsus – a Swiss physician of the Renaissance whose influence lasted well into the seventeenth century – saw man as the microcosm of the universe, the universe as the macrocosm of man. One great pattern went through all things – a conclusion reached by

nuclear physicists on very different evidence in the last fifty
years:

> Heaven is man and man is heaven, and all men together are one
> heaven, and heaven is nothing but one man. You must know this to
> understand why one place is this way and the other that way, this is new
> and that is old, and why there are everywhere so many diverse things.
>   (Paracelsus, *Selected Writing*)

Thus western science began, born from astrology, with a vision of
unity. All things had their correspondences. Paracelsus saw man
as subject to two influences: the heavens from which at birth he
drew 'the fundamental light, which includes wisdom, art,
reason', and that which 'emanates from matter' and includes
everything that 'relates to the flesh and blood'. But this theosophical and outwardly Christian astrologer-physician concludes
that the essential aim is unity:

> There is one single number that should determine our life on earth,
> and this single number is One. Let us not count further . . . It is true
> that the Godhead is three, but the Three is again comprised in the
> One . . . And because God transforms himself into the One, we men
> on earth must also strive for the One, devote ourselves to the One,
> and live in it.
>
>   (*Ibid.*)

Thus did modern science begin from a standpoint of unity and no
thought of development in time; and to some such standpoint
astro-physics and nuclear physics seem today to be returning.
'As above, so below'; as in the atomic world, so in the galaxies.
Infinity has become the only true measure of space.

But, suspended in a timeless and measureless continuum, how
can a person picture his position? The Buddha tells him that all is
the creation of mind: reality is such only to the extent that there is
a mind that sees it so. *Samsara*, the relative, is only distinguished
from Nirvana in so far as there are persons who see it so. But how
can one visualize eternity, when all one's imagery is built of
forms with colour, size and shape? The seventeenth-century poet
Henry Vaughan describes a visionary dream in terms of light:

I saw Eternity the other night
Like a great *Ring* of pure and endless light,
   All calm, as it was bright,
And round beneath it, Time in hours, days, years
   Driv'n by the spheres
Like a vast shadow mov'd, in which the world
  And all her train were hurl'd.

                              (*The World*)

The poem continues with an anatomy of the worldly scene, reviewing the many types of men who pursue various kinds of vanities. But when the poet is about to chide 'those who live in grots, and caves, and hate the day', he is reminded that eternity, the 'Ring' of the first lines, is not for everybody – it is reserved by the Bridegroom for the Bride alone. The echo of Ruysbroeck is no doubt unintentional. Vaughan was a neoplatonist, influenced by the ideas not only of the Greeks, but of Paracelsus and his new scientists.

Vaughan saw eternity in terms of light and associated it with the pure vision of childhood, thus anticipating Wordsworth:

I cannot reach it and my striving eye
Dazzles at it as at eternity.

Of all the English metaphysical poets, he is the most concerned with the relation of time and eternity, of the transient and the permanent.

With the eclipse of English mystical thought before the Reformation, the vision of eternity passed to the poets. With the exceptions of William Law and the egregious George Fox, the Protestant Churches produced few profound religious insights. Vaughan and Traherne, Blake and Wordsworth were the Protestant visionaries – and Keats, who, on the evidence of the letter quoted earlier, was not a Christian at all.

Keats' vision of eternity is a frozen moment of time, suggested by the figures painted around a Greek urn. Here there is no past and no future, nothing to tell whence these 'fair people' come or whither they are going. They play their pipes but no music sounds, the boughs blossom and it will always be spring. The contrast of this silent procession moving out from the empty town is with the world of suffering, of passion that brings only 'a burning forehead and a parching tongue'. Keats writes from his own experience of this suffering, whereas Vaughan and his contemporary poets gave only an objective and conventional picture of *samsara*, the relative world. Keats, as a romantic, was concerned with suffering and at times luxuriated in it. Many lesser romantic poets wrote only of suffering, seeing no alternative to it, except perhaps in fantasy or dreams of escape. Baudelaire, James Thomson, Heine and others lived always in the 'city of pain' and knew no other.

The first great modern poet of timelessness was the Austrian, Rainer Maria Rilke. For him the apprehension of eternity was an act of translation – human objects had to be elevated into ideas or essences that would be comprehensible in the higher world of angels:

> Angel: suppose there's a place we know nothing about, and there
> on some indescribable carpet, lovers showed all that here
> they're for ever unable to manage – their daring
> lofty figures of heart-flight,
> their towers of pleasure, their ladders,
> long since, where ground never was, just quiveringly .
> propped by each other, – suppose they could manage it there,
> before the spectators ringed round, the countless unmurmuring
> dead:
> would not the dead then fling their last, their for ever reserved,
> ever-concealed, unknown to us, ever-valid
> coins of happiness down before the at last
> truthfully smiling pair on the quietened
> carpet?   (Rilke, *Elegies*)

Thus life (symbolized by the band of acrobats in a picture by Picasso) is a continuous act in time that must be raised to the level of eternity, that 'place we know nothing about'. It is there that we perform what here 'we are unable to manage'. The whole set of Rilke's *Elegies* is an attempt to eternalize the transient, so that what is fragmentary on earth may be appreciated in the world of ideas. For Rilke's angels are not the denizens of heaven, but platonic beings who are nourished by the distillation of human experience.

In Rilke's world, the poet has replaced the priest, and his sheaf of newly forged symbols is man's new possession, now his only means of communication with higher levels of consciousness. No sooner, however, did the poets undertake to act as communicators between men and gods, between time and eternity, than they abdicated. The poets of the generation that followed Rilke were content to conduct mere tours of exploration around their own skulls.

Rilke's angelic world, like Blake's, was a world of private vision, in which, however, he made discoveries of general application. He was not, on the whole, concerned with common experience. Keats, on the other hand, in his 'Ode on a Grecian Urn', was describing in a completely original way a general experience – the moment at which time stops. 'It was immortality *now*', in the words of a contemporary; 'eternity palpably *present*':

There was little imagery but intense feeling. The whole experience was one of joy and gratitude which mounted at times to ecstasy and deepened at others into a vast, profound, illuminated peace. There was no negative emotion, no doubt, terror or struggle – only complete trust in life and the mystery sustaining life. It was immortality *now*; eternity palpably *present*. One wanted to go nowhere, change nothing, just gratefully *be*. The only urgency was that everyone else should realize the same beatitude, because it belongs to everyone by gift of whatever ineffable mystery is responsible for it. Not that pain and sorrow do not exist. They do, but on a more superficial, impermanent level – perhaps one could say on the training and testing level.

As the sensation came on after about twenty minutes of intercessory prayer, it gradually increased in intensity to a great glowing joy. I found myself drenched in gratitude for life ... I was overcome by excess of life. I could hardly bear it. I felt I might die of it, although I knew that to be impossible. I thought of Emily Brontë's 'Last Lines':

> There is no room for Death,
> Nor atom, that his might could render void:
> Thou – THOU are Being and Breath,
> And what THOU art may never be destroyed.

I was in labour with life immortal. I said 'It is strange to watch oneself being born'. I felt this vast excess of life must be what a baby senses coming into the great world from the womb. It was too much ... and like a baby, I cried out, gasping for breath ...

(RERU 1802)

Such a rebirth *can* happen in our present everyday world. But generally, awareness of the timeless moment is more closely concerned with the contrast between time passing and eternity. Sometimes such experiences are reported merely as 'time-slips'. In this category belong occurrences of the *déjà vu* phenomenon, in which time appears to split in two. A telling example of this was noted by Sir Walter Scott in his *Journal*:

I cannot, I am sure, tell if it is worth marking down, that yesterday at dinnertime I was strangely haunted by what I would call the sense of pre-existence – *videlicet,* a confused idea that nothing that passed was said for the first time, that the same topics had been discussed, and the same persons stated the same opinions on the same subjects. It is true there might have been some ground for recollection, considering that three at least of the company were old friends, and kept much company together: that is, Justice Clerk, Abercrombie and I. But the sensation was so strong as to resemble what is called a 'mirage' in the desert, or a calenture on board ship, when lakes are seen in the desert and sylvan landscapes in the sea. It was very distressing yesterday, and brought to my mind the fancies of Bishop Berkeley about an ideal world. There was a vile sense of want of reality in all I did and said. It made me gloomy and out of spirits, though I flatter myself it was not observed. The bodily feeling which most resembles this unpleasing hallucination is in the giddy state which follows profuse bleeding, when one feels as if walking on feather beds and could not find a secure footing. I think the stomach has something to do with it. I drank several glasses of wine, but these only augmented the disorder. I did not find the '*in vino veritas*' of the philosophers. Something of this insane feeling remains today, but a trifle only. (*Journal*)

The sense of unreality that accompanied Scott's mirage effect provides the chief clue to the experience. Some part of the novelist was standing outside the habitual diner and conversationalist, and outside the normal time-scale in which these discussions took place. The suggestion of lightness, as of walking on feather beds, relates the incident to certain out-of-the-body experiences which are discussed below.

The sensation of *déjà vu* that accompanies such moments can appear in reverse: the percipient may be aware (precognitively) of what is going to be said a minute later. Colin Middleton-Murry relates in his autobiography, *One Hand Clapping*, how as a child he unwittingly disconcerted grown-up company by forestalling what was about to be said. He could see a few seconds ahead and this prophetic knack did not surprise him; he took it for granted. However, when he found that others were embarrassed by his foreknowledge, he ceased to mention it. As he grew older it disappeared. Scott's experience was not of foreknowledge, but rather of unreality. He was for a while a witness of the temporal flow, which seemed to take place in the past, as if all this had happened before.

The same was the case in the following example, although here there was a sense of awe lacking in Scott's diary note:

[I was] standing at the back of my house one night and watching the lights of cars coming up the nearby main road. Suddenly I became aware that not only was this a highly significant experience, but that it carried with it an overwhelming conviction that it had happened to me before. I have never been able to ascertain whether it had or not, but the feeling has always remained with me, which is a familiar one to most people, and which was crystallized by J. B. Priestley in his play *I Have Been Here Before*. The experience was definitely spiritual in that it seemed to go deeper than ordinary experience. The car lights suddenly became enormously significant and the darkness took on an almost supernatural quality as though it had a life of its own.

(RERU 266)

The *déjà vu* is probably only a variety of the experience of deeper consciousness, of which we have recorded many examples in earlier sections. Physiologists have suggested physical explanations, such as a sudden lack of synchronism between the lobes of the brain. But this explains nothing. It only poses the further question: what prompts the physiological changes that undoubtedly take place in moments of altered consciousness? An electro-encephalogram will record variations in the electrical discharges of the brain during meditation. But this says nothing concerning the experience itself and its effects. As you read this book, your eye muscles move. But the mental effect of the book cannot be explained in terms of eye-movements.

The *déjà vu* has occasioned much speculation on the nature of time. Ouspensky saw this phenomenon as evidence for his theory of recurrent lives. The idea came to him from an experience shared with his sister in their Petersburg childhood. Sitting at the window, they knew who would next pass along the street, and told one another who it would be. His theory was that at death the identical life was repeated, with the same events and the same errors, and that this cycle would recur until and unless the person was able to 'remember himself' so clearly as to be aware of an approaching error before committing it. He wrote a short novel to illustrate this theme, *The Strange Life of Ivan Osokin*, whose hero's downfall began with his expulsion from school. During one life, the young man realized where his trouble had begun and went to a magician, resolving to alter his conduct 'next time'. But 'next time' there remained only a faint memory, and events once more took their inevitable course. Then he went back to the magician, who promised to rescue him if he would for a while surrender his will to him. Osokin agrees to do this and the story ends with his discovery of his own unreality: 'Osokin looks round, and suddenly an extraordinarily vivid sensation sweeps over him that, if he were not there, everything would be exactly the same.'

Escape from the recurrence of lives thus occurs, according to Ouspensky, only when the unreality of passing-time has been discovered, when one breaks into another dimension. The idea of recurrence played a considerable part in his teaching of the system, although Gurdjieff did not accept it and viewed it as a mere quirk of Ouspensky's.

What the *déjà vu* proves is that a person's relation to passing-time is a loose one. At certain moments of witnessing, one may stand slightly outside it and observe its passing.

Another case of *déjà vu* leads us into the territory of fore-knowledge:

One night I had a vision which was a forerunner of three deaths that did take place some months later. My vision was mounds of earth which looked much like graves which had just been filled and flowers were upon each grave. The vision was so real that I could almost read the names on the cards which were tied to the flowers; now this is what did happen. Just a few short months after, the first death occurred (my brother-in-law) ... Next came the death of my wife's older brother and within a year my wife also died ...

I had an idea that I would like to go to Canada. Here is what happened to me some months before I set sail: one night I had a vision of a landing pier ... As I later gazed upon the harbour in Halifax, everything that I had seen in my vision was the same as I stood and looked over the country that was to be my future home. Everything was as if I had been there before.   (RERU 239)

The percipient's first dream is purely prophetic: his vision symbolizes future events. The second, however, is a *déjà vu* in reverse: he recognizes the port of Halifax from a vision of it in the past. Such prophetic dreams and subsequent recognitions are extremely frequent but very hard to authenticate. As in all cases of prophetic knowledge, one has to ask whether the event actually fulfilled the prophecy, or merely reminded the percipient of something previously seen, heard or dreamt. His first sight of his future home city, moreover, may have occasioned a *déjà vu*, which he merely related to a past dream because of its dream-like quality.

Air Marshal Sir Victor Goddard's precognitive vision of an airfield not yet built seems to belong in the same category: while flying in mist and rain over Scotland in 1934, Goddard saw what should have been Drem airfield below him. But instead of the disused hangars among fields that Drem was at the time, the airfield appeared to be in full working order, with blue-overalled mechanics among four yellow aircraft. Four years later, the details of Goddard's experience were exactly fulfilled – the airport was rebuilt, training aircraft were then painted yellow, and blue overalls had become standard wear for flight mechanics.

G

Well-known and well-attested accounts of visions into the past, like the Misses Moberley and Jourdain's lapse into the eighteenth century while walking in the garden of Versailles, and Edith Olivier's vision of a long-ago fair held at Avebury, can only be accounted for as time-slips which occur at moments of expanded consciousness. On such occasions, the point *now* may expand to take in some secretly related instant of the past or future that is '*present*' at the place where the percipient '*sees*' it. The most that can be said of the copious but idiosyncratic evidence available is that in connection with moments of expanded consciousness, time loses its illusory linear nature and something lying in the 'past' or 'future' is perceived.

On the subject of this eternal now, we conclude this section with the Tibetan lama Chögyam Trungpa's answer to the question of how we are to become aware of this absolute *now* through a relative moment in time:

We have to start by working through the relative aspect, until finally this nowness takes on such a living quality that it is no longer dependent on a relative way of expressing nowness. One might say that *now* exists all the time, beyond the concept of relativity. But since all concepts are based on the idea of relativity, it is impossible to find any words which go beyond that. So nowness is the only way to see directly. First it is between the past and the future – now. Then gradually one discovers that nowness is not dependent on relativity at all . . . The past does not exist, the future does not exist – everything happens now.

(*Meditation in Action*)

8 Powers and 'Backdoor' Methods

Miraculous or supernormal happenings are well-attested in the records of the great religions and of shamanistic cults. They appear to occur spontaneously at a certain high level of spiritual attainment, although they occur also sporadically among people of low development. There are mediums, healers, hypnotists, black magicians, and certain children who seem to actuate poltergeist phenomena, who appear to have been born with strange powers that are largely out of their control. These often fade, leaving the medium or wonder-worker to fake for the remainder of his or her life.

It may be possible to associate the *siddhis* or psychic powers with that purity of the physical and nervous structure, attained by meditators, which endows the body with faculties unknown to the average person imprisoned by his coarse materiality and limited vision. It is reasonable also to suppose that some primitive and underdeveloped people, being less deeply immersed in the material clay, may preserve atavistic characteristics. Hence perhaps the legendary 'second sight' of some Celtic peasants and the clairvoyant claims of Eskimos. That all flesh is not identical is testified by the sweet-smelling incorruptibility of dead saints; that all minds are not identical is shown by the obvious difference between a holy person and a gangster. But to theorize on the *siddhis* is hardly necessary, since Patanjali has mapped them most adequately:

A man may attain extraordinary powers [*siddhis*] by birth, or by taking drugs, or by reciting mantras, or by austerities, or through *samadhi*.

The changes brought about in a man's body are the result of a natural influx.

Actions are not the direct cause of these natural transformations, but prepare the way for them by removing obstacles. Man differs from all other creatures by his power of choice. Like a farmer, he unblocks a stream and brings the water to his field.

Only those powers which are attained through *samadhi* are safe, for by them no new karma is incurred.

(Sutra IV, 1–6)

So supernormal powers can be obtained in five ways, of which only the last is safe, since only when acquired by deep meditation do the *siddhis* carry no fresh *karma*. Acquired in other ways they may be exercised for the subject's own advantage, or merely for display. There is also the danger that their possessor may use them, as Milarepa did, to destroy his relatives' crops. Black magic is not the invention of the gothic romancer. The use of magic powers that may well bring unpleasant consequences to the user may be illustrated by examples of known practitioners of the 'black arts': Gilles de Retz, once one of Joan of Arc's comrades, who later practised ritual murder, for which he was executed; Rasputin, who appears to have been endowed with healing faculties, but who exercised hypnotic powers over the Russian royal family; and Aleister Crowley, a sinister figure, half magician, half clown, whose power over his disciples drove more than one to kill himself. More recent cases of 'black magic' have been reported from drug-taking groups in California, and Carlos Castaneda's perhaps not entirely factual narratives also tell of psychic power exercised without scruples. If Castaneda's 'Don Juan' really existed, he cannot be said to have acted only for the good.

Patanjali insists that to possess the *siddhis* from birth or to acquire them through the back door via drugs or incantations is dangerous; and he does not expatiate on their advantages. He merely suggests that they accrue naturally to one deeply experienced in *samadhi*. They are then the result of changes that occur in one's body with meditation; and the impression one gets from various accounts of these supernormal manifestations is that they are accompanied by a corporeal lightness and the effulgence of light. They are related, no doubt, to the 'mystery of light', of which the Gnostics said Christ was the teacher. For, as his miracles adduce, he was indeed a supreme master of the *siddhis*.

The first of these twelve supernormal powers of which Patanjali speaks is that of entering another body:

When the causes of bondage are loosed and the subtle senses are free, then the yogin is able to enter into other bodies.

(Sutra III, 38)

There are two possible meanings of this statement: first, that a yogin may adopt another body, seemingly identical with his own, in order to appear at some other place to some absent person; and the second is that he may possess the body of another, speaking with his lips and acting with his limbs. Though there are innumerable anecdotes both of 'appearances' in two places at once and of possession in myths and legends, one can only say of them that since they conform to the popular imagination throughout the world, they may be considered to have a certain degree of reality.

The cardinal instances in the New Testament are the appearances of Jesus after his death. The meetings with the dead Jesus are of two kinds. On the road to Emmaus (*Luke* 24:13-34), the disciples met and walked with an apparent stranger. For 'their eyes were holden that they should not know him'. On the way, they told him of his own crucifixion and of other events in Jerusalem, and when they reached their destination persuaded him to eat with them. It was not till they sat at table that the disciples' 'eyes were opened, and they knew him'. Then he vanished, leaving them wondering. For each recognized that his heart had burned within him while this stranger walked with them on the road.

In the second appearance (*Luke* 24:36-53), and those in the Gospel of John, Jesus was instantly recognized. In *Luke*, his appearance at first terrifies the disciples; they fear that he may be a 'spirit', or ghost. In *John*, he twice comes among them, 'the door being shut', and insists in different ways on his corporeality, displaying the wounds in his hands and side. Everything is done to prove that he is *not* a spirit. Thomas, who plays the role of doubter, is not convinced that Jesus has risen, and the fact is proved to him in a very corporeal way (*John* 20:20-27).

It is significant that Thomas is the disciple whose authority is most frequently claimed by the Gnostic Christians, who saw Jesus primarily as 'the light' and were more concerned with the inward 'kingdom of heaven', than with the promised 'resurrection of the body' on the last day. Thus Thomas, in the canonical gospels, is made to contradict the beliefs with which he is credited in the apocryphal sayings of Jesus which bear his name. Here he speaks of Jesus as an omnipresent light or spirit:

> Jesus said:
>   I am the light
>   which is over everything.
>   I am the All;
>   (from me) the All has gone forth,
>   and to me the All has returned.
>   Split wood; I am there.
>   Lift up the stone, and you will find me there.
>
> (*Some Sayings of Jesus*)

Thomas is spoken of, without firm authority, as the apostle who travelled to India. Certainly he would have found thought in India similar to his own. But in comparing the sayings of Jesus attributed to him with those very similar sayings in the canonical gospels, we can only wonder which version is closest to Jesus' actual teaching.

The presence of an actually absent person, partiularly at that person's moment or place of death, is amply vouched for, although seldom in a way that can be substantiated. Rodney Collin Smith, for example, tells at the end of his *Theory of Eternal Life* of Ouspensky's presence with three of his followers at the moment when he was dying:

Lying in bed in Surrey he possessed with his own mind a young man flying over the Atlantic, whom he had already rid of an illusion. That morning dead, he walked with a traveller – crossing London Bridge;

and to another at the wheel of a car showed the nature of the
universe.

(The Theory of Eternal Life)

Another of Ouspensky's followers, Colonel Halsey, told one
of the authors of Ouspensky's presence beside him on one
occasion when he was walking in Kent. Another witness, however, who has no leanings towards the psychic, describes quite
factually the presence of a dead friend beside a stretch of water
where they had often fished together. This is Colin Middleton-
Murry, whose foreknowledge as a child of what the grown-ups
were going to say has already been mentioned. But such experiences are manifold and few can in any factual way be confirmed.

Certainly there can be no substantiation of the presence of
Mme Blavatsky's 'masters', who 'dictated' to her those two
unwieldy compendiums of theosophical theory, *Isis Unveiled* and
The Secret Doctrine. The manuscripts appear to have been written
in 'automatic writing', the form of script changing from time to
time as one 'master' took over from another. Mme Blavatsky
believed that the authors of the books to which she put her name
were hermits who lived in remote caves in Tibet and 'entered
into' her to promulgate the doctrines of theosophy. Certainly the
varied learning expressed in these books far exceeded the knowledge of this unlearned Russian lady, whose only education had
been from French governesses. With our present knowledge of
Tibetan Buddhism, we cannot attribute this east-west farrago of
theosophical theory to Tibetan inspiration. But a strong pre-
sumption remains that Mme Blavatsky was, as she claimed, no
more than the instrument of her incorporeal masters.

Although Tibetan masters may have played no part in the
birth of theosophy, there is much evidence from the writings of
the French traveller Alexandra David-Neel, Lama Govinda and
John Blofeld that, prior to the Chinese Communist take-over in
1959, the practice of 'influence at a distance', if not corporeally,
was known and widely credited. An experience of Lama Govinda's in an isolated monastery tells of the presence in the changing

shapes of the stones in a wall of a being whom he identified with Maitreya, the Buddha of the future:

I only felt that there was something about the surface of this wall that held my attention, as if it were a fascinating landscape. But no, it was far from suggesting a landscape. These apparently accidental forms were related to each other in some mysterious way; they grew more and more plastic and coherent. Their outlines became clearly defined and raised from the flat background. It was like a process of crystallization, or like an organic growth; and the transformation which took place on the surface of the wall was as natural and convincing as if I had watched an invisible sculptor in the creation of a life-size relief. The only difference was that the invisible sculptor worked from *within* his material and in all places at the same time.

Before I knew how it all happened, a majestic human figure took shape before my eyes. It was seated upon a throne, with both feet on the ground, the head crowned with a diadem, the hands raised in a gesture, as if explaining the points of an intricate problem: it was the figure of Buddha Maitreya, the Coming One, who already now is on his way to Buddhahood, and who, like the sun before it rises over the horizon, sends his rays of love into this world of darkness, through which he has been wandering in innumerable forms, through innumerable births and deaths.

I felt a wave of joy passing through me, as I had felt in the presence of my Guru . . .

(The Way of the White Clouds)

The experience might have been entirely subjective – the changing aspects of the Buddha Maitreya being suggested by the shifting rays of the evening light. One also frequently encounters the tendency to interpret experiences of this nature according to the person's cultural conditioning or religious presuppositions. Nevertheless, it could have been a living presence that 'entered into' the wall and brought joy to the German Buddhist traveller in search of deeper knowledge – which he indeed attained – and initiation into the mediations which were practised by recluse monks in those remote regions. In search of an Eckhart or a Ruysbroeck, where could one look in the middle of this century but to that surviving limb of an almost vanished culture, Tibet?

Consideration of the Patanjali sutra quoted earlier provides more questions than answers. But the Christian resurrection account sufficiently indicates that an appearance may convince reliable witnesses, although whether it is seen with the inner or the outer eye, corporeally or in the form of light, will be disputed between literalists and symbolists, immanentists and transcendentalists, Christians and Gnostics. In addition, there are many accounts of apparently authentic cases of appearances of the dying to their close friends or relatives, and a few instances, defying categorization, of influences like those on Mme Blavatsky and Lama Govinda. Exactly what these influences are, one is powerless even to guess.

Another sutra of Patanjali deals with levitation:

By directing the power of the breath towards the relationship between the body and the space around it, the body becomes as light as floating cobwebs, and through meditation on these he travels through space.
(Sutra III, 43)

But this *siddhi* has not always been welcomed by the saints, who had never set out to gain it. Santa Teresa, for example, described an unexpected levitation which greatly embarrassed her. She prayed that it might never happen again.

This has only happened rarely. Once, however, it took place when we were all together in the choir, and I was on my knees, about to take Communion. This distressed me very much, for it seemed a most extraordinary thing and likely to arouse considerable talk. So I ordered the nuns – for it happened after I was made prioress – not to speak of it. On other occasions, when I felt that the Lord was about to enrapture me again, and once in particular during a sermon – it was our patron's feast and some great ladies were present – I lay on the ground and the sisters came to hold me down, but all the same the rapture was observed. Then I earnestly beseeched the Lord to grant me no more favours if they must have outward and visible signs. For worries on this score exhausted me, and whenever He gave me these raptures I was observed. It seems that, of His goodness, He has been pleased to hear me. For I have never had them since, although it is true that this was not long ago.

It seemed to me when I tried to resist that, a great force, for which I can find no comparison, was lifting me up from beneath my feet. It

came with greater violence than any other spiritual experience, and
left me quite shattered. Resistance requires a great struggle, and is of
little use in the end when the Lord will otherwise, for there is no power
that can resist His power.

(Life of Santa Teresa)

Teresa's levitations were always the accompaniment of 'raptures' or ecstasies; and it is probable that levitation also accompanied the raptures of Suso and John of the Cross. Although they
were no doubt considered by simple people to be signs of very
great holiness, they were not valued among the religious. The
following account of the sprightly levitations of St Joseph of
Cupertino suggests that when such things happened they were
duly exaggerated by the ignorant:

He rose into space, and, from the middle of the church, flew like a bird
onto the high altar, where he embraced the tabernacle . . . Sometimes
too, he was seen to fly to the altar of St Francis and of the Virgin of the
Grotello . . . Another time he flew into an olive tree, 'and he remained
kneeling for half an hour on a branch, which was seen to sway as if a
bird had perched on it'. In another ecstasy he flew, about seven feet
above the ground, to an almond tree a hundred feet away.

(quoted in M. Eliade, *Shamanism*)

Although levitation has not been much recorded in the west,
and such accounts as are to be found in the lives of the saints are
hardly reliable, this skill was taught in the monasteries of Tibet
until the middle of this century. Alexandra David-Neel in her
book *With Mystics and Magicians in Tibet* describes the teaching
of levitation as she was told of it:

The student sits cross-legged on a large and thick cushion. He inhales
slowly and for a long time, just as if he wanted to fill his body with air.
Then, holding his breath, he jumps up with legs crossed, without using
his hands, and falls back on his cushion, still remaining in the same
position. He repeats that exercise a number of times during each period
of practice. Some lamas succeed in jumping very high in that way.
Some women train themselves in the same manner.

As one can easily believe, the object of this exercise is not acrobatic
jumping. According to Tibetans, the bodies of those who drill themselves for years, by that method, become exceedingly light; nearly

without weight. These men, they say, are able to sit on an ear of barley without bending its stalk or to stand on the top of a heap of grain without displacing any of it. In fact the aim is levitation.

A curious test has been devised, and the student who passes it with success is believed capable of performing the feats here above mentioned, or at least of approaching proficiency.

A pit is dug in the ground, its depth being equal to the height of the candidate. Over the pit is built a kind of cupola, whose height from ground level to its highest point again equals that of the candidate. A small aperture is left at the top of the cupola. Thus between the man seated cross-legged at the bottom of the pit and the opening, the distance is twice the height of his body . . .

The test consists in jumping cross-legged, as during the training exercises, and coming out through the small opening at the top of the cupola. I have heard Khampas declare that this feat has been performed in their country, but I have not myself witnessed anything like it.

(With Mystics and Magicians in Tibet)

To learn this skill the student must spend three years walled up in darkness; and even so levitation was only the preliminary to the ceremonial practice of 'trance-walking', which requires further long discipline. It would seem that certain monasteries specialized in the training of these spiritual athletes, but by the time Tibet became open to inquisitive westerners, such feats were rare.

The poet and writer Richard Church, who had not spent three years walled up in darkness, describes in his autobiography, how, as a boy, he one day just decided to 'take off':

But now I was free. Since time and space were deceivers, openly contradicting each other, and at best offering a compromise in place of a law, I was at liberty to doubt further, to carry on my exploration of the horizons of freedom. Still conscious of the warm blood whispering in my veins, I looked down at my wrist and saw the transparent flesh, the bird-bones, the channels of blue beneath the skin. All this was substance as fragile as a plant. It could not possibly outweigh the solid earth under my feet, where I and the rest of duped mankind walked with such docility.

. . . I sensed, with a benignancy deeper and more assured than reason, that my limbs and trunk were lighter than they seemed, and that I had only to reduce them by an act of will, perhaps by a mere change of physical mechanics, to command them off the ground, out of the tyranny of gravitation.

I exerted that will, visualising my hands and feet pressing downwards upon the centre of the earth. It was no surprise to me that I left the ground, and glided about the room (which was empty) some twelve or eighteen inches above the parquet floor. At first I was afraid of collapsing, of tumbling and hurting myself. But I had only to draw in a deep breath, and to command the air through the heavy portions of my anatomy, *watching* it flow and dilute the solid bone and flesh through the helpful chemistry of the blood, this new, released and knowledgeable blood, and I soared higher, half-way to the ceiling. This thoroughly frightened me, and I allowed myself to subside, coming to ground with a gentleness that was itself a sensuous delight.

(*Over the Bridge*)

It is interesting to note that the young Church spontaneously used the breathing technique always associated with the teaching of levitation.

In the west we have heard little of this practice until recently, but a related phenomenon – the 'out-of-the-body' experience – appears to be comparatively frequent, although most people to whom it occurs are generally shy of talking about it. A brief experience of this nature is recorded by a Jungian psychologist:

At seventeen I had an experience of nearly dying . . . I came out of my body and found myself lying about six feet above it, watching matron and a doctor caring for me below . . . It was an experience of intense 'livingness', expansion, of well-being. I thought, 'If this is death, how lovely, natural, easy.' Coming back was the reverse – very unpleasant, being cramped down into an ill physical body. Since then I have never been afraid of death. Also, from *experience* I know that this limited space-time, three-dimensional continuum is but a partial one and relative to that intense life I glimpsed . . .

There followed a lifetime of working on the personality, through psychological analysis (mainly Jungian).   (RERU 354)

This phenomenon of detachment from the body sometimes occurs in sickness, sometimes at a moment when the patient is close to death. Detachment is not always complete, however, as in the case of M.K., a friend of one of the authors, who described her experience to him:

M.K. was recovering from a throat operation, when she had a sudden relapse. She found herself floating above her hospital bed, while at the same time conscious of the pain in the throat of her grotesque self lying below her. She overheard the conversation between two nurses beside her. One was scolding the other for administering the wrong drug: 'I won't have you killing my patient'. She felt that she must go back to the bed, because M., her son, was too young to do without her. On coming round, she told one of the nurses that she shouldn't have considered her patient unconscious just because her eyes were closed. She told the story to her doctor, retelling the conversation she had overheard.

It may be remarked that this lady has suffered much illness since this experience and affirms that, as a result, she has never again been afraid of death. She is a person of no religious faith who has, however, at times practised TM. In the course of her experience she did not, as will be noticed, lose consciousness of her physical suffering. The detachment was far greater in the case of Beatrice Mayor, a writer who was long associated with Ouspensky. Seized with a sudden haemorrhage, she was hurried to hospital where she found herself drifting from her bed, out under the night sky, with feelings of great happiness, and only reluctantly returned to her body. Still happy from this confirmatory experience, she sent for various friends in order to tell them of it.

In a popular book entitled *Life after Life*, Dr Raymond Moody has made a collection of these experiences, gathered in America from people who have temporarily left the body at a moment of near-death. Several of these seem to have gone into that intermediate territory – called in Tibetan scriptures the *bardö* – even to the point of glimpsing the clear light, which, according to these writings, is the highest vision of the between-lives state. Moody shows from the title of his book, and by the excerpts from such scriptures as he appends to it, that he accepts the hypothesis of reincarnation. One of the most complete experiences related to him was of a man who, like Mrs Mayor, felt that he had actually experienced death, and yet came back:

'I heard the doctors say that I was dead, and that's when I began to feel as though I were tumbling, actually kind of floating, through this blackness, which was some kind of enclosure . . . Everything was very black, except that, way off from me, I could see this light. It was a very, very brilliant light, but not too large at first. It grew larger as I came nearer and nearer to it.

'I was trying to get to that light at the end, because I felt that it was Christ, and I was trying to reach that point. It was not a frightening experience. It was more or less a pleasant thing. For immediately, being a Christian, I had connected the light with Christ, who said, "I am the light of the world". I said to myself, "If this is it, if I am to die, then I know who waits for me at the end, there in that light." '

(Life after Life)

The 'kind of floating' with which the description begins is common to most of these experiences. In another gathered by Moody, the experiencer floats over the scene of a car accident in which he has been involved. Others, who have left their bodies during operations or in crises of illness, like M.K., hear and remember what is said by the doctors or nurses around them and, reporting the conversation afterwards, are able to gain some confirmation of the event. Moody in fact succeeds in supplying a fair amount of confirmatory material and manages to isolate a number of features common to those at the point of death. The feeling of emerging from a tunnel into the light is a frequent feature, as is the roaring or buzzing sound, recorded in *The Tibetan Book of the Dead*, which also seems to be associated with the 'universal hum', referred to by Patanjali in Sutra III, 42. In general the experients return to life reluctantly, and always with the conviction that death is not to be feared and that it is not the end.

It may be wondered whether some element of suggestion from Moody colours the narratives of those he interviewed. Were any of them familiar with eastern writings on death and reincarnation? The nature of their accounts makes this seem unlikely. They are written in simple language, showing no familiarity with oriental literature of any kind, and where any beliefs are revealed, these demonstrate a plain, unmetaphysical Christianity.

Another recent book on out-of-the-body experiences, which like Moody's has circulated widely both in Britain and America, is *Journeys out of the Body* by Robert A. Monroe. Here, as in the case of Castaneda, we are on treacherous ground. Mr Monroe, an American writer and journalist who has had a successful professional career, claims to be able to leave his body at will and to have travelled widely in what we may call the Swedenborgian borderland of astral beings and landscapes. Frequently in the course of his 'night flights' he visits his friends and reports to them the following morning what he has observed them to be doing or saying. Thus there is much confirmatory material, and in addition his book is introduced by an independent scientific investigator into this phenomenon, Dr Charles Tart, under whose guidance he has worked.

Other explorations take Monroe into a science-fiction country, which we must suppose to lie in future time or on another planet. These and other journeys that bring him in touch with angels or archetypes make one wonder whether these visions do not sometimes lead into dream states not easily distinguishable from them. More reliable, because more cautious in his claims and better versed in the literature of such things, is Professor Whiteman of Cape Town, whose account is published in the *Proceedings* of the Society for Psychical Research. Whiteman has been subject to out-of-the-body experiences throughout his life and his night journeyings have brought him more profound visions than those of Monroe. Here is an account of a 'flight' at the age of twenty-eight, which gave him a glimpse of the 'clear light'; during the night, but not in a dream, he saw himself 'separated' from the body and raised very quickly to a great height:

All at once, without any further change, my eyes were opened. Above and in front, yet in me, of me, and around, was the Glory of the Archetypal Light. Nothing can be more truly light, since that Light makes all other light to be light; nor is it a flat material light, but a creative light of life itself, streaming forth in Love and Understanding, and forming all other lives out of its substance . . .

Far below, as things can be seen at these times without turning away, there appeared something like the surface of the Earth. But this was only for a moment, in a representative vision, to make clear the immense height to which the soul had been raised, and her nearness to the Sun.

How can the source be described? How its direction? Though upwards and forwards, it was not a geometrical direction, more or less so, and in relation to something else, but an absolute direction, exactly so, by its own archetypal nature. Source it was, of Life and Truth, being the source of all ideas of life and truth; yet manifested as in space.

(The Mystic Life)

Professor Whiteman, like Ouspensky before him, is a mathematician; his cosmic vision, like the Russian's, is no doubt coloured by subsequent speculation. However, he reached a point where time and motion ceased; he was absorbed in the light. Perhaps such a vision of the light belongs with the other experiences of the light already discussed under that heading; but it began with an out-of-the-body experience, as did most of the accounts in this paper.

'Night flying' would appear to be a common occurrence, which the experient generally attributes to dreams. The man in the closet incident quoted earlier is someone who also had frequent night journeys over unfamiliar country. Others, such as Castaneda, write of night flying as if to a witch's coven. Granted the existence of an 'astral body', such happenings are not so hard to accept. The best evidence for them comes from the near-death, and even clinically 'dead', experiences methodically collected by Moody, and also from what is known of the *siddhis* formerly practised by monks and hermits in Tibet. In their judgement, no doubt, or in Patanjali's, Monroe would appear as one who possessed these powers from birth – a condition rather dangerous than advantageous.

An example of the 'trance-walkers' of Tibet is cited by Alexandra David-Neel:

. . . I noticed, far away in front of us, a moving black spot which my field-glasses showed to be a man. As I continued to observe him through the glasses, I noticed that the man proceeded at an unusual

gait and, especially, with an extraordinary swiftness. Though, with the
naked eyes, my men could hardly see anything but a black speck
moving over the grassy ground, they too were not long in remarking
the quickness of its advance. I handed them the glasses and one of
them, having observed the traveller for a while, muttered: '*Lama
lung-gom-pa chig da*' ['It looks like a lama *lung-gom-pa*'] . . .

The man continued to advance towards us and his curious speed
became more and more evident [Mme David-Neel was warned not to
speak to the lama or interrupt this trance state]. Now I could clearly
see his perfectly calm impassive face and wide-open eyes with their
gaze fixed on some invisible far-distant object situated somewhere
high up in space. The man did not run. He seemed to lift himself from
the ground, proceeding by leaps. It looked as if he had been endowed
with the elasticity of a ball and rebounded each time his feet touched
the ground. His steps had the regularity of a pendulum.

(*With Mystics and Magicians in Tibet*)

On two other occasions the same author came across these
trance-walkers and she was able to gather some information
about the practice. Its purposes were far from utilitarian, although
such rapid and apparently effortless travelling would indeed have
been advantageous in a country of such vast distances where
wheeled vehicles were unknown. The purpose of *lung-pa* trance-
walking was ceremonial, and these prodigious feats of travelling
were undertaken in connection with festivals that dated from
pre-Buddhist times. Training for this skill was very strict and was
open only to those who had passed the supreme levitation test.
The body had by then achieved such lightness that walkers would
sometimes hang chains around their necks, as Mme David-Neel
once observed in a lonely forest, to prevent their leaving the
ground.

Lama Govinda did not meet any trance-walkers in the course
of his journeys. He found himself, however, on one occasion
performing this feat spontaneously. Far from his camp, in
desolate country above the Blue Lake, he had stayed too long
painting and feared that he would not get back before nightfall;
moreover the homeward way was dangerous on account of
scree from a recent landslide:

It was no longer possible to pick my way between the boulders that covered the ground for uncounted miles ahead of me; night had completely overtaken me; and yet to my amazement I jumped from boulder to boulder without ever slipping or missing a foothold, in spite of wearing only a pair of flimsy sandals . . . And then I realized that a strange force had taken over, a consciousness that was no more guided by my eyes or my brain. My limbs moved as in a trance, with an uncanny knowledge of their own, though their movement seemed almost mechanical. I noticed things only like in a dream, somewhat detached. Even my own body had become distant, quasi-detached from my will-power. I was like an arrow that unfailingly pursued its course by the force of its initial impetus, and the only thing I knew was that on no condition must I break the spell that had seized me.

It was only later that I realized what had happened: that unwittingly and under the stress of circumstances and acute danger I had become a *lung-gom-pa*, a trance walker, who, oblivious of all obstacles and fatigue, moves on towards his contemplated aim, hardly touching the ground, which might give a distant observer the impression that the *lung-gom-pa* was borne by the air (*lung*), merely skimming the surface of the earth.

. . . I moved on with the certainty of a sleep-walker – though far from being asleep. I do not know how many miles of this boulder-strewn territory I traversed; I only know that I finally found myself on the pass over the low hills with the plain and the magnesium swamp before me . . . still under the influence of the 'spell', I went right across the swamp without ever breaking through.

(The Way of the White Clouds)

When Govinda found himself thus trance-walking he had not yet read Alexandra David-Neel's account, and only subsequently realized that he must have somehow learnt the technique unconsciously. Mme David-Neel witnessed various remarkable happenings during her travels, including a disappearance that can be explained only by the exercise of supernormal powers as described in another of Patanjali's sutras:

One afternoon, I was with my cook in a hut which we used as a kitchen. The boy asked me for some provisions. I answered 'Come with me to my tent, you can take what you need out of the boxes.'

We walked out and when nearing my tent, we *both* saw the hermit lama seated on a folding chair next to my camp table. This did not surprise us because the lama often came to talk with me. The cook only said 'Rimpoche is there, I must go and make tea for him at once. I will take the provisions later on.'

I replied: 'All right. Make tea and bring it to us.'

The man turned back and I continued to walk straight towards the lama, looking at him all the time while he remained seated motionless.

When I was only a few steps from the tent, a flimsy veil of mist seemed to open before it, like a curtain that is slowly pulled aside. And suddenly I did not see the lama any more. He had vanished . . . Upon another occasion he repeated the phenomenon. He utterly disappeared as I was speaking with him in the middle of a wide bare track of land, without tent or houses or any kind of shelter in the vicinity.

(With Mystics and Magicians in Tibet)

To this intrepid lady traveller we also owe a most dramatic account of the production of psychic heat – another *siddhi*, which is related to the production of light and its circulation through the body, and which was spoken of in an earlier section in relation to several accounts, including that of Richard Rolle of Hampole. This power too had its practical value in a country of such intense cold:

Upon a frosty winter night, those who think themselves capable of victoriously enduring the test are led to the shore of a river or lake. If all the streams in the region are frozen, a hole is made in the ice. A moonlit night, with a hard wind blowing, is chosen. Such nights are not rare in Tibet during the winter months.

The neophytes sit on the ground, cross-legged and naked. Sheets are dipped in the icy water; each man wraps himself in one of them and must dry it on his body. As soon as the sheet has become dry it is again dipped in the water and placed on the novice's body to be dried as before. The operation goes on in that way until daybreak. Then he who has dried the largest number of sheets is acknowledged the winner of the competition.

(With Mystics and Magicians in Tibet)

Mme David-Neel describes in detail the exercise for the raising of heat. Much seems to depend on the regulation of the breath. Indeed the attainment of most *siddhis* is by mastery of breathing.

As the last of these travellers' tales of what must in Tibet by now be a dead art, we give an account of an even more mysterious happening observed by the English Buddhist, John Blofeld, and others, during a visit to a distant monastery in western China, far out towards the Tibetan border:

As each one entered the little room and came face to face with the window beyond, he gave a shout of surprise, as though all our hours of talk had not sufficiently prepared us for what we now saw. There in the great open spaces beyond the open window, apparently not more than one or two hundred yards away, innumerable balls of fire floated majestically past. We could not judge their size, for nobody knew how far away they were, but they appeared like the fluffy woollen balls that babies play with seen close up. They seemed to be moving at the stately pace of a large, well-fed fish aimlessly cleaving its way through the water; but, of course, their actual pace could not be determined without a knowledge of the intervening distance. Where they came from, what they were, and where they went after fading from sight in the West, nobody could tell.

(The Wheel of Life)

For these fire-balls and the strange occurrences observed by Alexandra David-Neel, no 'scientific explanation' is possible. At most, one can say with her that in Tibet the power of thought, exercised by lamas of such skill and with such concentration, was so strong as to call up phantoms, apparitions and lights, which might be seen by one person and not by another. Telepathy was certainly practised between lama and disciple, who might have no other means of communication; and telepathic messages intercepted by chance might be interpreted in unexpected ways. Mme David-Neel was herself sceptical, and tended to find a material explanation where one was possible. But she had no doubt, after many years of travel in Tibet, that certain psychic skills, perhaps even then dying out, were practised, though for no purpose of display, in lonely monasteries and in the vast, thinly populated countryside.

Patanjali, besides cataloguing those skills productive of psychic or magical phenomena, gives a further list of those which bring deeper knowledge and subtler powers of communication. The following sutras belong in the first category:

By directing the power of breath towards a mind empty of thought, he becomes invisible. He is then pure intelligence and does not refract the light.

This appears to account for the vanishing mentioned by Alexandra David-Neel.

Another *siddhi* vouched for by Patanjali (Sutra III, 49) is the far more common phenomenon of clairvoyance. The well-known case of Swedenborg and the fire in Stockholm provides a good example of pure clairvoyance. Immanuel Kant was so impressed by the accounts that reached him that he carried out his own investigation. Here is his report:

The following occurrence appears to me to have the greatest weight of proof, and to place the assertion respecting Swedenborg's extraordinary gift beyond all possibility of doubt. In the year 1759 towards the end of September on Saturday at four o'clock p.m., Swedenborg arrived at Gottenburg from England, when Mr William Castel invited him to his house, together with a party of fifteen persons. About six o'clock, Swedenborg went out, and returned to the company quite pale and alarmed. He said that a dangerous fire had just broken out in Stockholm, at the Sodermalm, and that it was spreading very fast. He was restless and went out often. He said that the house of one of his friends, whom he named, was already in ashes, and that his own was in danger. At eight o'clock, after he had been out again, he joyfully exclaimed, 'Thank God! The fire is extinguished, the third door from my house.' . . .

On Monday evening a messenger arrived at Gottenburg, who had been dispatched by the Stockholm Board of Trade during the time of the fire. In the letters brought by him, the fire was described precisely in the manner stated by Swedenborg. On Tuesday morning the royal courier arrived at the governor's with the melancholy intelligence of the fire, of the loss which it had occasioned, of the houses it had damaged and ruined not in the least differing from that which Swedenborg had given at the very time when it happened; for the fire was extinguished at eight o'clock.

(I. Kant, *Documents Concerning Swedenborg*)

For Swedenborg it would have been quite inconceivable to regard such a gift as a psychic power divorced from spiritual reality. For him, as for Blake, it was a question of being 'informed in the world of spirits'. In an exchange of letters with John Wesley, Swedenborg correctly prophesied the date of his own death on the 29th March, 1772.

Swedenborg is exceptional. Yogins do not normally seem able to combine clairvoyance with what would be called precognition. It is always difficult to determine just how clairvoyant yogins are, or how much they can read another person's mind telepathically. Instances are manifold of a yogin trusting some obviously unreliable person, who will subsequently break his word to him. The case of Judas in the gospels is an obvious example. The yogin does not usually seem to know whether or in what manner his teaching will develop. There seems to be a large area of un-certainty in which unpredictable factors may interfere.

That the yogin normally has no exact knowledge of past and future seems probable. Nor does he usually have detailed know-ledge of his past lives. A Tibetan lama known to one of the authors is recognized as the reincarnation of a hermit who died shortly before he (the lama) was born. He refers to the years he spent in a cave in Nepal as if these were part of his present life, but he has no physical memory of his days as a hermit. Nor do yogins encourage their disciples to call up the memory of past lives. Indeed, this is the one *siddhi* that is firmly discouraged. The most likely reason is that too much interest in the past proves a fascination that deflects attention from the eternal now – the only moment in which enlightenment is possible.

Incidents of clairvoyance sometimes show not merely the acquisition of unknown facts, but a great deepening and widening of awareness as well. Indeed both the examples that follow convey more than a taste of 'cosmic consciousness':

My first conscious memory of seeing in an intense way was when I was a boy. I saw trees not only with ordinary perception, but was held in trance by them. There was something *between* me and them; something of them in me, perhaps something of me in them. The present moment opened. As a growing boy I lived in mystic participation with nature, yet I was an active boy, good at swimming, riding, boxing and fencing.

Once, at school, alone in a classroom doing extra work, I gazed out of the window at the swaying branches of fir trees; I had a vivid feeling that I had seen something similar in earlier lives. I knew no theory of reincarnation, but got a direct impression of an earlier, or many earlier, existences . . .

At Cambridge, I still had a trick of seeing things in a peculiar way. Once when I was dissecting out the mesonephros of a newt, I saw the creature, as it floated in its dish of water, as a *being* – not only of organs, skin, eyes, etc., but as a *form* that bore the mark of creative impulse. I was on the fringes of the mystery of life. That was as near as the quantitative evaluations of modern biology allowed me to get. The qualities of life were never mentioned. The restrictions of modern science were that they excluded, or tried to exclude, all subjective feelings. This I found was quite impossible, for no two men can see the same paramaecium, dogfish or caterpillar.

(RERU 1155)

In response to a questionnaire sent out by Marghanita Laski for her book *Ecstasy*, a reply advances a similar conclusion:

'When you suddenly discover a faculty working with effortless efficiency which enables you to hold in the forefront of conscious feeling both knowledge of the smallest bacteria in the field, how the blade of grass works, and the universe, in the same detail – all you know about nature, the whole thing, you can think about them all simultaneously and not in parts, that knowledge is almost limitless – one's aware objectively of what one's doing but not aware of anything else, not aware of yesterday or tomorrow, just of *the moment*, doing this now.'

(*Ecstasy*)

Patanjali is less precise in describing the advantages of some other *siddhis*. He merely generalizes on the powers gained by meditating upon friendship:

By directing the power of breath on friendship and compassion, the yogin acquires friendliness, compassion and equanimity in both joy and sorrow.

(Sutra III, 24)

However, the power that may emanate from this cultivation of compassion may also produce surprising results, not only in those who practise meditation, but also in those born with the skill of teaching or the gift of healing. The following account of a woman's spontaneous and unexpected power to heal demonstrates the meaning of compassion in Patanjali's sense – unemotional and undemanding:

Recently I was taken to a casualty ward [in a famous hospital] and put next to a young girl who had been in a serious car accident. Both legs and one arm were broken and she was in that twilight world, knowing no one, unable to speak or hear, with staring unseeing eyes. I asked the nurse about her and was told she was a perfect example for euthanasia ... her heart had actually stopped, she was taken to the resuscitation room, but there had been too long a delay and she was suffering from oxygen starvation to the brain. She was forcibly fed and had no control over bowel and urinary movements. Her one remaining arm was tied down because she became violent and tore and scratched the nurses or anyone who went near ...

For some inexplicable reason I became involved in this family, they treating me like one of them. One evening I prayed for this girl with a consuming force that I could not explain. I felt elevated in a horizontal position and filled with a strange power – a power in all my body which seemed to run out to my hands, and a knowledge that if I put my hands towards this girl I could cure her. It was a force that could bear no argument or doubt and as I pushed my hands towards this girl, I could hear her say 'Mummy, Mummy'. I then seemed to be a spent force, but with the realization that the girl would be whole once again. I did not mention this to anyone ...

The following morning, early, I was moved to the next ward. That evening the girl's mother came running in to say that her daughter was speaking and had recovered consciousness. The nurses were so surprised and amazed that they questioned her [on various details to which only she could reply. She answered all the questions correctly.]

I later had a letter from her mother at Christmas saying that 'Susan' had been home and was then going to a rehabilitation centre. She thanked me again for all I had done for her daughter – and yet I had never spoken a word about my prayers. (RERU 1169)

In the sutra already referred to (III, 42), Patanjali describes the comparatively common though seldom noticed phenomenon of the 'music of the spheres':

By mastering the powers of the breath, the yogin establishes a connection between his ear and the surrounding ether. Thus he acquires divine hearing.

The 'music of the spheres' is a phrase primarily associated with Pythagoras; it was also used by the seventeenth-century astronomer, Johannes Kepler, in his great work *Harmonius Mundi* (*World Harmony*). Plato, in the Myth of Er, describes the universe as a complicated musical machine in the shape of eight inter-related spindles:

Aloft upon each of the circles of the spindle is mounted a Siren; which goeth round with her circle, uttering one note at one pitch; and the notes of all the eight together do make one melody.

(Republic)

This music, from which according to Pythagorean theory our human octave is derived, is the fundamental harmony of the universe and as basic to man's experience as the colours of the rainbow. Patanjali says in *Sutra* 42 that it is possible to acquire 'divine hearing', in other words to be aware of this music with the inner ear. It is strange that this faculty of hearing the harmonics of the spheres, though not uncommon, has seldom been recorded. An account of this music is, however, provided by Rosalind Heywood, who refers to the sound as 'the singing':

The Singing seems to tell me something about my environment. It is best described as a kind of continuous vibrant inner *quasi*-sound, to which the nearest outer analogy is the noise induced by pressing a seashell against the ear, or perhaps the hum of a distant dynamo. This sounds like tinnitus to anyone else, but to the experient it does not appear to be heard by the ear or to be exactly located. Rather, like light, it pervades the whole atmosphere, though it is most clearly perceptible in a wide arc above and behind the head. And – I cannot explain what I mean by this – it does not appear to ring through outer space, yet neither is it far 'in'. The right word may be borderline, if, as I suspect, there is no sharp barrier between sensory and extra-sensory phenomena.

To hear the Singing in normal circumstances needs a deliberate switch of attention, for it is very delicate. By listening carefully I can just do so, sometimes, through normal conversation, and now I can hear it with an effort through the tapping of my typewriter. But I cannot pay attention to it through, say, the hubbub of a cocktail party or the blast of a road drill. On the other hand, there are places where it will force itself on one's attention. It makes the silence live.

(*The Infinite Hive*)

Rosalind Heywood adds that her husband could also hear 'the singing', as could others who have spoken to her about it. A doctor, who practises TM and himself hears the 'celestial hum', has this to say about it:

I find that whenever my surroundings are reasonably quiet, I can 'hear' a high-pitched sound, something like the singing of cicadas but much less definite – more ethereal. It certainly is *not* tinnitus, which is located *in* the ear (usually only one), whereas this is diffuse and quite unlocalized, though I agree with Rosalind Heywood that it does seem to be distributed in an arc above the head. Unlike R.H., I don't find that it increases or takes on different qualities in different places, such as churches; but it is certainly much easier to hear when things are very quiet. As far as I can remember I've been able to hear it all my life. I've usually put it down to neuronal 'noise' in the brain – i.e. rather analogous to the hum of a radio when nothing is coming through – but this may not be the real explanation.

Although in my case it doesn't seem to be related to telepathic impressions, it definitely gets much louder, just after meditation – indeed it can be almost deafening at these times, although the paradoxical thing about it is that, no matter how loud it may seem to be, it never interferes with the hearing of ordinary sounds – in fact, I suspect that my hearing is unusually acute at these times. When I was a boy, I used to think of it as the 'sound of the silence'.

(Dr A.C.)

This 'sound of the silence' calls to mind a moment described by Krishnamurti when the world seemed to stop turning and the morning was invaded by a silence which was not just the absence of noise:

That morning, especially so early, the valley was extraordinarily quiet. The owl had stopped hooting and there was no reply from its mate over in the distant hills. No dog was barking and the village was not yet awake. In the east there was a glow, a promise, and the Southern Cross had not yet faded. There was not even a whisper among the leaves, and the earth itself seemed to have stopped in its rotation. You could feel the silence, touch it, smell it, and it had that quality of penetration. It wasn't the silence outside in those hills, among the trees, that was still; you were of it. You and it were not two separate things. The division between noise and silence had no meaning. And those hills, dark, without a movement, were of it, as you were.

This silence was very active. It was not the negation of noise, and strangely that morning it had come through the window like some perfume, and with it came a sense, a feeling, of the absolute. As you looked out of the window, the distance between all things disappeared, and your eyes opened with the dawn and saw all things anew.

(*The Second Penguin Krishnamurti Reader*)

For Krishnamurti the essence of the moment of clarity is its spontaneity. He would be the last to advocate the inducement of the 'sound of silence', least of all the deliberate cultivation of any of the *siddhis*. In this passage he has clearly experienced something of a far more subtle and refined order than the usual accounts of such happenings suggest.

Although Patanjali set out to describe the many supernormal powers that may be attained and the ways of gaining them, the examples we have been able to gather of recent and contemporary happenings of this kind do not conform closely to his divisions, of which we have quoted only the more relevant. Moreover, four translations of his Sutras have been referred to and his meanings are still not entirely clear.

About some of his statements, however, there can be no doubt. First, he says categorically that the only safe way of acquiring the *siddhis* is through *samadhi*; they are in fact a by-product of meditation. If pursued for their own sake by means of drugs, spells or other mechanical means, they will be harmful, since by using them for the wrong reasons a person will accumulate bad *karma*. A small example of this danger is quoted by Alexandra David-Neel. One day a young man attached himself to her caravan who proved to be a student of trance-walking. He had given up his studies, however, and travelled with her as a bearer. On one occasion, she and one or two others had gone ahead to pitch camp and cook the stew for supper. The young man, left behind with the rearguard, sniffed from afar the smell of cooking and falling into a trance, set off with supernormal rapidity, to arrive before the stew was eaten. Thereafter he was bitterly ashamed of having practised *lung-pa* for such a profane purpose.

(One of the authors once asked a teacher about the *siddhis*, to receive the reply: 'Yes, we could teach them to you. But they would do you no good.')

The Tibetan tradition of teaching the *siddhis* for a religious purpose died with the Chinese conquest of 1959 and the dissolution of the monasteries. It was, as we have said, a survival of an ancient system of thought and action of pre-Buddhist origins, which had otherwise vanished from the world. In the present rebirth of Tibetan Buddhism under the Dalai Lama in India and further afield in the west, such things have no place.

Nonetheless, travellers on the path are never free from perils, for the 'little self' always remains with them and may at any moment lead them astray. What the little self chiefly demands are experiences. These are the tribute that she attempts to levy as her reward for the discomforts of the whole enterprise. Most of the contemporary occurrences so far described have been premonitory and have signified no more than that there is a way leading out of everyday existence into another life of reversed values, where emptiness is fulfilment and time is eternity. Premonitory experiences are usually pleasant, and sometimes the little self looks forward to a continuous diet of them. The world, it thinks, will now always be richer and brighter. But the road leads through many barren places. It climbs steadily, but seldom grants enchanting views of a promised land ahead.

These early experiences sometimes attract people to embark on the journey. They are the only evidence, apart from books, that there is a goal, that life is not exclusively made up of desires, frustrations, greed and suffering. So, *pace* Patanjali, perhaps an artificially induced foretaste may be no bad thing. A drug experience may be justifiable. Many religious cults have used narcotics and hallucinogens as an initiation into religious experience. If the subject is prepared and has a genuine desire to discover the spiritual way, all may be well.

But drugs are frequently misused. Perhaps the little self, enjoying this glimpse into another world, is enchanted and requires endless repetitions. Perhaps an insufficiently prepared person takes a drug out of curiosity and then has a 'bad trip'; the effect is then too strong for the subject's system. In any case drugs cannot help one to advance on the spiritual path. They only contribute to the little self's obsession with experiences; and experiences, although they may show evidence of progress, do not help one forward on the path. At best they may encourage one, but when mechanically obtained they deflect one utterly.

There appears to be no superficial difference between the sudden expansion of consciousness that arises spontaneously and that induced by drugs. In either case, the mirror is suddenly clean and a world of far greater subtlety is reflected in it. The same thing may happen to an epileptic, who immediately falls into unconsciousness, since the light revealed is too strong for his impaired nerves. Schizophrenics also know this sudden light, which is, however, generally clouded by their delusions.

Sceptics basing their arguments on the similarity between hallucinated and spiritual experience may contend that the mystical vision has no more validity than that induced by mescalin or LSD. In a sense, it has not. But the mystical experience marks a stage on the path; and when the subject is advancing towards higher consciousness, it brings with it knowledge that cannot be gained by a series of mechanical experiments.

That an isolated taking of LSD may not differ from the common 'picking up of sixpence' is shown by the fact that the account quoted on pp. 189–90 was in fact the account of an 'acid trip' (RERU 1802). The chief clue that this was not a natural but an artificially contrived experience lies towards the end of the narrative: 'It was too much.' This repeats the burden of an earlier passage: 'I could hardly bear it. I felt I might die of it.' Furthermore, the experiencer is surprised at the absence of terror and of negative emotion. He had feared a 'bad trip' and one can see how the trip might have turned bad by excess.

The danger of the drug experience is that the doors of perception may be opened a little too wide and the percipient be blinded by excess of light. One is reminded of the warning to the meditator who was bathed with light, seemingly from his closet (see p. 146), not to open his eyes too wide. There is in this particular account of an 'acid trip' an excitability, a pressure to communicate that which can never be told.

This is also found in one of the first writers to speak of drug visions, Thomas de Quincey:

If in this world there is one misery having no relief, it is the pressure on the heart from the *Incommunicable*. And if another Sphinx should arise to propose another enigma to man – saying, 'What burden is that which only is insupportable by human fortitude?', I should answer at once – *It is the burden of the Incommunicable*.

(*Confessions of an English Opium Eater*)

William James, a more philosophical investigator, having experimented with nitrous oxide, reached a clearer understanding of the nature of this 'incommunicable' revelation:

Our normal waking consciousness, rational consciousness as we call it, is but one special type of consciousness, whilst all about it, parted from it by the filmiest of screens, there lie potential forms of consciousness entirely different. We may go through life without suspecting their existence; but apply the requisite stimulus, and at a touch they are there in all their completeness, definite types of mentality which probably somewhere have their field of application and adaptation. No account of the universe in its totality can be final which leaves these other forms of consciousness quite disregarded.

(*The Varieties of Religious Experience*)

Such a conviction is probably the optimum benefit that the open-minded enquirer can derive from the use of drugs. A friend of one of the authors, a Mexican scholar and critic, by eating an hallucinogenic fungus, derived a similar assurance that other modes of consciousness existed. Emotionally, the experience gave him a great release. Going to the university next morning, he felt an unexpected warmth towards all his colleagues; and this warmth remained many months later. Indeed, he felt that he would never be the same. But, long afterwards, asked whether he would like to take the drug again, he answered coolly, 'Perhaps; some day.'

A peculiar feature of this Mexican experience was that it was a joint experiment by a number of intellectuals and that all but one was content with the revelation. One woman alone had had a bad trip. But in answer to the suggestion that this was an approach by the back door and that a permanent change of consciousness could be attained by meditation, none was interested. The revelation was sufficient.

Another peculiar aspect of this mushroom-eating was that the experiencer did not apparently go deep. One of them in fact dictated an account of his sensations to his wife, stage by stage as they occurred. This would of course be impossible for anyone using nitrous oxide, or to anyone in a state of deep meditation. It is clear, therefore, that experiences under certain types of hallucinogenics differ in an important way from the mystical states which we have been considering. The witness, in fact, is far more alert, even in command of the external situation, than he would be if in a state of *samadhi*.

Aldous Huxley, gazing at a vase of flowers an hour and a half after taking mescalin, describes his thoughts and sensations to friends, who are taping the conversation:

I continued to look at the flowers, and in their living light I seemed to detect the qualitative equivalent of breathing – but of a breathing without returns to a starting-point, with no recurrent ebbs but only a repeated flow from beauty to heightened beauty, from deeper to ever deeper meaning. Words like Grace and Transfiguration came to my mind, and this of course was what, among other things, they stood for. My eyes travelled from the rose to the carnation, and from that feathery incandescence to the smooth scrolls of sentient amethyst which were the iris. The Beatific Vision, *Sat Chit Ananda*, Being-Awareness-Bliss – for the first time I understood, not on the verbal level, not by inchoate hints or at a distance, but precisely and completely what those prodigious syllables referred to. And then I remembered a passage I had read in one of Suzuki's essays. 'What is the Dharma-Body of the Buddha?' (The Dharma-body of the Buddha is another way of saying Mind, Suchness, the Void, the Godhead.) The question is asked in a Zen monastery by an earnest and bewildered novice. And with the prompt irrelevance of one of the Marx Brothers, The Master answers, 'The hedge at the bottom of the garden'. 'And the man who realizes this truth,' the novice dubiously enquires, 'what, may I ask, is he?' Groucho gives him a whack over the shoulders with his staff and answers, 'A golden-haired lion'.

(*The Doors of Perception*)

Huxley begins with vision and seems to come close to revelation. But all the time there is an active commentator, a brilliant intelligence at work, which seems to be guiding the experience rather than yielding to it. There is no terror, but neither is there a 'Beatific Vision'.

The experiment was successful as far as it went; perhaps as successful as any experiment can be that approaches by the back door. Huxley was, however, not only intellectually adventurous. He was a man of truly religious bent. His crowning achievement is *The Perennial Philosophy*, which traces the 'Highest Common Factor' that runs through the mystical traditions of all the great world religions. He desired both rational knowledge and the highest intuitive apprehension. A friend of Krishnamurti and member of a Vedantist centre in California, Huxley was far more than an intellectual explorer. But he was a man with limited training in meditation, who relied not on a spiritual guide but on a friendly doctor skilled rather in treating schizophrenics than mystics. This doctor knew what was a tolerable dose, but even so, at a later sitting, Huxley went too far. External reality seemed to be dissolving and he was afraid:

Confronted by a chair which looked like the Last Judgement – or, to be more accurate, by a Last Judgement which, after a long time and with considerable difficulty, I recognized as a chair – I found myself all at once on the brink of panic. This, I suddenly felt, was going too far. Too far, even though the going was into intenser beauty, deeper significance. The fear, as I analyse it in retrospect, was of being over-whelmed, of disintegrating under a pressure of reality greater than a mind accustomed to living most of the time in a cosy world of symbols could possibly bear. The literature of religious experience abounds in references to the pains and terrors overwhelming those who have come, too suddenly, face to face with some manifestation of the *Mysterium tremendum*. In theological language, this fear is due to the incompatibility between man's egotism and the divine purity, between man's self-aggravated separateness and the infinity of God. Following Boehme and William Law, we may say that, by unregenerate souls, the divine light at its full blaze can be apprehended only as a burning, purgatorial fire.

(The Doors of Perception)

Huxley understood even this. Knowledge derived from books rather than experience is a helpful guide, and Huxley always had a sure sense for literature. He knew what writings to trust:

An almost identical doctrine is to be found in *The Tibetan Book of the Dead*, where the departed soul is described as shrinking in agony from the Clear Light of the Void, and even from the lesser tempered Lights, in order to rush headlong into the comforting darkness of selfhood as a reborn human being, or even as a beast, an unhappy ghost, a denizen of hell. Anything rather than the burning brightness of unmitigated reality – anything.

(The Doors of Perception)

He knew that he had confronted the Clear Light of the Void and that it was too bright for him. But at the time of his wife's death, and afterwards of his own, he was able to make practical use of this lesson.

Huxley published his account of the mescalin experiments in 1954, and research into the effects of mescalin, LSD and other drugs continued on an increasing scale, particularly in American universities. By 1962 Huxley was alarmed at the claims made for the drugs and the unscientific way in which some researchers were using them. Also, the theories of some of his fellow-explorers in the field perturbed him. 'He talked nonsense', he wrote of an unnamed 'Irish researcher' – perhaps Dr Timothy Leary – in a letter to Dr Humphrey Osmond, his original

H

collaborator, about the conscious mind being merely a robot, about true intelligence residing only in the DNA: 'I have told him repeatedly that the only attitude for a researcher in this ticklish field is that of an anthropologist living amidst a tribe of potentially dangerous savages' (*Letters*).

The English intellectual reasoned in vain with the psychedelic cowboys of the pioneering west coast. They saw a vast new terrain lying ripe for conquest and did not listen to any words of restraint. But Huxley is often blamed for what followed.

There are many approaches through the back door among those offered by the competing hucksters at the entrance to the path. Some of them are proclaimed to be short cuts that lead to enlightenment far more quickly than the ways advocated by the old religions. 'This', cry the hucksters, 'is the jet age. Buy our guide today and follow the modern way to enlightenment.'

The need is certainly great; and the age, according to the Vedanta theory of cycles, is fitting. For we are approaching the end of the Kali Yuga and at such a time, according to the theory, all the phases of the past age are repeated in speeded-up succession. This is certainly borne out by the rapid changes of style and re-vivals in our current arts and thinking. Astrological reckoning also supports this reading of history, for at the end of the century we shall be passing from the 'age of Pisces' into the 'age of Aquarius'.

It is this great need that impels some people to seek out paths as strange as that of the Argentinian anthropology student, Carlos Castaneda, in following the Mexican shaman (witch doctor) 'Don Juan'. Drugged or hypnotized, Castaneda underwent pos-session by evil spirits, night-flying journeys over haunted moun-tains and many other terrors in order to be accepted by a teacher of a primitive tradition, whom most seekers would not have trusted. Reading *The Teachings of Don Juan* and *A Separate Reality* one wonders where fact ends and imagination takes over.

In general the shaman demands the complete surrender of the will to the experience. One may say that Gurdjieff demanded a similar surrender. He told the tale that among the group in which he learnt the system there was a practice of standing adepts in a dry water-course and then releasing the lock gate higher up, so that the water rose steadily up to the person's head. Only when he was about to drown was he pulled out of the water. Such was the initiation into the Work at its beginnings. None of the rigours suffered by Gurdjieff's early followers at his centre at Fontainebleau came near to that.

This feature of shamanism, perhaps adopted by Gurdjieff but never by Ouspensky, is the demand for the abdication of reason. The adept surrenders his will to the master as to a god. Thus the perhaps fictional procedures of 'Don Juan' belong to the cults of shamanism common among primitive peoples, which survive in modernized versions among the Negro and *mestizo* populations of Brazil, Venezuela and the Caribbean.

A survey of shamanism lies outside the scope of this book and the competence of its authors. It can be said in general, however, that the purpose of shamanism is to induce ecstasy in its followers by mechanical means, which may include drugs, persistent drum-beating combined with dancing, singing, shouting and other violent movements. Such procedures undertaken in groups have the result of inducing ecstatic trance among the participants, who see visions, foretell the future, speak with the dead and appear to assume different personalities. On the one hand, shamanism borders on spiritualism; on the other, it sets out to remove by violent means those 'blockages' which prevent the common consciousness from realizing its unity with the absolute.

An account of the shamanistic cult as it exists today in Brazil will suffice to demonstrate both its power and limitations. One of the authors had the opportunity of attending 'healing festas' conducted by a Brazilian shaman:

The medium had taken over the local inn for the occasion and hired a four-man samba group. But this was no ordinary *festa* in the usual Latin American sense. It turned out to be a mixture of solo drama, *agapé*, healing, interspersed with music, singing, dancing, laughing, sudden tense silences and much talk. The guests ranged from high officials, army officers, bank managers and businessmen, to fishermen, truck drivers and banana porters.

The religious ingredients consisted of the kind of metaphysical cocktail at which Brazil excels, all taking place within the framework of the long-standing synthesis between Catholicism and Spiritism. This particular shaman had evolved his own unique blend within a blend, claiming membership of the exclusive 'Roman Cult' – an aristocratic form of mediumship involving the psychic influence of such dubious historical characters as the emperor Nero, whose restless soul seeks to atone for his earthly brutalities and sins by repossessing the medium and supplying healing force.

We were told that the first patient was suffering from kidney cancer. He was taken to an adjoining room and the next I saw of him he was lying on the bed apparently unconscious, with his intestines exposed to view. Within an hour, he was dancing a samba of thanksgiving. The next patient underwent an 'eye operation' in the presence of all the guests (there were about sixty of us), with a qualified doctor standing by. I later asked what he thought about it all. He was cautious, replying: 'I saw what I saw.' The healer inserted an ordinary, unsterilized knife between the eyelid and the eyeball and removed something from the man's eye. The patient remained standing and did not even flinch. Next in the queue was a nun. A similar but more elaborate 'operation' was publicly performed on both her eyes. She too was soon dancing and her eyes and whole facial expression were transformed. The shared joy of this particular 'operation' was great and moving, for it seemed quite clear to all of us that a straight, immediate cure had taken place. She responded well to a simple eye test and mentioned that she had felt nothing.

The fourth patient, a young man who suffered from violent fits of uncontrolled aggression, underwent a 'brain operation' in the adjoining room. With some misgiving, I heard a loud hammering noise. I was allowed to see him after the 'operation'. He too was lying unconscious on the bed, with a whitish substance protruding from both sides of his head. A long steel needle had apparently been driven from one side to the other, presumably passing right through the brain. I saw short lengths of steel protruding from both temples. By rights, he should have died on the spot, but a couple of hours later I helped carry him back into the *festa* room, where he came to, began to talk quite coherently and smoked a cigarette. I subsequently heard that he was doing well.

(J.-F. P., Brazil, 1968)

The miracle seems to be not that some patients are apparently cured by these exotic shamanistic ministrations, but that they survive such 'operations' at all. Following up cases is particularly difficult in Brazil, where the truth is apt to be elusive. One heard of some patients relapsing to their previous conditions, while others claimed complete cures. At such 'healing festas', power is undoubtedly drawn from those participating. In a sense, it is group treatment, with the medium acting his role literally, as the vehicle through whom the cure is effected. After such sessions, one feels that one has contributed in some undefined way; one also feels completely drained of energy.

It is fair to say that shamanism, like the modern drug cult, aims at the production of phenomena. The shaman, medium, or cult leader appears to display supernormal faculties. Not only healing, but prophecy, clairvoyance and far stranger and more spectacular powers seem to be in evidence. At the same time, the medium acquires great influence over his adherents, some of whom he will invest with his skills, while others only follow him out of superstitious fear.

Although contemporary shamanism often contains Christian elements, it does not take from Christianity any belief in enlightenment. Its highest aim is the inducement of ecstasy, in short, almost epileptic spasms. Outbursts of 'speaking with tongues' and other excitable practices were reported by a hostile Church as common practice among the many heretical cults of the Middle Ages. Christianity has always contained some shamanistic or charismatic elements and even so orthodox a mystic as Ruysbroeck sees 'spiritual inebriation' as a natural condition:

Spiritual inebriation is this: that a man receives more sensible joy and sweetness than his heart can either contain or desire. Spiritual inebriation brings forth many strange gestures in men. It makes some sing and praise God because of their fulness of joy, and some weep with great tears because of their sweetness of heart. It makes one restless in all his limbs, so that he must run and jump and dance; and so excites another that he must gesticulate and clap his hands. Another cries out with a loud voice, and so shows forth the plenitude he feels within; another must be silent and melt away, because of the rapture which he feels in all his senses. At times he thinks that all the world must feel what he feels: at times he thinks that none can taste what he has attained.

Often he thinks that he never could nor ever shall, lose this well-being; at times he wonders why all men do not become God-desiring. At one time he thinks that God is for him alone, or for none other so much as for him; at another time he asks himself with amazement of what nature these delights can be, and whence they come, and what has happened to him. This is the most rapturous life (as regards our bodily feelings) which man may attain upon earth. Sometimes the excess of joy becomes so great that his heart must break.

(John of Ruysbroeck)

Foreign though the idea would have been to Ruysbroeck that 'blockage' may be dispersed under the impact of the sudden lifting of the heart, he accepts this experience – only advocating a sober humility, grounded in the consciousness that one is not worthy of such gifts. But there is a danger, he says, that the recipient may turn away from the world prematurely. In this state, hoar-frost and fog often harm such men, for it is 'just in the middle of May', according to the course of the inward life. Thus Ruysbroeck warns against the temptations that may accrue from spiritual drunkenness.

One cannot make an exaggerated comparison between this spiritual enthusiasm and shamanism. The Church exercised in the past too strong a discipline to allow such outbursts to carry the faithful away. When such over-enthusiastic movements arose they were liquidated as heretical. This is no longer true today and shamanism appears in various forms throughout the 'civilized' world.

Not only do some of the more excitable West Indian congregations resort to violent hymn-singing which culminates in a 'babble of tongues', but more sophisticated cults seek to remove 'blockages' in comparable ways. The Subud cult, like the Shakers of the seventeenth century, practise convulsive movement and cries, shouts and groans, in order to induce a moment of calm when the mind's mirror may suddenly become cleared of mist.

The Gurdjieff cult practised 'super-effort' in order to exhaust the body and release the deeper consciousness. A follower once told one of the authors how, returning home after a tremendous walk on Salisbury Plain, he was instructed by his companions, senior to him in the Gurdjieff hierarchy, to set out again, exhausted though he was, and repeat the same walk without so much as resting or taking a meal. The adherent did as he was told but reported no remarkable result. A retired naval officer, on the other hand, who submitted himself to months of rigorous discipline in a Burmese monastery, was rewarded by a momentary revelation when he disembarked from his returning ship at the first European port.

The rigours of asceticism in Christian monasteries were no doubt directed to the same end. They deteriorated, however, into an obsession with the foulness of the body, which was far removed from their original purpose. Brooding on the evils and temptations of sex contributes as fatally to a blockage as overindulgence in the pleasure itself.

The clearance of blockages is a serious problem for the contemporary meditator. The great traditions have usually followed the threefold path of meditation, physical practice and right action. Thus the yogin meditates, performs Hatha Yoga and pursues wisdom (Jnana Yoga). The Sufi meditates, performs the Dervish exercise of whirling or turning and behaves honourably as merchant or householder. The Buddhist, on the other hand, follows the eightfold path of right view, right aim, right speech, right action, right living, right effort, right mindfulness and right contemplation. No great teaching has ever resorted to 'blowing the mind' with the aim of speedy results. Nor is there any single-track route to enlightenment. The yogin who spends weeks in *samadhi* can go no further unless he comes out to teach. The Hatha yogin may hibernate in a pit, slowing down his metabolism to that of a dormouse, or learn to walk on burning coals, but with these skills alone he is at a dead end. The Vedantist scholar who has all wisdom finds his own wisdom to be a blockage.

The blockage problem is not solved by strong-arm tactics. 'From the days of John the Baptist until now', said Jesus, 'the Kingdom of Heaven suffereth violence, and men of violence take it by force' (*Matt.* 11:12). Jesus was not against John, for had he not been baptized by him in the Jordan before beginning his mission? But was he perhaps referring to some shamanistic elements in John's teaching? Violent methods are always possible. Perhaps Yogananda's sudden initiation by his master into higher consciousness is an illustration of this possibility. Zen also suggests parallels. But this was not Jesus' method. Even when his disciples slumbered around him in the garden of Gethsemane, he did nothing to rouse them. These last remarks, however, are purely speculative. The passage quoted from *Matthew* is one of the very many in the gospels which can no longer be interpreted. The key to their meaning was lost long ago.

The problem of blockages remains. According to Zen, a well-timed blow by the master may be enough to disperse them. Ouspensky believed that if the master were to tell his follower the nature of his 'chief feature', the whole of his false personality, which hung on that feature, would dissolve. In this way, if a disciple really understood that his whole persona revolved around a false picture of himself as, let us say, a shrewd man of the world, and if he could accept that this was a mere self-comforting fiction, then the disciple would become, in Gurdjieff's phrase, 'realized man'.

Recently, a number of more or less violent new techniques for attaining self-knowledge have been introduced in the west. These contain elements drawn from psychoanalysis, Gurdjieff's system and sociological theory. Their aim is by confrontation of conflicting personalities to compel a person to recognize his or her 'chief feature' and adapt relationships accordingly. Some of these encounter-therapy and confrontation groups are specifically concerned with marital problems; some with self-realization in general; while others aim only at smoothing out 'personality conflicts' between colleagues in a business or public organization. In week-end courses and meetings, those who participate are forced to reveal themselves to one another by means of contrived situations; and after some degree of explosiveness, a certain amount of warmth is sometimes engendered between participants. No doubt some blockages are removed by such methods. The following account shows that considerable benefit may be received even from a managerial week-end get-together of this kind:

I [once] participated in a managerial grid course. I was a prisoner of sorts, confined in a hotel along with fifty-nine others – men and women from the company I worked for. We played group games all week, solving problems alone, then together, mostly in one group of six. During the week, which was purposefully full of frustrations and long hours, the group I was part of became very closely interdependent. The penultimate day of the course was spent evaluating each other and this highly emotional activity was followed by a party to loosen up. I was highly rated by my group and drank a lot of wine at the party.

Next morning at the final session, in the middle of a psychology lecture, I found myself looking in at myself from the outside. I was literally beside myself. I liked what I saw. At the same time I was aware of a physical adjustment in my head – a sort of fitting together of two pictures that had been slightly out of focus.

Following this came a feeling of liberation; utter contentment, delight, ecstasy. Whatever it was, I have never felt so wonderfully happy in all my life. I could feel a smile spreading over my face and my eyes lighting up. It was obviously apparent to others too – they must have sensed something, for I found them looking at me with something akin to awe . . .

It seemed as if I had lifted the corner of a carpet and could see the beautifully ordered pattern that went into making the universe. I felt I was not ready for more, so I let the carpet fall again. But the glimpse I had was enough to give me a sort of cornerstone of faith in the rightness of the universe.

(RERU 1148)

The theory of blockages is well known to Buddhism, which, however, reduces them to one principal cause – the human habit of self-cherishing. Central to the meditation on compassion is the prayer to Avalokiteshvara, the Buddha of compassion, to remove one's 'obscurations'. One learns to visualize the nectar flowing from his image and circulating through one's *chakras* or psychic centres, to stream out as a wave of compassion for all living beings. Thus the blockages are slowly dissolved and the practice of advanced meditation or Tantra becomes possible. But how wise was the experiencer just quoted to realize after her moment of liberation that she 'was not ready for more'? Only a competent guide will recognize the moment at which the meditator is strong

I

enough to go further. Then will come the sudden realization of Zen, the initiation into the Tantra of Mahayana.

Modern teachers in the west, dazzled by the prospect of a large organization and world influence, try to computerize their teachings. Without personal contact with their followers, they offer new material and practices broadcast to all with the time and money to purchase them. As a result, there are many failures and defections, although those with the necessary inner strength may not be harmed. Our own conclusion is that none of the 'backdoor' methods detailed in this section will lead the seeker one inch nearer to true enlightenment.

9 Death and Rebirth

The doctrine of rebirth, accepted by all eastern religions, was current among the ancient Greeks, among Jews of the pre-Christian era, among the Sufis and among Christians also, particularly the Gnostic wing of the faith until the third century, when belief in reincarnation was proclaimed heterodox. A simple statement of this belief was made by the great Church Father, Origen, who did not consider himself to be making any strange pronouncement:

Every soul comes into this world strengthened by the victories or weakened by the defeats of its previous life. Its place in this world as a vessel appointed to honour or dishonour is determined by its previous merits or demerits. Its work in this world determines its place in the world which is to follow this . . .

This plain enunciation of the law of *karma* was traditional in Origen's day, though it was already unacceptable to the 'linear' Christians, who believed that each child was born anew with his own burden of original sin, from which he could be freed by virtue of the redemption on the cross, but only if he had undergone baptism. Pagans, Jews and members of other faiths were automatically debarred from the redemption, and those children of Christians who had not survived to be baptized were equally excluded from participation in Christ's gift.

Two passages are quoted from the gospels, perhaps inconclusively, to prove that the idea of reincarnation was not foreign to Jesus himself. In the first he asks his followers: 'Whom say they that I am?' The answer variously given was Elijah, Jeremiah or John the Baptist. Already John the Baptist has been identified with Elijah. But here is no proof that the people were thinking of reincarnation. Elijah, according to the Bible, had not died but had been assumed into heaven, and Jesus' life had overlapped with John's. Rather the question seems to refer to a transmitted prophetic inspiration.

Again, the passage in *John* 9 concerning the blind man does not lead in this direction either:

> And his disciples asked him, saying, Master, who did sin, this man, or his parents, that he was born blind?
>
> Jesus answered, Neither hath this man sinned, nor his parents: but that the works of God should be made manifest in him.

Jesus appears to be saying that 'it was in this man's *karma*' that he should be born blind, in order that the works of God should be demonstrated by his cure. Jesus, like other holy men before and since, uses any questions for his own purposes, and his purpose at that moment was to emphasize the opportunities of that time when he was with them:

> I must work the works of him that sent me, while it is day: the night cometh, when no man can work.
>
> As long as I am in the world, I am the light of the world.

It might be said that the introduction of the blind man into the narrative served as an excuse for a reference to 'the light of the world'. The question about *karma* in general remained unanswered. The reason is clear: Jesus did not wish to discuss past causes or their future working out. He repeatedly drew his disciples' attention to the immediate moment at which the chain of *karma* could be snapped.

Reluctance to talk about the succession of rebirths is common among yogins, particularly those who address western audiences. Fascination with the past sharply deflects a person's attention from the possibilities of escape from the wheel of rebirth *now*, in *this* life. The past cannot be altered. The future does not exist. Opportunity lies in the present.

Nevertheless it is necessary to try and comprehend the laws of *karma*, as they apply to rebirth, in order to take advantage of the unique opportunity to escape from the wheel that occurs at death. It is significant that many spiritual teachings stress the need to live in the awareness that we may die at any moment. The Greeks, the Hindus and the Buddhists treasured secret teachings concerning the cycles of rebirth. The Egyptians too had such teachings, as did many primitive religions. The mystery tradition of early Greece survives in a funerary tablet of the Orphic cult, which tells the dead man how he shall conduct himself on his passage to the underworld:

> To him who, purified, would break this vicious round
> And breathe once more the air of heaven – greeting!
> There in the courts of Hades wilt thou find
> Leftward a beckoning cypress, tall and bright
> From out whose root doth flow the water of Oblivion
> Approach it not: guard thou thy thirst awhile.
> For on the other hand – and further – wells
> From bottomless pools the limpid stream of Memory,
> Cool, full of refreshment. To its guardians cry thus:
> 'I am the child of earth and starry sky:
> Know that I too am heavenly – but parched!
> I perish: give then and quickly that clear draught
> Of ice-cold Memory!' And from that fountainhead divine
> Straightway they'll give thee drink quaffing the which
> Thou with the other heroes eternally shalt rule.
>
> (Golden tablet found in an Orphic tomb)

The draught from the stream of memory restores the dead man's knowledge of who he eternally was and is, and so joins him with the heroes – those who have never to be reborn.

Such at least is the meaning, if one refers the tablet to the Pythagorean tradition to which it belongs. This tradition of eternal recurrence and the secret of release from it survives only in references in later writings. In the previously quoted passage from Plato's Myth of Er, we are shown the vast interlocking spindles on which the universe turns to the sound of the divine and fundamental harmony. Plato describes the afterworld as seen by Er himself, who, like some of Dr Moody's patients, had almost died but returned to the world:

He said that when his soul went out, it journeyed together with a great company, and they came unto a certain ghostly place wherein were two open mouths of the earth hard by each other, and also above, two mouths of the heaven over against them: and judges were seated between these, who, when they had given their judgements, bade the righteous take the road, which leadeth to the right hand and up through heaven; and they fastened tablets on them in front, signifying the judgements; but the unjust they sent by the road which leadeth to the left hand and down, and they also had tablets fastened on them behind, signifying all that they had done. But when he himself came before the judges they said unto him that he must be for a messenger unto men concerning the things there, and they charged him straitly that he should give diligence to hear and see all the things in the place.

Now, he told how that he beheld the souls departing, some by one of the mouths of heaven, and some by one of the mouths of earth, when judgement had been given unto them; also how that he beheld souls returning by the other two mouths, some coming up from the earth travel-stained covered with dust, and some coming down from heaven, pure. And he said that all, as they came, being come belike from a long journey, turned aside with joy into the meadow and encamped there as in a congregation; and they that were acquaintances greeted one another, and they questioned one another – they that were come from the earth questioned them that were come from heaven concerning the things there, and in like manner they that were come from heaven questioned the others concerning the things that had happened to them. So they discoursed with one another – some of them groaning and weeping when they called to mind all the terrible things they had suffered and seen in their journey under the earth – he said that their journey was for a thousand years; and others of them to wit, those which were come from heaven, telling of blessings and marvellous fair sights.   (*The Myth of Er in the Republic*)

Plato's scenario is poetic. But this elaborate myth is no doubt closely related to the more precise teachings, now lost, of the Pythagorean tradition and the mystery cults. The central drama is the judgement, in which the dead are divided into just and unjust, and consigned to a sojourn either in heaven or in the underworld of hideous sights and sufferings. Thus, between life and life is a time of rewards and penalties, which for those in Hades may be of a thousand years.

The measure of time in this myth and in the more precise narrative of *The Tibetan Book of the Dead* can only be symbolic. The Tibetan writings speak of forty-nine days as the period of the sojourn in *bardö* – the intermediate state between death and rebirth. The ceremonial prayers for the dead were spaced over that time and the stages of the dead person's passing from life to life were followed in the minds of the living during this period. But what can time be to a discarnate being, of whom only the essential experience survives? Discussing time and the *bardö* with a Hindu yogin, one of the authors drew the sharp comment: 'Oh, much quicker than that!'

The doctrine of the after-death state is set out by the death-guide in words addressed to the dying man, who appears to be clinging to his departing life:

O nobly-born, at that time, at bridge-heads, in temples, by *stupas* . . ., thou wilt rest a little while, but thou wilt not be able to remain there very long, for thine intellect hath been separated from thy body. Because of this inability to loiter, thou oft-times wilt feel perturbed and vexed and panic-stricken. At times, thy Knower will be dim: at times, fleeting and incoherent. Thereupon this thought will occur to thee, 'Alas! I am dead! What shall I do?' and because of such thought the Knower will become saddened and the heart chilled, and thou wilt experience infinite misery of sorrow. Since thou canst not rest in any one place, and feel impelled to go on, think not of various things, but allow the intellect to abide in its own state.

(*The Tibetan Book of the Dead*)

The reluctance of the dying man to 'go on' contrasts strangely with those out-of-the-body experiences that we have noticed, in which people on the frontier of death appear reluctant to turn back. However, the Tibetan book has already spoken of those who have prayed to the compassionate one, and who have earned an easy, even a happy transition.

In the Tibetan tradition, as in the Greek, the dead person now comes to judgement, whereas in the contemporary *bardö* experiences that we have recorded, of those who have almost passed over the border, they were seemingly brought directly to a vision of the dazzling light. As for the judgement, there are many tales

current of those who, when almost drowning, or when a para-
chute delays in opening, see the whole of their lives pass as on a
film before them. The judgement is therefore no more than an
acceptance of one's own *karma*. Thus in the Tibetan book, the
dead person gazes into a mirror:

'O nobly-born, [so-and-so], listen. That thou art suffering so
cometh from thine own *karma*; it is not due to any one else's: it is by
thine own *karma*. Accordingly, pray earnestly to the Precious Trinity;
that will protect thee. If thou neither prayest nor knowest how to
meditate upon the Great Symbol nor upon any tutelary deity, the
Good Genius, who was born simultaneously with thee, will come now
and count out thy good deeds [with] white pebbles, and the evil genius,
who was born simultaneously with thee, will come and count out thy
evil deeds [with] black pebbles. Thereupon, thou wilt be greatly
frightened, awed and terrified, and wilt tremble; and thou wilt
attempt to tell lies, saying, 'I have not committed any evil deed'.

Then the Lord of Death will say, 'I will consult the mirror of
karma'.

So saying, he will look in the mirror, wherein every good and evil
act is vividly reflected. Lying will be of no avail.

(The Tibetan Book of the Dead)

'The lords of death are thine own hallucinations', the death-guide
reminds the dead man and at the same time the living mourners.

Swedenborg speaks of such a moment when he describes his
own near approach to death, from which he fortunately returned:

As to the senses of the body I was brought into a state of insensibility,
thus nearly into the state of the dying, but with the interior life and
thought remaining unimpaired, in order that I might perceive and
retain in the memory the things that happened to me, and that happen
to those who are resuscitated from the dead. I perceived that the
respiration of the body was almost wholly taken away; but the interior
respiration of the spirit went on in connection with a slight and tacit
respiration of the body. Then at first a communication of the pulse of
the heart with the celestial kingdom was established, because that
kingdom corresponds to the heart in man. Angels from that kingdom
were seen, some at a distance, and two sitting near my head. Thus all
my own affection was taken away although thought and perception

continued. I was in this state for some hours. Then the spirits who were around me withdrew, supposing that I was dead . . .

(Heaven and Hell)

Swedenborg was a professional scientist; however wayward his visionary ramblings, he appears always to be aiming at an objective exactness. Here, in describing his own descent into near-death, he tries also to be precise about the stages of his sinking. Only in the last phrase of this extract does he stray into fantasy. For if the angels, who stand for the clear light of the Tibetans and so many modern experiencers, retreated, it could hardly have been because they supposed that he was dead. Rather, they vanished because he was withdrawing from their realm back to the life of the material world.

We have already noted the appearance of light to those near death, and devoted a section to the nature of this light of the void or the absolute which confronts a person at death. In *The Tibetan Book of the Dead*, the death-guide accompanies the dead man in thought and prayer to this supreme experience. He may in death attain perfect enlightenment, which will bring him freedom from the necessity of rebirth:

O nobly-born, listen. Now thou art experiencing the clear light of pure reality. Recognize it. O nobly-born, thy present intellect, in real nature void, not formed into anything as regards characteristics or colour, naturally void, is the very reality, the all-good.

Thine own intellect, which is now voidness, yet not to be regarded as of the voidness of nothingness, but as being the intellect itself, unobstructed, shining, thrilling, and blissful, is the very consciousness, the all-good Buddha.

Thine own consciousness, not formed into anything, in reality void, and the intellect, shining and blissful – these two – are inseparable. Their union is the state of perfect enlightenment.

One is told that, in order at this moment to face the light, it is necessary to have experienced it already when living, in medi-tation. For most – as we saw with Plato's cave analogy – the light is too bright, and people easily slip back into a realm of good and bad visions, personalized for the Tibetans as blissful and angry deities. Thus they fall again under *karma*. Their previous deeds take effect and soon, to escape from this limbo, they begin to long for a new birth.

The Myth of Er also speaks of the choice of a rebirth, the lots being drawn among the waiting souls as they rest in the meadow of pre-birth:

Truly it was a sight worth looking at, he said, to see how the souls severally chose their lives – yea, a pitiful sight, a laughable, and a wonderful; inasmuch as they chose mostly after the custom of their former life; for he told how he saw the soul that had been Orpheus's choosing a swan's life, for that, hating womankind because women murdered him, it would not be born of a woman. Next came the soul of Agamemnon; which also, out of enmity towards mankind because that it went evil with him, took in exchange the life of an eagle. The soul of Atalanta, which had gotten her place between the first and the last, perceiving the great honour which belongeth to the life of a man who contendeth at the games, was not able to pass by but took it . . . and amongst the last he saw the soul of Thersites the jester putting on an ape. Also it chanced that the soul of Odysseus, which had gotten the last place of all, came forward to choose, and having abated all her ambition because she remembered her former labours, went about seeking for a long while, and after much ado, found the life of a quiet private man lying somewhere despised of the others, and when she saw it said – 'Had I come first I would have done the same'; and took it with great joy.   (*Republic*)

Thus an ordinary life is preferable to a hero's. But the life of a teacher or philosopher is chosen by no one. Nor were any of these heroes concerned for the future benefit of 'all sentient beings'.

There is little in the Christian tradition that teaches one how to prepare for death, and nothing that speaks of the after-death state with any clarity. The author of the medieval text *Horologium Sapientiae* offers instruction in the art of dying, which, he claims, is known by few:

Thou shalt understand that it is a science most profitable, and passing all other sciences, for to learn to die. For a man to know that he shall die, that is common to all men; as much as there is no man that may ever live or he hath hope or trust thereof; but thou shalt find full few that have this cunning to learn to die ... I shall give thee the mystery of this doctrine; the which shall profit thee greatly to the beginning of ghostly health, and to a stable fundament of all virtues.

(*Horologium Sapientiae*)

But this priest is unable to accompany his penitent beyond the point at which his former life comes before him in foreshortened review: 'The bitterness of pain that we now feel in one hour', he writes, 'seemeth as great as all the sorrows of the passing world in a hundred years.' But he does not see this as the judgement, for that has yet to come.

Another medieval scripture of the same kind, *The Book of the Craft of Dying*, touches on another thought that is present in greater concentration in *The Tibetan Book of the Dead* – that the art of dying must be learnt in life, and that it enhances life:

Against his will he dieth that hath not learned to die. Learn to die and thou shalt learn to live, for there shall none learn to live that hath not learned to die. (*The Book of the Craft of Dying*)

For a western guide to the state 'across the border' we have no alternative but to turn once again to Emanuel Swedenborg. In his account, we meet the light and find ourselves surrounded by spirits, with whom it is possible to have direct telepathic communication:

Whereas spirits converse with each other by a universal language ... Every man, immediately after death, comes into this universal language ... which is proper to his spirit.

The speech of an angel or a spirit with man is heard as sonorously as the speech of a man with a man; yet it is not heard by others who stand near, but by himself alone; the reason is, because the speech of an angel or spirit flows first into the man's thought ...

(*Compendium*, quoted by Moody, op. cit.)

Swedenborg's limbo world is one in which the dead behave much as if they were still alive. Their friends come round them and they find themselves possessed of bodies. But soon they begin to wonder whither they are bound, and to reflect on the possibilities of heaven and hell.

One might guess that, in describing the after-death state, Swedenborg drew on his own out-of-the-body experiences, telepathic communication and clairvoyance. *The Tibetan Book of the Dead* depicts the various stages of the *bardö*, as remembered by one who can recall his own lives and deaths. One must, however, always distinguish between those features that are coloured by the Tibetan tradition and their basis in 'the common experience'. The condition of a person who turns away from the clear light is that of one haunted by the forms of deities, first beneficent, then malign. And throughout his sojourn in this limbo, the opportunity to escape into the light is repeatedly presented to him, though in ever-diminishing strength. On each successive day, the death-guide reminds the dead man of the teachings he has received from his guru, in preparation for the ordeal ahead. He tells him that all these visions are illusions:

O nobly-born, the possessor of that sort of body will see places [familiarly known on the earth plane] and relatives [there] as one seeth another in dreams.

Thou seest thy relatives and connexions and speakest to them, but receivest no reply. Then, seeing them and thy family weeping, thou thinkest, 'I am dead! What shall I do?' and feelest great misery, just like a fish cast out of [water] on red hot embers . . . But feeling miserable will avail thee nothing now. If thou hast a divine guru, pray to him. Pray to the Tutelary Deity, the Compassionate One. Even though thou feelest attachment for thy relatives and connexions, it will do thee no good. So be not attached. Pray to the Compassionate Lord; thou shalt have nought of sorrow, or of terror, or of awe.

O nobly-born, when thou art driven [hither and thither] by the ever-moving wind of *karma*, thine intellect, having no object upon which to rest, will be like a feather tossed about by the wind, riding on the horse of breath. Ceaselessly and involuntarily wilt thou be wandering about. To all those who are weeping [thou wilt say], 'Here I am; weep not'. But they not hearing thee, thou wilt think, 'I am dead!' And again, at that time, thou wilt be feeling very miserable. Be not miserable in that way . . .

O nobly-born, at about that time, the fierce wind of *karma*, terrific and hard to endure, will drive thee [onwards] from behind in dreadful gusts. Fear it not. That is thine own illusion. Thick awesome darkness

will appear in front of thee continually, from the midst of which there
will come terror-producing utterances . . . Fear these not.
(The Tibetan Book of the Dead)

But as the days pass, the beneficent deities retreat and the wrathful
deities increasingly terrify the lonely spirit in his grey half-world,
lit no longer by clear white light, but by murkier effulgences of
baleful colours. The dead man is caught up by the chains of his
own *karma*. He must seek a new body. Only in the womb will
he be safe from the mounting horrors of the *bardö*.

So the death-guide must instruct him in the choice of a new
body, a human body:

If, however, a supernormal birth be not possible, and one delighteth
in entering a womb or hath to enter, there is a teaching for the selection
of the womb-door of impure *Sangsara*. Listen:

Looking with thy supernormal power of foresight over the continents, choose that in which religion prevaileth and enter therein.

If birth is to be obtained over a heap of impurities, a sensation that
it is sweet-smelling will attract one towards that impure mass, and
birth will be obtained thereby.

Whatsoever they [the wombs or visions] may appear to be, do not
regard them as they are or seem; and by not being attracted or repelled,
a good womb should be chosen. In this, too, since it is important to
direct the wish, direct it thus:

'Ah! I ought to take birth as a universal emperor; or as a brahmin,
like a great sal tree [or *boddhi* tree]; or as the son of an adept in *siddhic*
powers; or in a spotless hierarchical line; or in the caste of a man who
is filled with faith; and, being born so, endowed with great merit so as
to be able to serve all sentient beings.'
(The Tibetan Book of the Dead)

Thus, although all birth is impure, a womb must be sought in a
land where the *dharma* is taught, and the newly-born must vow
to devote his or her life to the benefit of all creatures. Even so,
many are so terrified by the *bardö* that they seek any place where
they 'hear the sound of copulation', and are then born again to
fresh suffering in a further round of life and death.

Stripping away such detail as belongs only to the Tibetan
tradition, one sees a spirit driven back to rebirth by his own

inability to recognize the essential void in himself. For in everyday life we escape a confrontation with this void by incessant bustle, by 'killing time', by social and other activities that give us an illusion of our own reality. Stripped of all this at death, we gaze into the mirror, which shows our true reflection, and turn away. The clear light dazzles us. We are haunted by our own guilt and suffering. In this grey *bardö*, we have bad dreams and there is no reassuring morning to wake up to. So we seek refuge in the womb – Freud saw its attractions, although from an opposite standpoint – and are reborn into the world so hurriedly that most of us have made no choice of 'a country where the *dharma* is taught', nor of a religious or spiritually-minded family to be born into. The whole of another life may pass before we discover our purpose. But because today we are living at the end of one epoch and the beginning of another, our chances this time are, as we have said, particularly good.

The Tibetan Book of the Dead has been known in English only since 1927. Before that, no such authoritative rebirth teaching was available, except from such rare teachers as came to the west earlier in the century. Theosophical theory on the subject gave the impression of a more personal survival, although it was emphasized that after the dissolution of the physical body, the psychic or astral and mental bodies also broke up, leaving only the causal body, which carried the *karma* like some sort of DNA code from the old being to the new. But over-concern about past lives deflected the theosophists' attention from the central theme of escape from the wheel of rebirth.

One finds Aldous Huxley during his mescalin experiments speculating rather dubiously on the possibility of seeking and holding the clear light in the drugged state:

'Would you be able', my wife asked, 'to fix your attention on what *The Tibetan Book of the Dead* calls "Clear Light?"'
I was doubtful.
'Would it keep the evil away, if you could hold it?'
I considered the question for some time.
'Perhaps', I answered at last, 'perhaps I could – but only if there were somebody there to tell me about the Clear Light. One couldn't do it

by oneself. That's the point, I suppose, of the Tibetan ritual – someone sitting there all the time and telling you what's what' . . .

I took down my copy of Evans-Wentz's edition of *The Tibetan Book of the Dead*, and opened it at random. 'O nobly born, let not thy mind be distracted.' That was the problem – to remain undistracted.

(*The Doors of Perception*)

The mescalin vision and the *bardö* vision did not correspond. For the drug heightened Huxley's awareness of the physical world, which in the *bardö* state has fallen away. His delight in objects seen in greater subtlety and heightened colour was that of a physical being whose doors of perception have been cleansed. But in the *bardö* mirror one sees not objects but oneself in all one's emptiness.

When his wife was dying, Huxley attempted to help her over the threshold by reading to her from the Tibetan book and from Eckhart. Here he was acting as the author of *The Book of the Craft of Dying* would have recommended, although substituting their own personal eclectic choice of scriptures for the formal Christian prayers for the dying. One learns from one of his subsequent letters that the reading was helpful:

This matter of death – how badly we handle it! . . . My own experience with Maria convinced me that the living can do a great deal to make the passage easier for the dying, to raise the most purely physiological act of human existence to the level of consciousness and perhaps even of spirituality. The last rites of Catholicism are good, but too much preoccupied with morality and the past. The emphasis has to be on the present and the posthumous future, which one must assume – and I think with justification – to be a reality. Eileen told me that, in one of her contacts with what she was convinced was Maria, there was a message for me to the effect that what I had said had helped to float the soul across the chasm. (This message, incidentally, contained two items which I felt to be evidential – one a reference to something which Eileen could not understand, something she heard as 'the Bardle' – which was obviously the Bardö, which M. knew well and from whose spirit and whose techniques I had borrowed when talking to her in the last hours. The other word which Eileen heard was 'Ecker' which referred to a quotation from Meister Eckhart which I used once or twice). (*Letters of Aldous Huxley*)

That this reading was comforting we cannot doubt. The curious misreading of the clairvoyant provides some confirmatory evidence, which is hardly necessary. When Huxley himself was dying, he left the hospital, refusing an operation, and was helped out of the world in the same way that he had helped his wife.

Evidence suggestive of reincarnation is of two kinds. The first, quite common in the east, takes the form of children's memories of a past existence, of which some details can be confirmed. In Tibet, after the death of a Dalai Lama or the head of a monastery, his successor was sought throughout the country. The humblest peasant home was not neglected by travelling monks in search of a boy born shortly after the deceased lama's death. Then, if the physical signs were promising, the boy, who might be four or five years old, was subjected to strict tests. He was shown a collection of objects, a few of which had belonged to the deceased; and these he had to recognize without hesitation as his own property. Sometimes the child's memory would stretch further back, and he would recognize in the visiting monk a former friend or servant. By this method, *tulkus*, or reincarnations, were discovered and there was until 1959 no gap in the succession to the principal lamahoods. Only seldom was there a disputed candidature.

Memories of former lives, frequent also among children in the west, are seldom checked. Western parents often ascribe them to childish fantasy, to the point of even convincing their children that they are imaginary. These memories do not normally persist far into childhood and they seldom provide facts that can be verified. At best there is a half-recognition, an intuitive feeling of having seen some hitherto unknown place before. This occasionally goes much deeper than a casual fleeting feeling of *déjà vu*.

Dr Ian Stevenson has spent many years of research methodically investigating cases suggestive of reincarnation, cases where other explanations of the evidence seem less plausible than the survival hypothesis. He did not by any means confine his researches to India, and has carefully examined accounts from all over the world. Here are two examples, one from Japan and the other from Cuba:

A Japanese boy called Katsugoro, when about eight years of age, stated that he had been called Tozo in a preceding life a few years earlier. He claimed to have then been the son of a farmer called Kyubei and his wife Shidzu and to have lived in a village called Hodokubo. He further stated that Kyubei had died and that his mother had then married a man called Hanshiro. He said that he himself, Tozo, had died of smallpox at the age of six, a year after his father had died. He gave details of his burial and described the appearance of his former parents and their house. Katsugoro was eventually taken to the village he named, and the persons he named were found and identified as having lived there. In the village (unaccompanied by anyone from the village) he led the way to his former parents' house and recognized it and them. He pointed to a shop and a tree in the vicinity, saying that they had not been there before, which was true. Altogether, Katsugoro's statements provided sixteen items correctly matched with the verified facts. Responsible witnesses made numerous affidavits respecting the facts of this case.

A four-year-old boy, Eduardo Esplugus-Cabrera, who lived in Havana, told his parents about a home and different parents he claimed to have had in a previous life. The parents were sure the boy had never been to the house he named. To test the matter they made a long detour to reach the street where the house was, this house being quite unfamiliar to them and, so they firmly believed, should have been to the boy also. On arrival at the street, the boy immediately recognized the house as the one about which he had been talking . . . The parents then made further inquiries about the previous occupants of the house and found that out of the eight statements made by the boy which it was possible to verify, seven correctly matched the facts and one (his father's Christian name) did not.
(*The Evidence for Survival from Claimed Memories of Former Incarnations*)

It might be possible to explain these children's knowledge of previous existences in some way other than that of memory. But theories involving telepathy or clairvoyance would require an effort of belief even greater than that of accepting the story at face value. To believe that such anecdotes are pure 'flukes' would be to stretch the laws of probability far beyond the credible.

Sometimes in rejecting the marvellous, critics will swallow the incredible.

Evidences of the second type present more difficulties for the theorist and are rather less conclusive. These are memories of past lives produced in dreams or under hypnosis, which have been checked by historians and found to be accurate in many details, some of which were unknown at the time of the dream or hypnotic state. A collection of such trance-memories, published under the title of *More Lives than One*, provides some convincing evidence, but at the same time raises some puzzling problems.

The 'Bloxham Tapes' record conversations between Arnall Bloxham, a healer and hypnotist of Cardiff, and certain of his patients; also one or two other people, previously unknown to him, brought in by a television producer, Jeffrey Iverson. Beginning to investigate Bloxham's recordings for a possible television programme, Iverson, after producing the programme, published a selection of the tapes in the book just mentioned. The published recordings are of course the most dramatic. Much other material, excluded from the book, might have thrown greater light on the whole question of these trance-memories, since these were perhaps less perfect than those chosen and edited for the book. They probably contained less detail that could be checked on the ground by historians or other experts.

Bloxham's star performer was a young woman of modest education and little reading or travel, who produced memories of several previous lives, all of which were passed in places and at times that provided good opportunities for checking. She was by turns a Romano-British woman, a Jewess in twelfth-century York, a girl from Egypt living in the house of a well-known French merchant of the fifteenth century, Jacques Coeur, and a humble seamstress in Queen Anne's London. Only her last life was too obscure to allow of much checking; the others were lived in epochs amply documented.

As an example of Bloxham's method, we will quote the crisis in Rebecca's story, when she and some others have taken refuge in a church from the populace of York who are killing the whole Jewish population of the city:

'*Bloxham*: Is Rachel with you?

'*Rebecca*: Yes and my son. And we managed to get out – somebody helped us – somebody my husband paid to help us. We got out of the castle and we took shelter in a Christian church and we – there was a priest and a clerk in this church and we held them and bound them and told them we wouldn't hurt them as long as they didn't tell people we were there – and we were down in the cellars – down below the church – and we were so hungry and we had to eat – all we could find was wine and they called us infidels and Jewish pigs for drinking the wine – it was sacrificial wine – and we had to drink – we were thirsty – we were thirsty and hungry. And we are all here, we can hear the screams – terrible things. And the priest told us that there had been riots in London and Chester and that Jews were being killed. And John had ordered that all Jews be killed – all Jews be killed.'

(*More Lives than One*)

Bloxham's prompting is sometimes helpful, but often irrelevant. It would appear that the hypnotized woman is viewing a film of a past life, with which she feels utterly involved. Refuge in the church becomes more precarious, and finally she is killed. But all that the subject says at this point is: 'Dark . . . dark.' She had never visited York but under hypnosis had a fair knowledge of the city in medieval times. She located the house in which she lived, but the location cannot be verified, for the site of the medieval Jewish quarter is not known. At first the church in which Rebecca hid presented equally formidable difficulties. She was sure that it was not York Minster and that it had a crypt. The church of St Mary's answered best to her description but it has no crypt. Some time later, however, excavations revealed that an old crypt had in fact once existed.

The Jacques Coeur story brought similar confirmations of local detail that could not have been known to the hypnotized woman, who had never been to Blois, the scene of this particular past life.

Other subjects produce similar material, always in rather banal modern English, except for one, a soft-spoken Swansea man who described his former life as a gunner on a ship that was blockading an unnamed French port at some unspecified time in the eighteenth century. He used a rich nautical vocabulary full of technical jargon about guns and a seaman's life at the time – all of which was quite unfamiliar to everyone in Bloxham's room. It turned out to be authentic, however, when naval histories were referred to. But the man's ship could not be identified, nor could the exact place or time at which a French ball shot off his leg.

A strange feature of these sittings is that the hypnotist is able to implement a change of scene by merely asking the sitter to go on in time. It would seem that some of these stories had been told before and were repeated for the benefit of the television team. Such control might suggest a carefully rehearsed performance by hypnotist and sitters, a collaborated deception. But this explanation seems harder to accept than any other. For it would have required very considerable research and invention by Bloxham and his partners, to say nothing of a willing deceit on the part of BBC officials who also told their stories when hypnotized. One had witnessed the execution of Charles I from across the street. An elaborately staged performance being ruled out, we are left with the question: from what mind did these historical dramas originate?

That mind had access to information possessed by no one in that room, in fact to no one but a historian. And the details were checked by historians. Yet these stories seem to be reflected through a modern intelligence. Not only does Rebecca speak modern English but she speaks in a modern way. The twelfth-century Jewess would have called on God in her hour of need and would have recited prayers in Hebrew. She is not a credible inhabitant of that time and place. In fact, these trance narrations would appear to be a reflection of past events mirrored in a contemporary mind. They have a strong flavour of the historical romance.

Perhaps another way of looking at the Bloxham tapes is to view them within the perspective of a more profound understanding of the philosophical implications of telepathy. Some years ago, the English philosopher H. H. Price observed that telepathy demands a revision of our traditional notion that minds are temporally and spatially separate entities, in the same way that bodies are. If at an unconscious level there is no division between one mind and another, and if there is indeed some form of racial memory or collective unconsciousness where the current laws of time and space do not apply, then it would be possible, even likely, for such phenomena to occur. The French philosopher, Henri Bergson, in fact supplied a framework capable of containing such occurrences. His view of the brain as a 'reducing valve' (a term used by Aldous Huxley in relation to Bergson's theory) is particularly significant.

Another hypothesis would be that the mental world is full of memories, that violent events in particular may leave a vortex that can affect the unconscious minds of people many centuries later. Some such explanation might account for the seeing of ghosts. Such correspondences are inexplicable in terms of science as at present constituted and they neither prove nor disprove reincarnation.

Such evidence as there is that man is born and dies many times before he finally emerges from the stream rests on eastern religious documents like *The Tibetan Book of the Dead*, composed by men who had memories, as have many yogins, of their former lives, and on the confirmed memories of children. Since all matter is essentially indestructible, there is no logical reason why the 'spark' in man should be extinguished at death, while his body, his belongings and clothing are 'recycled' and appear in new forms in other times and places.

That the idea of reincarnation is philosophically respectable is clear from the writings of Plato, Socrates and the pre-socratics, from the Vedanta, the Buddhist scriptures and the Gnostics – from all of whom we have quoted – and also from certain western philosophers of this century, notably J. M. E. McTaggart, the dominant figure in Cambridge philosophy prior to the hegemony of Bertrand Russell and Wittgenstein. Any form of survival of bodily death, McTaggart argues, logically entails existence prior to physical birth:

The self's eternal existence, which appears as enduring throughout all time, implies pre-existence no less than post-existence. The self must have existed before the event appearing as the birth of its present body, and it will exist after what will appear as the death of this body.

Now that which appears, *sub specie temporis* [under the form of time], as our present life is probably very short as compared with our life future and past. And this longer stretch of life is probably divided into many lives of which each is terminated by events that appear as births and deaths of different bodies. Even were the memory of each earlier life beyond recall in each later one, this would not destroy the self's identity. Memory is not lost, it is dormant.

('Human Immortality and Pre-existence', *Some Dogmas of Religion*)

McTaggart deliberately refrained from using the emotive word 'soul'. Had he used a capital S for the self in this passage, it would be indistinguishable from classical Vedanta philosophy.

Western philosophy has since turned away from these questions and often seems bogged down in linguistic disputes over meanings: the more refined the qualifications of any proposition become, the more impossible it is to ask any significant question. This was not so when Nachiketas, in the *Katha Upanishad*, compelled Death to grant him the triple boon of an answer to three questions, the third of which Death endeavoured to avoid, although in the end he had to grant it:

The knowing Self is not born, it dies not; it sprang from nothing, nothing sprang from it. The Ancient is unborn, eternal, everlasting; he is not killed, though the body is killed.

If the killer thinks that he kills, if the killed thinks that he is killed they do not understand; for this one does not kill, nor is that one killed.

The Self, smaller than small, greater than great, is hidden in the heart of the creature. A man who is free from desires and free from grief, sees the majesty of the Self by the grace of the Creator.

Though sitting still, he walks far; though lying down he goes everywhere. Who, save myself, is able to know that God who rejoices and rejoices not?

The wise who knows the Self as bodiless within the bodies, as unchanging among changing things, as great and omnipresent, does never grieve.

That Self cannot be gained by the Veda, nor by understanding, nor by much learning. He whom the Self chooses, by him the Self can be gained. The Self chooses his body as his own.

But he who has not first turned away from his wickedness, who is not tranquil, and subdued, or whose mind is not at rest, he can never obtain the Self even by knowledge.

Who then knows where He is, He to whom the Brahmans are but food, and death itself a condiment?

(Katha Upanishad)

The question of death and rebirth itself becomes secondary; life and death are the creation of mind, and he who attains freedom from illusion thinks no more of death and rebirth, since he has then reached the further bank of Heraclitus' ever-flowing stream.

It thus becomes clear why the great religions have never been preoccupied with the question of rebirth as such. For the aim is not survival, but transcendence of repeated birth and death. The Vedanta and Buddhism do not preach rebirth so much as cessation of birth and death, breaking out of the iron circle. Sufis, Gnostics and Taoists accept rebirth but say little about it. Yet Christian orthodoxy, by actually denying it, entangles itself in logically untenable linear eschatologies, which, together with its claim to an exclusive revelation, have for many centuries alienated it from its own mystical roots. What Eckhart, Suso and Ruysbroeck knew could never be reconciled with what their Church taught. That the Kingdom of Heaven is within each person is the supreme secret that poets in the west have been able to proclaim much more freely than priests, who have owed a literal conformity to a rigid creed.

To reach the break of day entails plunging into the burning sunset, Blake's 'gates of wrath'. Then Avalokiteshvara, the Buddha of compassion, will lead one up behind the sunrise to full day. Blake's poem below was long ago explained to one of the authors in this sense, although with no Buddhist connotation, by Mansfield Forbes, with whom he studied at Cambridge. It is as fitting a poem with which to end this traveller's guide to the opening stages of the way as any to be found.

There is no dividing line between the true poet and the true philosopher. Both in different ways are telling us the same thing: the mystical path is not mysterious, but open to all. Blake, the most prophetic of English poets, compressed into two verses a complete parable concerning the way of enlightenment:

> To find the Western path
> Right thro the Gates of Wrath
> I urge my way
> Sweet Mercy leads me on
> With soft repentant moan
> I see the break of day
>
> The war of swords and spears
> Melted by dewy tears
> Exhales on high
> The Sun is freed from fears
> And with soft grateful tears
> Ascends the sky

It is not only creatures that die and are reborn. Religious traditions too may disappear from their original homes, to be transformed and to arise again in other places and among other people. They too undergo rebirth. Uprooted from its own land after more than a thousand years, Tibetan Buddhism lives again in India, Europe, America and Australia. Of the necessity for such death and rebirth, Lama Govinda writes:

We are transformed by what we accept. We transform what we have accepted by understanding it. We are transformed by the act of giving, and we contribute to the transformation of others by what we are giving.

He who opposes the process of transformation will die the death of rigidity; he will be expelled and rejected from all that lives, like dead matter from a living organism. Death is a deficiency of the faculty of transformation.

(*Creative Meditation and Multi-dimensional Consciousness*)

Truth cannot die. But its forms seem to disappear utterly from the place in which they flourished. Elsewhere, however, it will be reborn in new forms. When death is accepted, rebirth is certain.

Bibliography

A list of books from which quotations have been drawn

AL GHAZALI, *The Alchemy of Happiness*, tr. C. Field (John Murray, 1930)
AL GHAZALI, *Confessions*, tr. C. Field (John Murray, 1909)
ALLEN, W., *The Timeless Moment* (Faber, 1946)
The Apocryphal New Testament, ed. M. R. James (OUP, 1926)
Attar, The Persian Mystics, tr. M. Smith (John Murray, 1932)

BERENSON, B., *Aesthetics and History* (1950)
BLAKE, W., *The Life of William Blake*, A. Gilchrist (Dent, 1906)
William Blake, ed. A. Ostriker (Penguin, 1977)
BLOFELD, J., *The Wheel of Life* (Rider, 1969)
BOEHME, JAKOB, *The Signature of All Things* (Dent, Everyman, 1912)
BUBER, MARTIN, *Tales of the Hassidim* (Thames & Hudson, 1956)
A Buddhist Bible, ed. D. Goddard (Harrap, 1956)
Some Sayings of the Buddha, tr. F. L. Woodward (OUP, 1939)

CAPRA, F., *The Tao of Physics* (Fontana, 1976)
CHUANG TZU, *Musings of a Chinese Mystic* (John Murray, 1906)
CHURCH, R., *Over the Bridge* (Heinemann, 1960)
CLARK, K., *The Other Half* (John Murray, 1977)
The Cloud of Unknowing, ed. Wolters (Penguin, 1961)
COLLIN SMITH, R., *The Theory of Eternal Life* (Vincent Stuart, 1950)
CONZE, E., *Buddhist Meditation* (Allen & Unwin, 1956)
COSTA, G., *Yoga and Western Psychology* (OUP, 1934)

DAVID-NEEL, A., *With Mystics and Magicians in Tibet* (Penguin, 1936)
DE QUINCEY, THOMAS, *The Confessions of an Opium Eater* (Dent, 1907)

DOSTOEVSKY, F., *The Possessed*

Meister Eckhart (2 vols.) tr. Evans (Watkins, 1924)
ELIADE, M., *The Two and the One*, tr. J. M. Cohen (Harvill, 1962)
ELIADE, M., *Shamanism*, tr. Trask (Routledge, 1964)

FOX, GEORGE, *Journals* (2 vols.), ed. N. Penney (Cambridge, 1911)

GOVINDA, LAMA, *Creative Meditation and Multi-dimensional Consciousness* (Allen & Unwin, 1977)
GOVINDA, LAMA, *The Way of the White Clouds* (Rider, 1966)

HAWKES, J., *Man on Earth* (Cresset, 1954)
HEYWOOD, R., *The Infinite Hive* (Chatto, 1964)
HILTON, WALTER, *The Scale of Perfection* (Watkins, 1923)
Hindu Scriptures, tr. Max Müller (Dent, 1938)
HUXLEY, A., *The Doors of Perception* (Penguin, 1959)
HUXLEY, A., *The Letters of Aldous Huxley*, ed. G. Smith (Chatto, 1969)

ISRAEL, M., *Precarious Living* (Hodder, 1976)
IVERSON, J., *More Lives than One* (Souvenir, 1976)

JAMES, W., *The Varieties of Religious Experience* (Collins, Fontana ed., 1974)
JOSEPHUS, *The Jewish War*, tr. A. G. Williamson (Penguin, 1959)
JULIAN OF NORWICH, *Revelations of Divine Love*, ed. G. Warrack (Methuen, 1901)

KAUSHIK, R. P., *Light of Exploration* (Journey Publications, 1977)
KEATS, J., *The Letters of John Keats* (OUP, 1931)
KOESTLER, A., *Dialogue with Death* (Hutchinson, 1966)
KRISHNAMURTI, J., *The Second Penguin Krishnamurti Reader*, ed. M. Lutyens (Penguin, 1973)

LAO TZU, *The Way and its Power*, ed. A. Waley (Allen & Unwin, 1934)
LASKI, M., *Ecstasy* (Cresset, 1965)
LAW, WILLIAM, *Selected Mystical Writings of William Law*, S. Hobhouse (Rockliff, 1948)

LAWRENCE, BROTHER, *The Practice of the Presence of God* (Epworth, n.d.)

LEVY, G. R., *The Phoenix' Nest* (Rider, 1961)

MCTAGGART, J. M. E., *Some Dogmas of Religion* (Cambridge, 1906)

MARVELL, ANDREW, *Poems of Andrew Marvell*, ed. G. A. Aitken (Routledge, n.d.)

MILAREPA, *Tibet's Great Yogi, Milarepa*, ed. Evans-Wentz (OUP, 1951)

MOODY, R., *Life After Life* (Bantam, 1975)

OUSPENSKY, P. D., *A New Model of the Universe* (Routledge, 1934)

OUSPENSKY, P. D., *Strange Life of Ivan Osokin* (Faber, 1948)

PARACELSUS, *Selected Writings*, tr. & ed. Jacobi (Routledge, 1951)

PASCAL, B., *Pensées*, tr. J. M. Cohen (Penguin, 1961)

Persian Poets, ed. A. J. Arberry (Dent, 1954)

PHILOKALIA: *Writings from the Philokalia*, tr. E. Kadloubovsky and G. E. H. Palmer (Faber, 1951)

PIRSIG, R. M., *Zen and the Art of Motorcycle Maintenance* (Bodley Head, 1976)

Pistis Sophia, tr. G. R. S. Mead (Watkins, 1947)

PLATO: *The Myths of Plato*, J. A. Stewart (Centaur, 1960)

PLATO: *Republic* (Penguin, 1955)

PLOTINUS: *The Enneads*, tr. S. McKenna (Faber, 1956)

RAMANA MAHARSHI: *Ramana Maharshi and the Path of Self-Knowledge*, A. Osborne (Rider, 1954)

Richard of St-Victor, tr. C. Kirchberger (Faber, 1957)

RILKE, R. M., *Duino Elegies*, tr. S. Spender and J. B. Leishman (Hogarth, 1942)

ROBINSON, E., *The Original Vision* (RERU, 1977)

ROLLE, RICHARD, *The Fire of Love* (Methuen, 1914)

RUMI: Jalal-uddin, *Maihnawi*, tr. R. A. Nicholson (London, 1925–40)

RUMI: Jalal-uddin, *Poet and Mystic*, tr. R. A. Nicholson (Allen & Unwin, 1950)

RUYSBROECK: *John of Ruysbroeck, The Adornment of the Spiritual Marriage*, tr. C. A. W. Dom (Watkins, 1951)

SCUPOLI, L., *Unseen Warfare*, tr. E. Kadloubovsky and G. E. H. Palmer (Faber, 1952)

The Secret of the Golden Flower, tr. R. Wilhelm (Routledge, 1931)

The Secret Sayings of Jesus According to the Gospel of Thomas (Collins, 1960)

SOLZHENITSYN, A., *The Gulag Archipelago* (Collins, 1974)

SUSO, HENRY, *The Little Book of Eternal Wisdom*, tr. J. M. Clark (Faber, 1953)

SUZUKI, D. T., *Essays in Zen Buddhism* (Rider, 1950)

SUZUKI, D. T., *Manual of Zen Buddhism* (Rider, 1950)

SWEDENBORG, E., *Heaven and Hell* (Swedenborgian Society, 1966)

TAULER, JOHANN, *Life and Sermons* (London, 1907)

The Ten Principal Upanishads, tr. S. P. Swami and W. B. Yeats (Faber, 1937)

ST TERESA: *The Life of Santa Teresa*, tr. J. M. Cohen (Penguin, 1957)

Theologia Germanica (Gollancz, 1937)

The Tibetan Book of the Dead, ed. Evans-Wentz (OUP, 1927)

TRAHERNE, THOMAS, *Centuries, Poems, and Thanksgiving* (OUP, 1958)

TRUNGPA, C., *Meditation in Action* (Stuart & Watkins, 1969)

VAN DER POST, L., *The Night of the New Moon* (Hogarth, 1970)

VAUGHAN, HENRY: *The Works of Henry Vaughan*, ed. L. C. Martin (OUP, 1914)

The Way of a Pilgrim, tr. R. M. French (SPCK, 1941)

WILMHURST, W. L., *Contemplations* (quoted in R. C. Johnson, *The Imprisoned Splendour* (Hodder, 1953))

Wisdom of India, ed. Lin Yutang (Michael Joseph, 1949)

WORDSWORTH, *William Wordsworth* (2 vols.), ed. J. O. Hayden (Penguin, 1977)

YOGANANDA, P., *Autobiography of a Yogi* (Rider, 1969)

Zen Flesh, Zen Bones, ed. P. Reps (Penguin, 1971)

Note of Acknowledgement: We thank those publishers who have given us permission to use material from those of the above books that are in copyright.

In addition, certain quotations have been translated by the authors from French or Spanish. Those of Miguel de Molinos from a recent

Spanish edition (Barral, Barcelona, 1974). An English translation of *The Spiritual Guide* was, however, made in 1687 and was reprinted, with an introduction by Kathleen Lyttleton, in 1907. There is no translation of his *Defence of Contemplation*, selections from which are included in the Barral edition. There is a complete translation of the works of St John of the Cross, by E. Allison Peers (Burns Oates, 1953). For the *Diwan* of Mansur Hallaj we have used a French edition (Cahiers du Sud, Paris, 1955). In the case of some eastern texts, we have modified existing translations in the interests of clarity.

Index of Passages Quoted